I0199706

THEN CAME THE FIRE
PERSONAL ACCOUNTS FROM THE PENTAGON, 11 SEPTEMBER 2001

Stephen J. Lofgren
General Editor

MILITARY INSTRVCTION

Center of Military History
United States Army
Washington, D.C., 2011

CONTENTS

*Names in bold indicate the first excerpt; italics signal a subsequent excerpt.

ILLUSTRATIONS

Illustrations courtesy of the following sources: pp. 34, *Army* maga-
zine; 60, photographer unknown but copy provided by Lincoln
Leibner; 89, 93, David J. King Jr.; 125, 178 (*center*), 312, *Pentagram;*
246, 247, Information Management Support Center; and 297,
Stephen J. Lofgren. All other illustrations, except when the source
is noted in the caption, are from the files of the Department of
Defense.

FOREWORD

The horrific events of 11 September 2001, now ten years in the past, are seared into the memories of all who witnessed the attacks that fateful day. To observe the fires in the Twin Towers in New York City and the towers' ultimate collapse was heart-wrenching. This was further compounded for many who watched in nearly equal horror as a black plume of smoke arose from the Pentagon after it too was struck by suicidal terrorists in a hijacked commercial airplane. Although not as dramatic or as deadly, the attack on the Pentagon that day was almost as shocking as that on the World Trade Center. The terrorists, apparently inspired by a twisted version of Islam and a deep hatred of the United States, had successfully struck the nerve center of American military power.

The attack on the Pentagon on that clear September day will not soon be forgotten by any who watched it, but even less so by those near or inside the building as the jetliner slammed into the side of the structure and its lethal cargo of jet fuel ignited, burning through offices and hallways. The intense heat, fire, and smoke killed many instantly and drove thousands into the corridors of the five-sided headquarters to save themselves and to locate and aid coworkers. Still others, first responders and health care professionals, rallied to the building from nearby medical, police, and fire facilities to find survivors, triage and treat the wounded, and bring a semblance of order to the chaos.

Each individual directly affected by the attack on the Pentagon has his or her own unique and important story to tell, and it is vital as every year goes by that each voice is heard and remembered. This collection of oral histories highlights the personal accounts of over fifty such participants who witnessed some aspect of the events in the Pentagon that day: those wounded, the first responders, medical personnel, rescuers, those rescued, those who moved through the rubble for days afterwards hoping to find more alive, and building occupants who began picking up the pieces. This volume, assembled by the diligent efforts of the historians at the U.S. Army Center of

Military History, seeks to ensure that the voices of all those involved will continue to be heard now and for years to come.

Washington, D.C.   RICHARD W. STEWART
11 September 2011   Chief Historian

PREFACE

On 11 September 2001, Middle Eastern terrorists hijacked four passenger airliners along the east coast of the United States. They flew two of the aircraft, American Airlines Flight 11 and United Airlines Flight 175, into the World Trade Center in New York City, causing the collapse of the Twin Towers and the deaths of almost three thousand people. Another aircraft, United Airlines Flight 93, crashed in Pennsylvania after passengers fought back against the hijackers.

The fourth airplane was American Airlines Flight 77, which had departed from Dulles International Airport at 8:20 a.m. on a cross-country flight carrying six crew members and fifty-eight passengers. The passengers included five hijackers who seized control of the plane over Kentucky about one-half hour after departure. Flight 77 flew back across West Virginia and into northern Virginia. Flying on a northeasterly course low to the ground and parallel to Route 244, Columbia Pike, in Arlington County, Virginia, it dived and crashed into the Pentagon at approximately 9:37 a.m.

Flight 77 was traveling some 530 miles per hour when it struck the fortress-like Pentagon at ground level between the fourth and fifth corridors, creating a giant ball of fire and punching more than 200 feet through three of the building's concentric rings. For those people in the offices along the path of destruction inside the Pentagon, as Dalisay Olaes would remark, "then came the fire." As Flight 77 smashed through walls and supporting columns, it released thousands of gallons of jet fuel that ignited in a series of explosions inside the building. The crash, ensuing fire, and choking, black smoke killed 125 military personnel, Department of Defense civilians, and contractors in the Pentagon in addition to those on American Flight 77. Thousands of the building's occupants quickly evacuated. For hundreds of others, the period after the crash was a struggle to help themselves and coworkers escape and survive.[1]

---

[1] The official Department of Defense history is Alfred Goldberg et al., *Pentagon 9/11* (Washington, D.C.: Historical Office, Office of the Secretary of Defense, 2007).

At the U.S. Army Center of Military History (CMH), the significance of the attack was immediately understood, and the Chief of Military History, Brig. Gen. John S. Brown, directed the Chief of the Histories Division, Richard W. Stewart, to document the historic event. On 13 September, oral historians from the Histories Division conducted their first interviews with Army patients at the Virginia Hospital Center in Arlington, Virginia. These were the start of hundreds of interviews with a broad range of participants that would be carried out over the next year by fourteen historians, military and civilian, assigned to or affiliated with the Center. The interviewers were Alan T. Bogan, Military District of Washington; Capt. George K. Dover, 46th Military History Detachment, CMH; Capt. Timothy R. Frambes, Histories Division, CMH; Leo P. Hirrel, Histories Division, CMH; Kim B. Holien, Fort Myer; Sfc. Dennis Lapic, 305th Military History Detachment, CMH; Stephen J. Lofgren, Histories Division, CMH; M. Sgt. Donna K. Majors, 46th Military History Detachment, CMH; Lt. Col. Robert Rossow, Office of the Deputy Chief of Staff for Personnel; Cpl. Austin Shellenberger, 305th Military History Detachment, CMH; Frank R. Shirer, Histories Division, CMH; Maj. Robert G. Smith, 305th Military History Detachment, CMH; Pfc. Kelly A. Strand, 46th Military History Detachment, CMH; and Erik B. Villard, Histories Division, CMH.[2] Parallel efforts were performed by the U.S. Army Corps of Engineers Office of History (John C. Lonnquest), the Historical Office of The Office of the Surgeon General (John T. Greenwood), the 90th Military History Detachment (Capt. Suzanne L. Summers), and the U.S. Army Chaplain Center and School historian (then-Col. [CH] John S. Brinsfield), as well as by the historical offices of the Office of the Secretary of Defense, the U.S. Air Force, the U.S. Marine Corps, and the U.S. Navy.

The accounts presented in this anthology are excerpts from the interviews and written recollections gathered by the Center of Military History. Due to considerations of space, only some of the accounts at the Center could be included. This volume, therefore, does not offer every story or even, in most cases, complete stories. *Then Came the Fire* is a mosaic of individual accounts and impressions, arranged in an approximately chronological order, that reflects the reality of 11 September as understood and remembered by the people who experienced it.

The interviews have been lightly edited, but the intent has been to retain the voices of the individuals as much as possible. Four asterisks within an interview indicate that a significant portion of text has been omitted. Many interviews were conducted with a

---

[2] Ranks and affiliations as of October 2001.

floor plan of the Pentagon at hand so that interviewees could more easily explain their movements. Readers will discover references to such diagrams. Readers will also encounter some stories that seem impressionistic or disjointed as speakers try to relate what they felt, saw, and did amid the turmoil and danger. My hope is that these personal accounts, taken together, will convey a sense of what so many people experienced in and around the Pentagon on that day ten years ago.

Many people helped create this anthology, beginning with those who willingly sat for interviews or wrote down their memories and those historians who conducted the interviews and collected the accounts so that they would be preserved for history. At the Center of Military History, William M. Donnelly, Stephen W. Lehman, and Kathleen J. Nawyn helped select and excerpt the accounts. Nawyn also made a number of suggestions that improved the organization of the volume, and she assisted the production process by subjecting the manuscript to a close scrutiny. Michael R. Gill obtained many of the photographs and designed the cover and layout of the volume. Joel D. Meyerson and Richard W. Stewart approved the project and supported it through the publication process. Robert M. Mages helped review the index. Beth F. MacKenzie provided substantial advice and assistance. Finally, Keith R. Tidman edited the manuscript, and Diane Sedore Arms and Alexander O. Camarota expertly guided it through production in a remarkably short time.

Washington, D.C.   STEPHEN J. LOFGREN
1 August 2011

THEN
CAME
THE FIRE

PERSONAL ACCOUNTS FROM THE PENTAGON, 11 SEPTEMBER 2001

Brig. Gen. Clyde A. Vaughn was the Deputy Director of Operations, Readiness and Mobilization, as well as the Deputy Director of Military Support, in the Office of the Deputy Chief of Staff for Operations and Plans. He was interviewed at the Pentagon by Stephen Lofgren of the U.S. Army Center of Military History on 12 February 2002.

BRIG. GEN. VAUGHN: I was scheduled to sit in on the Reserve Forces Policy Board meeting for [Maj.] General [Philip R.] Kensinger at the Army-Navy Country Club, and so sometime after the morning brief, I left here and went to the Army-Navy Country Club. I would say probably I arrived out there around 0800, and sat in on the opening sessions and the opening remarks. We were waiting at that time, I think, for . . . the Assistant Secretary of the Army for Manpower and Reserve Affairs. We were waiting for him to show up and deliver his remarks, and General Davis, Lieutenant General [Russell C.] Davis, the Chief of the National Guard Bureau, came in the back of the room and motioned for myself and Lieutenant General [Roger C.] Schultz to come out in the lobby. So, I went outside with him and he gave us the information then, the breaking news was that the [World Trade Center] towers—and I don't remember whether it was one tower or both, but I think at that time it was both—had been hit by an airplane or by airplanes.

And so I called in here to talk to my exec who was at that time Lieutenant Colonel Jerry Ketcham, and he told me that [Maj.] General [Peter W.] Chiarelli had already gone to the CAT [Crisis Action Team] floor. The CAT was being stood up, and I told him that I would be there quickly. So, from that point I just picked up my materials and went outside and got in the vehicle and drove down Glebe Road for [Interstate] 395. I turned to go on 395 north and was listening to the radio. At that time, of course, they had it on about the towers being struck and I remember thinking then that I was probably driving towards a target. It was pretty obvious that it was a terrorist incident because I do remember either earlier or at the time I turned on the radio that both towers had been struck, so it was definitely a terrorist action.

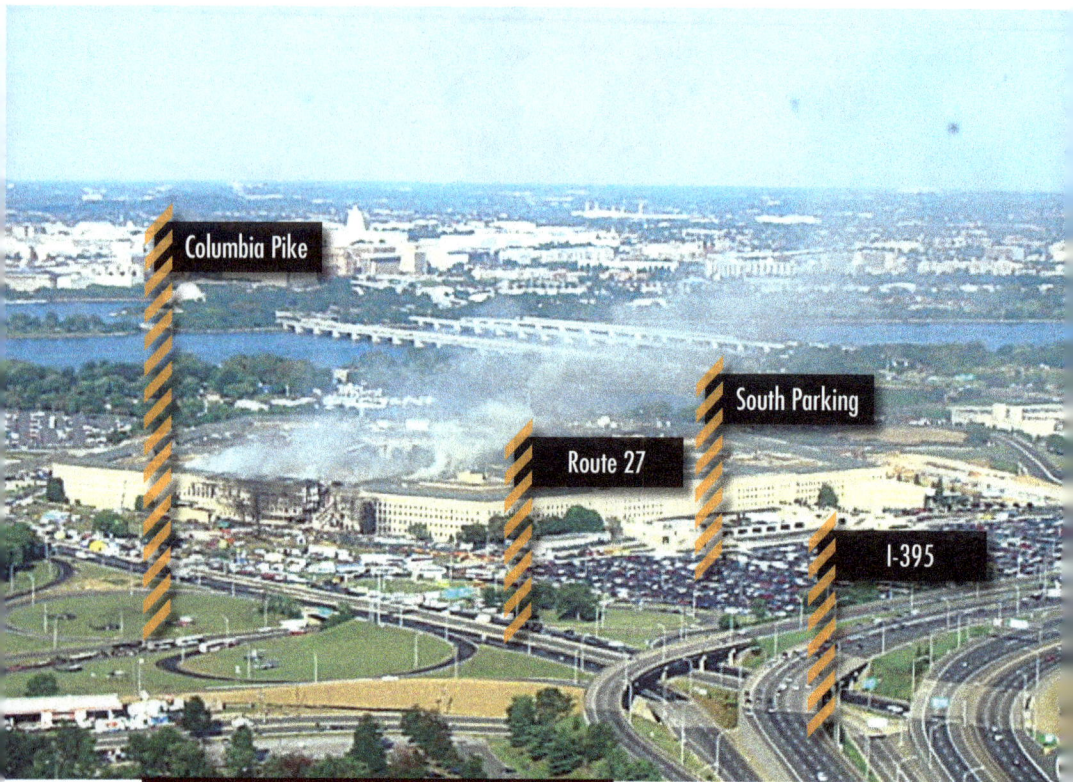

Columbia Pike

South Parking

Route 27

I-395

Pentagon and surrounding area

I remember very vividly there wasn't anything in the sky, and again, thinking about, as I came up 395 and over the top of the hill, you know, somewhere down in there you think about what a target the capital would be. You know, that's kind of what you think when you come up 395. So, as I was going north on 395. I remember seeing an airplane, a liner, that to me it seemed a little bit out of, you know, out of sorts. There was only one aircraft in the sky that I could see, and I didn't—I didn't, of course, didn't hear anything else. And that aircraft from where I was coming up 395 at that time appeared to be in a straight line up over maybe the Georgetown area or something like that, and I watched it kind of bank slowly and head west, and then you're kind of down in a defilade area coming up 395, you can't see back to the left or the right. . . . But as I came up 395, I got to the top of the hill where from that point you had a really good view of the Pentagon and the city . . . and right as I got to the top of that hill, the hijacked airliner was out my left window. . . . The highway

Pentagon, 1st Floor, map showing corridors, rings, and A-E Drive

was full of cars and vehicles, and so it was slow traffic, but the airliner . . . it was very low, and it probably had to be in close proximity or over the top of the Navy Annex. It may have been even over Columbia Pike, but very, very close, very low, and there was no doubt instantly what was going on, because it was—it must have just barely missed the Sheraton and the landing gear was up, I mean, there was no doubt it was . . . if anything, it was accelerating, and it was on a collision course, it was aimed for the Pentagon. There was just no question at all.

And I saw it. Of course, you know, traffic had come to, I mean, a slammin' stop right then, even before it hit the Pentagon.

From where I was I had probably as good a vantage point as you could have on 395, and it appeared that it may hit short, I mean it was so close. . . . At some point, as you come off the hill, you're somewhat in a defilade there, your view gets a little obstructed by . . . Washington Boulevard, where it turns and goes under 395. There's a little ramp in there, or an underpass, but I saw it track all the way in to the Pentagon. . . . I saw it all the way in and if I lost it at all it was just in the last split second before it hit. From there I don't know. During that time we may have moved a hundred feet and traffic was stopped, and I had trouble—I have had trouble with a particular brand of cellular phone that they had given General Chiarelli and me probably that week, and so . . . I didn't have my phone with me. . . . There was a young lady in a car next door to me. It was a hot day, and windows were down, and she was on her cell phone so I yelled at her to see if I could borrow her cell phone real quick, and I called in here to the AOC [Army Operations Center], into this office, and talked to a Major George Sterling at that time, and my first question I asked him, I said, "George, are you all right?" and he said, "Yeah." I think he said that Jerry, my exec, had already gone into the CAT and they were all in the CAT, opening the CAT up, and I said, "You know that you've been hit by an airplane," and I think he said, "Is that what happened?" Because, you know, there are many, many, many people that didn't find out for some time it was an airplane. He said everybody down here was okay, and they were headed for the CAT. So I told him to tell General Chiarelli I was on top of the hill and I would be there as quickly as I could get in.

Alan Wallace was a firefighter with the Fort Myer Fire Department. He was at the Pentagon heliport on the morning of 11 September 2001. He was interviewed at the Fort Myer Fire Station by Cpl. Austin Shellenberger of the 305th Military History Detachment on 30 October 2001.

CPL. SHELLENBERGER: Could you tell me a little bit about what you were doing and what led up to that incident? Did you hear about the World Trade Center at the time?

MR. WALLACE: Yeah. We had heard about the World Trade Center attacks. . . . I was reading a book in the back of the apparatus

Images from a Pentagon security camera showing American Airlines Flight 77 approaching and striking the building

area. The apparatus door for the firehouse was up, it was open. Mark Skipper comes into the room and tells me that there's been a—a plane has crashed into one of the World Trade Center buildings in Manhattan. . . .

Mark and I had been working at the rear, the right rear of the fire truck. Mark was showing me something about the foam-metering valves in that compartment there. It was just the fire-fighting system compartments. And we had just left that—he had jumped down out of there and he closed the door of the compartment and he and I began to walk up along the right side of the crash truck, the fire truck that's assigned there at the Pentagon. And we were walking to the front of the truck. And sometime after we passed the right front corner of the truck we were just—I don't know what we were talking about, we were very close, you know, within an arm's reach of each other—and somewhere in that area in front of the truck I just happened to look up to my left and see the airplane right there just a couple hundred yards away. And it was coming after us. It was coming at us. So I yelled to Mark, "Let's go." . . . As I was running I thought to myself, "Now it's happening here. Now we are being attacked here in the Washington area."

In addition to that—we're talking about a second and a half here now, okay? They talk about having your life go by, you know, as you see something like this happen, in slow motion. I don't think I experienced that. But it seemed like I had a lot of time to think about things. And, in fact, I had about a second and a half, from the time we saw the plane and until it hit the building. So during that time that's one of the things that crossed my mind. The other thing that crossed my mind is I knew I was going to be on fire very soon. And my thoughts were to run as far as I could until I caught on fire and then I would hit the ground, and then after that I would do whatever I thought of, you know, whatever came to mind.

At that point when I felt the blast and the fire and everything, that's when I did dive forward and it just happened to be right beside a nine-passenger Ford van which was parked beside the firehouse facing north. I immediately crawled underneath the van and crawled to the front of the van. As I recall, there was an enormous amount of pressure and a lot of heat that was coming underneath the van so I decided maybe I better get out of there. So I continued on out the front of the van. And I guess probably about that time that was about the end of the explosion and the amount of debris that was being projected away from the building. So I ran out into the field where Mark was. I don't think he moved until I got out there where he was. And I asked Mark if he was okay and he asked me if I was okay. . . . After I said, "Are you okay?" he said, "Yeah." I said, "Get your s——t on, I'm going to the fire truck. We've got a lot of work to do. I'm going to the fire truck." So I left Mark and ran back to the fire truck, jumped in the passenger side door. . . .

My intentions were to get the fire truck because that's what it's there for, is fire protection; pull the fire truck away from the building and turn it over to the left and take it over to the impact site where the blast occurred and dump the foam and water agent that's carried on the truck into the blast site. I at some point picked up the radio headsets and put those on, pushed the buttons to start the truck. It started immediately. I pushed the brake off, yanked its gear and tramped the accelerator and it just wouldn't—the engine speed never left idle. It just set there. It never moved. So I did this several

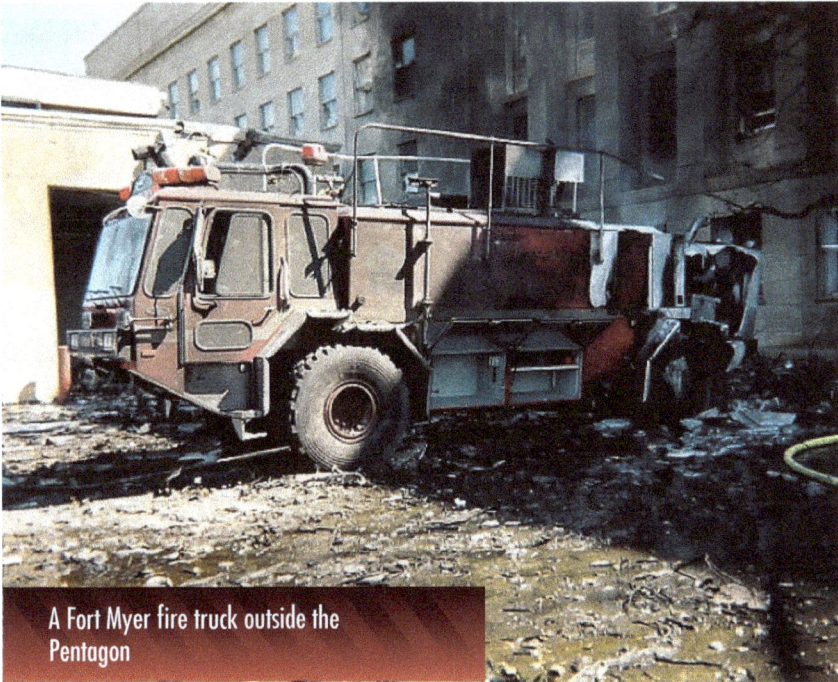

A Fort Myer fire truck outside the Pentagon

times. I moved the transmission selector several times thinking I'd done something wrong or out of sequence. And at some point while I was in there I called Fort Myer to tell them that we had had a commercial airliner strike the west side of the Pentagon. This is exactly what I said. Once again I said, "Foam 61 to Fort Myer. We've had a commercial airliner strike the west side of the Pentagon at the heliport. The heliport crew is okay with minor injuries. The aircraft was a 320 airbus or a 757 Boeing." I immediately took the headsets off, threw them into the dash, stepped over the radios and began to get out of the truck. At that point there was a—maybe a police officer who was wearing black, like the Pentagon SWAT Officers, the guys that wear black.

They asked me if we had a breathing apparatus. So I handed him one. My friend Mark was there and he had been yelling for me to get out of the truck. The whole back of the truck was blazing. There was an enormous amount of smoke coming through the cab of the truck. And I think the seat that I was sitting on, the side of the seat was on fire. So I gave Mark a breathing apparatus and there was still a third one in the truck. And I eventually removed it but not for probably about a half-hour. I took my helmet at that point and threw it out of the truck. I grabbed a lantern and set it on the floor, or on the seat beside the officer's seat, and I grabbed my mask out of the cab and I got down out of the truck and I reached around and took the lantern, my face piece, picked up my helmet and put them in an area over by the corner of the firehouse that was relatively out of the way. I mean, it was a place where I could put it until I needed it later. I went into the firehouse to

Alan Wallace's fire coat

put my fire pants and boots on, and about this time I heard a man who was at the Pentagon working—as it turned out, he was helping people get out of the building there, out of these first floor windows. And as I ran into the fire station I heard this man yell, "We need help back here." So at this point Dennis and Mark and I, I believe, were together and stayed together until we pretty much removed the people from this area or helped them get out of the building. So when I saw that my boots were full of rocks and trash and everything else, quite a bit of debris, I chose to—maybe more so because I heard this guy yelling that he needed help—I chose to leave the boots. I figured I could put them on later.

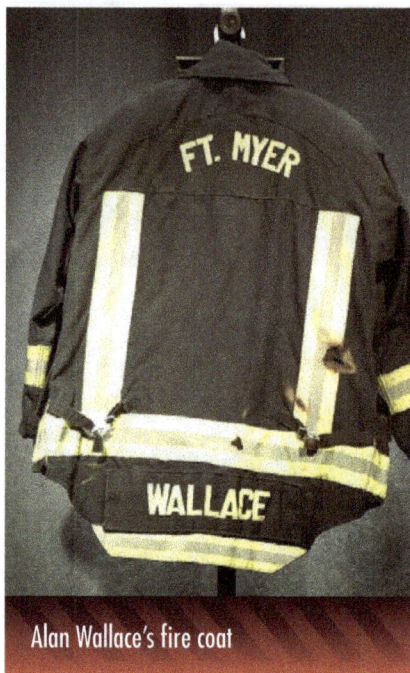

Michael DiPaula was Area Coordinator for Pentagon Wedge One, with PENREN, the Pentagon Renovation Team. He was interviewed at the Pentagon by Sfc. Dennis Lapic of the 305th Military History Detachment on 29 October 2001.

Michael DiPaula was in a trailer outside the E-Ring.

SFC. LAPIC: Where were you that morning?

MR. DIPAULA: I was, how do I explain it?—I was in the trailer. . . . We call the outside area here the lay-down area. It's the heliport area, and out there . . . we have all of our construction trailers. We were in the process right prior to September 11 cleaning out the area. We moved all the trailers. Actually, on the 10th we had some other trailers that were just leaving because we were getting ready to turn them back over to the building. And we had one trailer left, which was the—we had the singleton trailer out there. . . . So that's the lay-down area, where the plane actually came over. I was in the trailer when the plane was coming, and not knowing what the noise was. I mean we always hear planes come over. The helicopters always land there, so it's always loud. You never know when they're going to come in, and when there is a plane coming around it usually comes around the north portion of the building and goes around down the Potomac. But sometimes, depending on the weather, you can hear the plane. And on this morning we heard the plane coming, and I just thought it's another normal plane. You know, then—kind of weird, it's kind of loud, and it was getting louder and louder, and I couldn't figure out exactly what was happening. And I guess. . . . I would say like ten seconds maybe. It seemed like it was forever as you were hearing—you're hearing it approach us, but it was just coming right—right towards us. I mean—

SFC. LAPIC: And yet you couldn't see it? You were inside the trailer?

MR. DIPAULA: We . . . couldn't see it. We couldn't—we just—we heard it. And we were like, "Okay, what is that?" And then all of a sudden it seemed like the whole roof was just being peeled off because what was happening is the wing was probably about two feet above, and there was a generator outside where the engine had hit. The engine hit the generator, the wing clipped the generator and tilted it up. But it sounded like . . . it was just like a can opener. Like just peeling off. . . . And it just—it happened in a matter of seconds, but as it was going over is when it was hitting. So the nose is already going into the building. We still were freaking out not knowing exactly what was going on.

At this point, none of us knew about the incident in New York. So we had no idea what was happening up there with the Trade towers. So when—I mean we got all shaken up and we got out, and as we opened up the door there was nothing but—it was like complete darkness. It was just flames everywhere, metal falling out, and the smoke, and—it was just—you can hear the roar of the—of the fire, of the fireball as it was going down the hall. I mean everything was just so loud, but you can literally hear the fireball going. It sounded like a missile when it first came in, but when it hit it was like three thumps. It was just like a bang, bang, bang. I mean it was—and you could hear the metal crushing. You could just hear this—but it was only a matter of seconds that it was—that it hit. . . .

It was pitch black, and people were just screaming and running, and—like I said, it seemed like it took forever, but it really wasn't. It was just a matter of minutes, because I—I think I was—I was so scared and petrified of knowing what really took place because I think I was still—I was in so much shock knowing that this is really happening. I mean I'm standing right there. I'm here, and there's nothing but fire and metal falling down on us. And we couldn't—it was just—you couldn't accept what really just happened because this is real. This is really happening, and you're seeing people running and screaming from the building. What we tried to do is we tried to run back into the building here. There is an entrance here between—in the apex. The apex is basically where the building meets. . . . At the end, we call that the apex of the wedge. And I tried to go back into the door but the flames—it was just too hot to get back in, and the blast had pushed the wall down going into that entrance. So we couldn't get back in to try to get people out.

Yvette Buzard, an Acuent contractor in the Office of the Director of Information Systems for Command, Control, Communications, and Computers. She submitted the following account of her experiences to the U.S. Army Center of Military History on 8 April 2002.

On September 11th, at 9:38 I was going up the ramp onto [Route] 27 from [Route] 110, which is my normal route to work. All of a sudden there was a huge ball of flames that went up into the sky behind the row of trees that lines the exit and blocks the view of the Pentagon. There was a cement truck in front of me who jammed his brakes and skidded out of control and slammed into the guardrail. He was very shaken and confused as to what he just saw. I pulled up next to him to ensure that he was okay, after confirming that he was indeed okay, I ventured forward warily to see what had happened. When I saw the ball of flames, I figured it was either an explosion from an overturned fuel truck or possibly a gas pump from a gas station had exploded.

I was not prepared for what I was about to see. The side of the Pentagon facing 395 [*sic*] was blackened and windows were blown out. There was a small fire on the ground near the heliport pads. At first I thought that a helicopter had crashed either landing or taking off. There was a large light pole laying across 395 on top of a cab car and there was debris on the road. There was an SUV [sport utility vehicle] that had run into another car. Everyone appeared okay, they were out of their vehicles and on the side of the road. There were people streaming out of the Pentagon very quickly—the scene reminded me of when in the movies rats are shown escaping out of a flooded sewer system in the city. Pedestrians were abandoning their cars on northbound 395 and running across the southbound lanes heading for shelter. There were still other pedestrians who stepped out of their cars staring in disbelief at the Pentagon, hugging each other.

Richard M. Hudnall was a contractor in the Office of the Assistant Secretary of Defense (Command, Control, Communications, and Intelligence). He prepared these notes on 12 September 2001.

The office I am in is across I-395 from the Pentagon South Parking lot. Our ninth-floor window looks out over the Pentagon, and our office is here, because the Pentagon is under renovation one "wedge" at a time and we were moved out but not back in yet. The space that got clobbered yesterday was the wedge that had just been finished recently. This is the three-four wedge as it has both the third and fourth corridor in it. We here in the office were watching CNN in disbelief about the NYC [New York City] attack, when the explosion at the Pentagon sent a large amount of smoke, dirt, and debris into the air. We watched this massive plume go up and up until it covered the Pentagon. We assumed the building had taken a massive hit. The plume seemed to go up in slow motion. A very large funnel shape—and there were objects embedded everywhere in it, which then began to rain down. I ran immediately downstairs and rode across the South Parking lot on my bike toward the smoke (I commute to work by bicycle). The smoke was thick and black typical of jet fuel and was coming from the west side of the Pentagon toward the helipad. As I got closer there were many small aircraft parts on the parking lot and grass, most of them small twisted pieces of aluminum with that typical zinc chromate paint used on the inside surface. Some had a few rivets here and there. Some torn composite pieces. Scattered like a tornado had gone through the place. As I turned the corner at the helipad I was somewhat relieved to see the fire centered *outside* the building. Very black smoke rising in a column maybe a hundred feet in diameter at the base. A firetruck and ambulance from the Arlington fire station were the first ones to get there. You could not get close to the fire—it was very hot—and looked like an oil well fire you see on TV. The fire crews went to work immediately. They were very fast. I can't say enough about them. They were on their feet working very close to that fire. The building itself looked intact, but the entire helipad side was covered in soot and white ash. I could not see any hole in the building at that point, although obviously there was one. The wall right behind the fire was obstructed by smoke. There were sure not any airplane parts of any size on the ground in front of the Pentagon. Hand-sized airplane parts were strewn all over the place but nothing of any size. I picked up a few to examine them to see if I could figure out what kind of airplane hit. Then I came across a larger piece, about a foot long section of wing leading edge, and knew right away this was a jet. It was heavy construction—not a light airplane or helo part.

There is an overpass that goes over Columbia Pike and the overpass is maybe thirty feet higher than the Pentagon Helipad, so I walked up on it to overlook the scene. I noticed the light poles at that point. They had been bent over or clipped off about three feet from the ground so I knew then the plane had come from the west. There was a lady very shaken up standing on the overpass. Her small grey Chevy car was stopped in the middle of the roadway, and she had had to slam on her brakes as the plane went right in front of her car and slammed in. She said it was an American Airlines jet. I took her to talk to a policeman who had just arrived.

In some places, the basement just below ground is larger in diameter than the Pentagon above the ground, so it occurred to me the plane either skipped off the ground and went into the E-Ring, or slammed through the ground into the basement. It was in a dive when it hit—but it could not have been excessively steep if it clipped the light poles on the overpass. I'd estimate twenty degrees nose down. They were laid over flat toward the Pentagon, so they did not get blown back by the blast—they got hit by the plane on the way in.

More police began to arrive and immediately made us all get away from the building, which no one where I was wanted to do. I think everyone wanted to try to help out. But the police began to arrive in force and made everyone get away from the Pentagon all the way across South Parking to 395. There was no way to get into the Pentagon as both doors I know of near there were too hot to get to. It was a very helpless feeling to just stand there and watch it burn so I left, and went back to my office to let folks there know what had happened.

Maj. Lorie A. Brown was the Chief Nurse of the DiLorenzo Clinic at the Pentagon. She was interviewed at her Pentagon office by Lt. Col. Robert Rossow of the Office of the Deputy Chief of Staff for Personnel on 29 November 2001.

MAJ. BROWN: We were watching the TVs in the clinic, with the CNN showing the Twin Towers on the TVs, and kind of still going about clinic business—patients in the clinic, you know, normal busy day—when about 9:42—the crash happening at 9:40—we had somebody run in the clinic and say to evacuate, evacuate, something horrible has happened—a lieutenant colonel Air Force type. He continued to run down through the clinic, and I caught him in a hallway, and I just knew what happened. . . . So that man had gotten down two or three hallways deep into the clinic by the time he had found me, but he was running full bore, so it wasn't more than thirty seconds from when he came into the clinic.

I ran to dental, to get dental, trying to—on radio—because we carry radios—trying to get DPS [Defense Protective Service] to

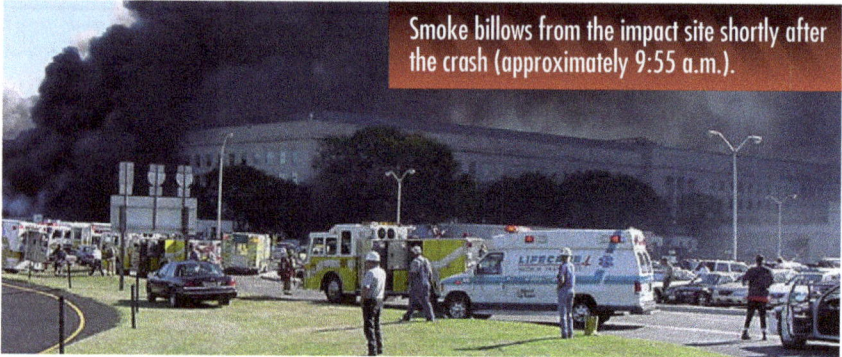

Smoke billows from the impact site shortly after the crash (approximately 9:55 a.m.).

confirm. "DPS, I need confirmation. I need confirmation." You know, "This is TRICARE Clinic, do you copy, do you copy?" as I'm running to dental to get the triage officers. Dental officers in the Navy are trained for triage . . . they have triage equipment back there, and so I ran—while I was trying to get confirmation—to them, to get the equipment, get them forward. . . .

So within three minutes of the crash, we knew what had happened. We had no physical impact. Many people that were much closer to the scene heard the plane coming in, heard the loud bang, heard the fireball. We heard nothing. Our lights didn't flicker. We didn't lose phones. We had no physical impact. The ground didn't shake. Nothing happened. Our first inkling was that man running in, saying, "Evacuate, evacuate, evacuate."

So as I was trying to muster our MASCAL [Mass Casualty] [personnel]—getting more organized—just within two minutes, just hundreds and hundreds of people running down the hallways, bringing patients, carrying patients. And very quickly the smoke started piling in. Still on the radios, trying to get DPS.

In our MASCAL plan, how we manage our emergency teams is standardized. We already have two emergency teams, so immediately we sent one team forward to center courtyard. They would have run down eighth corridor on the first floor, into the center courtyard, and then they came around to either Corridor 3 and 4 or 5 and 6—I'm not sure which corridor they set up at—outside [within the courtyard]. Captain [Jennifer] Glidewell was one of the first to arrive, with a sergeant, as well, and then the ambulances that we have parked in the corridor, they came after, but the runners got there faster than the ambulance. There were already patients there. . . . And that was probably no more than five minutes in, because as soon as the man came running in, they picked up their bags and went, so to run down eighth corridor—maybe another minute or two—not long.

So they were there and I was here in the clinic, still organizing. By that time we had patients, you know, as I said, hundreds of people were bringing patients to us or just running out the doors, straight out eighth corridor, into the parking [lot]. So what we had was several of our folks, when that gentleman had run in to say evacuate, they evacuated out with everyone else before I came forward. They had radios, though, so they called immediately and said, "Hey, we've got patients out here by the POAC [Pentagon Officers' Athletic Club]." . . . So then I sent more people out here to . . . what we called the POAC scene. So we set up a patient-collecting triage here, we set up one inside the clinic. We had the one already going inside the center courtyard. Then DPS started calling, saying, "I need a team," you know, "TRICARE Clinic, I need medics here. Corridors 5 and 6. Corridors 3 and 4." Different floors, different exact locations, they would give me, you know. And then I would make up new teams. The way our triage plan works is . . . the manpower pool gathered. And then we have blue vests, medical equipment, MASCAL equipment all ready, and then I make teams. "Okay, you"—one doc, one nurse, three medics—grab vests, grab radios, grab this. "Go, you're going to three and four. Call me when you get there and let me know what you want."

And then in the meantime, I'm getting reports—"I need O_2 (Oxygen)," "I need splints," "We've got burns," "We need this," "We need that"—all via radio. And then I'm, "Okay . . . you get this," "You can do that," "You do this," "You go here," "Send this there"—making up more teams. Then volunteers coming in—"I'm a doc," "I'm a nurse," "I'm here to help. What can I do?" "Okay, here's a vest, here's a bag. You're going to"—you know—"Corridor 6. I haven't heard from my team on Corridor 6. You need to run to Corridor 6 and then you need to run back here and tell me what's going on. I need to know." In my head I am thinking, "Are they dead? Do they need equipment? Do they have patients? What do they need?" "You run, and you come

back, and then you let me know." So all of this coordination was
going on from the clinic here—managing—sending more drugs.
"We need morphine." "We need this." "We've got"—you know—
"we've got shrapnel." "We need O_2, O_2, burns, burns, burns." So
that's kind of what the different scenes were then. . . .

Then the report for the second plane came in. DPS: "You've got
to get out. Evac, evac. You got to get out. You can't stay." So we
evac'd the clinic. We evac'd Center Court. All the firefighters
that were there by that time—I can't even tell you—and the
patients were all evac'd out Corridors 1 and 2 down and out.
So everybody that was here in the clinic and the teams that I
could get hold of via radio were told to evac. From the clinic,
we evac'd out Corridor 8 to North Parking. We had a lot of
patients in the clinic and we had maybe another twenty or
thirty outside by the POAC. So this is all simultaneous. We're
trying to get the patients out of the clinic, get every little scrap
of equipment that we could, throwing them on blankets and
gurneys and anything, just grab them and go. Like I say, I had
lots of volunteers by that time, who could make a big difference,
because all my medicals were out then . . . so then I was using
volunteers to empty out equipment. "Now we're getting out,
we're getting out, evac, evac, evac"—I had to clear the clinic.
So everyone's evacing out—because DPS said, "Second plane's
coming. Get out, get out"—including, like I say, by that time,
the firefighters who got there [to the courtyard] very fast. . . . So
we evac'd and then from there, we evac'd our patients further
back from the building. You know, we picked up all our triage
and all our patients and moved them back. All the while, we've
got radio comms saying, "I need evac," "I need help," you know.
"What's the status on the plane?" We weren't getting, obviously,
good communication at that time. We weren't getting a lot of
answers from DPS. Obviously, they had their hands full.

But what had happened was there were ambulances lined up
over here [on the other side of the building] and no patients
or few patients, and patients here with us and no ambulances
in North Parking. (We have already done our after-action with
Arlington [County] and have worked on trying to improve our
communication.) So what I did here was I evac'd by civilian
means. I stood up on top of a car and yelled, "Anybody!" I said,
"Stop that car. Stop it now." Anybody with their keys, anybody
with an SUV. Because we had lots of litter patients that were
very critical and had to get out. A plane coming in—I've got

critical patients and I've got no evac—no air evac—and I kept trying but could get nothing. So we had the cars lined up, threw seats out of them, and put the patients with a doc or a nurse, you know, had medical go with, and sent them all to Arlington, which is the closest hospital, in order to try and keep accountability of them, because there was no time with a plane coming in to get names and ranks. . . . And people afterwards have said, "You don't know how many? You don't know who?" That would be no. Let's see. A plane coming in. I'm bagging them. He needs to go. I don't need his name. He needs help and I can't get it, so he needs to get to it.

So we evac'd all of these patients. . . . By that time [we were] trying to get DPS to give—"Is it all clear?" "Can we go back in?" "Can we go back in?" And they would not give an all clear. [Eventually] we gathered up our medical supplies, and went back in. And we went back in through Corridor 8, branched off teams again to go around, trying to find anybody else and see what else we could do. . . . We had lots of volunteers, lots of folks who stayed to help—amazing stories of volunteerism, it's a wonderful staff here. It's just incredible. I can't say enough about them. But we gathered up supplies, threw them on blankets and anything we could carry, and then moved back in to make more teams and go back in and see if there was anybody left. But by that time the corridors had collapsed. We had teams that had gone into some of those areas and had gotten folks out before they collapsed, but once they collapsed—and the smoke was so thick that, you know, we had medics crawling on their knees, getting lost in the smoke themselves, and trying to find anybody and get themselves out.

So we did that. And by that time the Center Court was filling back up with firefighters. They would be respiting inside—dehydration, smoke inhalation for the firefighters. We were treating those kinds of patients here in Center Court again. And then I went out to the crash site itself and continued to set up—I was working with Lieutenant Colonel Patty [Patricia D.] Horoho . . . Army nurse. . . . Patty works very close, and she came out and went directly to the heliport. So they were set up there. And again, that's where fire rescue went to. They had medical there really fast, because they were just down the road. The response time for Arlington Rescue to the building is three to four minutes, and that's a standard. That's a normal. Not when a plane flies in the building. That's every day. When we call, they get here in three to four minutes when we have a patient to evac, and we do that on a daily basis. So it wasn't long out here where medical got out to this scene and formalized that. After the second evacuation—maybe within forty minutes or so, half-hour, once I had come in to make sure all the teams were doing what they were supposed to be doing—then I came back out, joined Patty Horoho here. Arlington Rescue was here—the chief in charge. And we had worked on, for the past year, coordinating with him—our lane, his lane, how we worked together. So then I was put in charge of the acute-care area. We had already set up our different triage areas, not just one. I set up all the different areas and then worked on getting the volunteers organized, getting our equipment organized, getting ready for patients. "We're ready, we're ready," you know, just waiting for them to find anybody when they went back in after the evac. So that's what we did out on the heliport.

Assistant Fire Chief James H. Schwartz was Assistant Chief of Operations for the Arlington County Fire Department. He was interviewed at the Arlington County Fire Department in Arlington, Virginia, by Stephen Lofgren of the U.S. Army Center of Military History, Sfc. Dennis Lapic of the 305th Military History Detachment, and Randy Papadopoulos and Senior Chief Kathy Wright of the Naval Historical Center on 17 April 2002.

CHIEF SCHWARTZ: I was sitting in the office . . . on September 11th. And actually, my wife called me . . . to say that an airplane had just flown into the World Trade Center. And so I immediately . . . turned on the television. And for me, when I looked at the first visuals of the World Trade Center I already had a pretty good idea that that was an act of terrorism, that that was a deliberate act, because for me, when you looked at those initial pictures, that airplane hit that building just too squarely. You know, there were no indications to me that it was trying to divert its path or to get away and clip a wing or something along those lines. So the thought definitely entered my mind that it was a deliberate act.

Our emergency communications center, which is a dual center for police and fire—they serve both police and fire for emergency call-taking and dispatch—our administrator at ECC at the time, a man named Steve Souter . . . called me on the telephone and asked if I was watching the events that were on the television. And I said that I was. And he said, "Okay, I'm going to check a couple of things and I'll be back to you." And it was shortly after I hung up the phone with him that the second airplane went into the building. Well, by that time, he was receiving calls in the 911 center from people in the *USA Today* building. *USA Today* was headquartered here in Arlington on September 11th. . . . If you've ever come into National Airport on an airplane down along the river, you know that sometimes, at least pre-September 11, the airplanes are actually below the height of the building. And people that are in the building are looking out or are looking down on the airplanes. So we were receiving 911 calls from people in the *USA Today* building with a lot of concern about stray aircraft, which was all they knew at the time. Steve and I had a conversation just briefly about what was going on, in a second phone call, including the possibility that clearly this appeared to be now an attack, and did we have a vulnerability here, given our proximity to the District, as well as the many government facilities that we have here.

I hung up the telephone and there was then a call dispatched for the *USA Today* building for, if I remember correctly, alarm bells going off in the building, which is a relatively frequent event around here. And because . . . one of [my battalion chiefs] at that particular moment was at a doctor's appointment . . . and asked me to cover for him for that period of time . . . I got assigned to the *USA Today* building. I got my radio and walked down the hallway to the elevator. And when I got to the elevator is when Engine 101 came up on the air and said that they had just seen an aircraft go down in the area of the 14th Street Bridge. I never made it to the *USA Today* building. I diverted and went directly to the Pentagon and arrived at the Pentagon incident, you know, within ten minutes of the aircraft going down.

DR. PAPADOPOULOS: How did you know to go to the Pentagon and not to the 14th Street Bridge?

CHIEF SCHWARTZ: Well, because the 14th Street Bridge is directly adjacent to the Pentagon. And interestingly, where the units were that saw the aircraft go down, they didn't have a visual on the Pentagon. They were on [Interstate] 395. But if you've been around this area any time, you remember 1983, when we did have an aircraft that hit the 14th Street Bridge and went down. . . . I've always taken that to have come from their memory of that event in 1983, as well as the approximate geographic location. It wasn't too much longer after that that we recognized where it was. And interestingly enough, at least in my own mind, I had a pretty good idea that it was into the Pentagon, again, simply because we had been watching the events of the World Trade Center and this clearly was an attack by that point and the attack wasn't going to—in my mind, terrorists weren't going to do much by hitting the 14th Street Bridge.

DR. PAPADOPOULOS: What route did you take coming into the Pentagon?

CHIEF SCHWARTZ: I actually got onto Washington Boulevard. . . . It was an interesting sight because as I was going down Washington Boulevard I had probably two dozen police cars in front of me. If you looked out my windshield it was just a wave of emergency response vehicles going down the road. There were a couple of fire trucks and ambulances in that parade also. And then we all just jumped down off of Washington Boulevard, where Washington Boulevard loops under 395 and goes down into South Parking [at the Pentagon]. . . . In fact, many of the police vehicles were sort of parting the way for us as we were coming through. And I went down into the South Parking lot, where I met on the scene there one of my battalion chiefs, Robert Cornwell.

DR. PAPADOPOULOS: Were you in communication with these people—or with anybody—as you were driving to the Pentagon?

CHIEF SCHWARTZ: Well, in fact, there was a tremendous amount of radio communications going on, for obvious reasons. I mean, people were giving all sorts of reports. Our communications center—the dispatchers were inundated with telephone calls. And as the radio reports went back and forth and as they tried to give information—in fact, it was in that travel to Washington Boulevard that they had other reports that the plane had gone into the Pentagon. They were asking if anybody could verify. You know, I guess that's where we were picking up on what our real destination was going to be. . . .

SENIOR CHIEF WRIGHT: From the time of impact to the time you arrived, can you estimate how long that took?

CHIEF SCHWARTZ: Less than ten minutes. Less than ten minutes. I arrived on the scene probably—the battalion chief who was first on the scene who arrived within a three- to four-minute time frame had not gotten from the front of his vehicle to the back of his vehicle, which is where we typically operate our initial command setup from. You know, he was in the process of moving back. So easily within the first ten minutes. . . .

At the point that I arrived, I saw, obviously, a tremendous amount of fire and a tremendous column of smoke that had come from the tremendous amount of jet fuel that was burning. At the point when I first arrived, we had not yet had structural collapse. So there was simply a hole where the airplane had gone in. And then, of course, there were hundreds of people on that west lawn of the Pentagon, both military and civilian, that were assisting those that were injured, as well as the injured themselves, who were strewn, you know, across that lawn. From my vantage point there, which was along the curb at South Parking that looked out on that west lawn . . . you could make out body parts, you know, those sorts of things that, obviously, you know, the fatalities that came from the airplane and also from inside the building. And what you really saw was a sea of people that were trying to assist the injured. A lot of military folks that were trying to mobilize themselves into small groups to make entry into the Pentagon. And then, of course, our initial first responders on the first alarm assignment who had come in on the response.

* * * *

I tasked Chief Cornwell with an interior position, assigned him several companies. And he moved towards the interior of the Pentagon. I then established several other divisions to deal with the EMS [Emergency Medical Services] needs. We were already working the EMS portion of the incident, patient care, medical management. But we hadn't yet established the groups and the divisions that were necessary under incident command systems to deal with that.

It was within that time frame, and I mean a few minutes after we started giving those taskings, that I was met at the command post by Chris Combs, who was a special agent with the FBI [Federal Bureau of Investigation]. And Chris' job is, he is on the National Capital Response Squad out of the Washington field office. But his special responsibility, in addition to his other normal job duties, is he is the fire liaison to the FBI. In other words, it's his responsibility to interface with those of us in the local fire and EMS agencies about what the FBI is doing and how it relates to our particular role. . . . He was one of the first to arrive on the scene. And I don't know the time frame, but I'd have to guess, you know, it was within the first twenty minutes or so. Shortly after that—and again, we're talking five-, ten-minute pieces here—is when Chris got word and came to me and said, "There's another aircraft that's unaccounted for that we know has been hijacked, and it is believed to be headed this way." Now, [pause] under normal circumstances, the degree of risk that firefighters take would probably have caused me, you know, in my risk-based decision-making, to minimize that somewhat and not necessarily alter our tactical actions at that point. However, because less than an hour before I had watched this second airplane go into the World Trade Center, my frame of reference now was that this was an imminent possibility. And since Chris was telling me that this hijacked aircraft was twenty minutes out, I had to make a decision. And the decision did not come instantaneously, I will tell you that. In fact, I still remember, and Chris remembers, too, looking at me, saying, "You've got to do something." So, you know, we made the decision that we were going to call essentially an evacuation from the incident ground and pull everybody back and position them underneath the highway overpasses that were there. . . .

So we repositioned underneath the overpass and essentially waited. Chris was getting constant updates, over his radio, because he was connected with the FBI's command center who was, you know . . . they've got all sorts of connection with the federal agencies, including FAA [Federal Aviation Administration], who can give them accurate information. And that's an important point, which we'll get to shortly here. But he was standing next to me underneath the overpass and he's telling me, you know, "Fifteen minutes out, eight minutes out, three minutes out." And when we reached the twenty-minute point he received a communication that said, "It is no longer a problem." And, in fact, what he was told was that the aircraft had crashed into Camp David. Now, one of the things that I found out subsequently. . . . [is] that because the transponder had been turned off on that aircraft, they were pretty much guessing, based on where it last was, and using, you know, essentially a guess as to what its path would have been were it headed directly this way. I didn't know that on that morning. Okay. On that morning he was saying it's headed towards us. And so that's what we based our decision on. It now looks like it never even came close to us. You know, it now looks like that was, in fact, the plane that crashed in Pennsylvania and not Camp David, which obviously wasn't hit. But at the time there was a lot of confusion and that was the best information that we had available at the time.

Capt. Thomas Panther was the Acting Deputy Chief of Police for the Operations Division, Arlington Police Department, at the time of this interview. He was interviewed by M. Sgt. Donna Majors and Capt. George Dover of the 46th Military History Detachment on 28 May 2002.

CAPT. PANTHER: I was standing out in front of my house in Springfield [Virginia] on a street corner with my dogs, getting ready to take the dogs for a walk, when a woman I had never seen before in my life, with a Walkman, walked by me and said, "My God, did you hear they've had planes crash into the World Trade Centers," and she said, "and now something may have happened at the Pentagon?" Well, I ran—ran the two blocks home, and ran up to my bedroom, turned on the TV, and they were reporting that they had known planes had hit the World Trade Centers, and it was believed they were just getting a report on one that had hit the Pentagon. I immediately dressed. I'm assigned a police cruiser that I take home with me, an unmarked car. I went red light and siren the whole way. The minute I got in my car I could hear units on the police radio responding, talking about a major fire, an airplane impact. I went red light and siren from Springfield to the Pentagon, made it in record time, I might add. . . .

I checked in. I was tasked with a few tasks. I drove down to the impact site and stood on the lawn. I made contact with the FBI scene commander. We had made a decision very early on that we needed to sweep the lawn and the landing pad there around the heliport for any evidence that could be located quickly, knowing that the rescue and recovery response that was coming would eventually obliterate any evidence that might be found on the outside of the building. So we got together really quickly and organized teams of FBI agents, ATF [Alcohol, Tobacco, and Firearms] agents, and Arlington Police to sweep the lawn on the heliport side of the building. . . . Everyone was literally lined up shoulder-to-shoulder. I observed it. I did not take part in it. Everyone was given a . . . paper bag, and they were instructed if they found anything that looked like it may be related to the aircraft or anything having to do with the crash, to pick it up. Aircraft parts and human remains were located during that sweep.

Ceci Mayhew was a budget analyst in the Office of the Assistant Chief of Staff for Installation Management. She was interviewed by Stephen Lofgren of the U.S. Army Center of Military History on 7 March 2002. Also present were Andrea Seabrook of National Public Radio and Martha Rudd of the Office of the Chief of Public Affairs.

MS. MAYHEW: My office was located in the first floor [of the Pentagon]. . . . That particular day was just a normal day for me, so I was there no later than seven o'clock, and went around the normal routine-type business. Then around nine o'clock one of my coworkers stopped by my cubicle, and, addressing everybody who was there, asked if we have seen the attack on the Twin Towers in New York. We were surprised to hear what she was talking about, so she went ahead and continued to elaborate the details and so forth. So around 9:30 we all proceeded to go to one of the local offices and watch what was happening at the moment on national television. . . .

We were all watching TV at the moment and . . . it was like a dream. We couldn't believe what we were seeing. First, as they continued to repeat the attack of the first airplane, then all of a sudden the other airplane came and attacked the other tower. I can't remember the exact sequence of events, but then almost at the same—I did notice that while we were watching TV there was like a vacuum in the room where I had to swallow and clear my ears. You know, it's like an impression like when you're in an airplane and either you are descending or ascending like your ears get clogged or whatever? So I have to swallow—I thought for a second, how strange. I mean, I never experienced this. And probably a second later we heard this noise going through the corridor. It sounded like a storm, like the wind was very strong and to the point that it just slammed the doors open. Then, at the same time, it felt like a vacuum because you could hear the wind going through or the noise going through and at the same time it opened the door and you hear this suction noise. And one of our lieutenant colonels who was watching the news with us—evidently it was like a second reaction for him; he knew what was happening—he went and looked in the corridor and turned around, and very strongly he directed us to just leave the building. I mean, nobody even asked him any questions. We just did what he told us to do. Because, by second nature, I think we knew what had happened. We didn't understand it, but we knew. And so we all decided to leave the building but I did stop by my office, by my desk, before I left to pick up my purse and specifically I wanted to make sure I had my cellular phone with me so I could communicate with my husband. . . .

Once we all went into the hallway then we met with the rest of the people that were leaving the building. And we all left, you know, not so much in a single row but we all were just trying to get out of the building. Once we were out of the building—I mean, I was just following the crowd—my car was parked on the South Parking lot and I ended up in the North Parking area. And as soon as I got out of the building, I looked up and I saw all this very dark, black smoke coming out of the building and I thought, "All right, that's when I call my husband." And evidently the news of the airplane hitting the Pentagon had not hit the media yet, so it wasn't on TV, so when I told him I said, "I am leaving the Pentagon because of a bomb"—I mean, we didn't know what was happening— he said, "Ceci, you mean the Twin Towers, you were watching something on TV." I said, "No, I'm watching the roof of the Pentagon and all this black smoke is coming out of there. . . ." And then, at that moment, it hit the news and he was really relieved that I had contacted him.

Leona G. Shaw *worked in the Office of the Assistant Chief of Staff for Installation Management. The following excerpts are taken from an account she prepared on 24 September 2001 titled "Noteworthy Efforts During the Pentagon Attack."*

Lt. Col. Janet Hodnett kept a very clear head and took charge of the office evacuation. Once the persons in the office realized we were in danger, for some reason we ran to the E-Ring door of DAIM-MD. Once in the E-Ring hallway, we stopped momentarily (less than five seconds, and far too long) to figure out the direction we should run in. Colonel Hodnett, with an amplified and commanding voice, quickly organized the evacuation, and kept the personnel from moving in the wrong direction (toward the sixth corridor). Many people were confused and temporarily disoriented, especially after just having watched the events in New York. Personnel did not know at the time the impact we experienced was a plane. We were all under the impression we were being bombed, felt there could be a succession of bombs, and also felt that at any second our path of egress could be cut off. This was very frightening to those of us evacuating. I shall never forget the fear that a second blast would cave in the structure and trap us.

Colonel Hodnett kept a clear head, and moved—very fast—with us to the outside through the North Parking entrance/exit. This very easily could have been a panic situation without her guidance. . . . I literally ran out of energy, and my running strides then became small steps. When Colonel Hodnett looked back and saw that I was coming to a stop—all of us still thinking the building was being bombed—she turned back in my direction and repeatedly yelled for me to keep going and not stop. Otherwise, I would have temporarily stopped at that point, and there was no time to waste.

I remember right after that Colonel Hodnett stopped to use both hands to beat on a door on the right side of the E-Ring hallway just after passing the seventh corridor. She noticed a combination lock on the door. These offices are generally secure areas that may not have access to a television or radio, and personnel within may not have been aware of the New York tragedy or the Pentagon's imminent danger. She yelled very loudly while beating on the door, "Evacuate, evacuate!" I did not see anyone else in the nearby crowd, to include myself, stop to warn personnel behind secure areas who may not have known what was going on. There were very few seconds to waste when you thought you were being bombed. As I think back, the personnel assigned to that room could have already departed, and Colonel Hodnett used precious seconds that she could have used to save her own life to make sure they were aware of the impending danger. . . . In my view,

[she] displayed tremendous courage and leadership, clearly putting the safety of others ahead of her own.

Col. Joseph M. Tedesco Jr. was the Chief of the Focused Logistics Division, Office of the Deputy Chief of Staff for Programs (DAPR-FDL). He submitted the following account of his experiences to the U.S. Army Center of Military History on 8 November 2001.

0815—I returned from our routine Tuesday morning video teleconference (VTC) and asked my deputy if we could gather our folks for a staff meeting. . . .

0830—We began the meeting in our tiny conference area across the office from the massive 1942-era steel-framed Pentagon windows. We normally met in my office next to the windows, but my desk and adjoining conference table were cluttered with briefs and staff actions. My deputy, Sheila Striegel, recommended we move to our conference area. One of our people (Tom Bortner) placed a loaf of his famous sweet bread in the middle of the table as we sat down. As we munched and drank our coffee (some of the 30,000 cups served that morning in our five-sided home) FDL folks grew weary of listening to my boring guidance. Answering phones during meetings was taboo in FDL, so little did we know that the world had totally changed by the time our meeting came to an abrupt and violent end. . . .

0938—Bob Dotson, a civil servant from Redstone Arsenal, Alabama, and frequent visitor to FDL, pushed the cipher door buzzer to our office. He was thrown back. Gene Summerlin (a retired colonel who now continues to serve his nation as a civilian) first heard a whooshing sound reminiscent to him as a missile. Kia Batmanglidgi (a former 82d Airborne Division trooper of Iranian descent, and now hard-charging young American contractor) then heard the rumbling of an apparent earthquake, followed by violent shaking of the floor. Major Jay Bienlien (our youngest active duty soldier) then looked up to view the initial blast. The windows across the office from us shattered and sprayed against the old, heavy three-inch 1942 steel Venetian blinds (thank God for American steel) and crashed to the floor. The second wave, a deafening explosion, then proceeded to cause those same heavy blinds to protrude from the wall horizontally. John Huber (a celebrated and well-liked civil servant and sixty-year-old Pittsburgh native) then saw the concrete wall next to Jim Randazzo's desk heave inward about three feet only to snap back, causing Jim's feet to jerk from his desktop, where moments earlier they rested while he "listened" intently to "guidance." At that moment, the three solid "particle board" book shelves descended on Jim, pinning him to his chair. All of the actions noted above happened within less than five seconds. I looked at my comrades in a surreal moment. I saw them sway left, then right. Denise Rawlings (my wonderfully caring admin assistant and quasi-mom to all in FDL) fell first into Sheila's lap, and then was thrust into mine. As I reached for and held Denise, my senses became starkly real. I barked commands from the pure instinct of thirty years of military training: "Everyone leave now! Go straight out the ammo door!" (referring to my war reserve ammunition office's door, closest to us). The ceiling buckled above us. "Do *not* go to your desks! Do *not* get your hats or purses! Go right now!" Of course, it did not take much to convince FDL to leave their home. The smoke from the raging fire below filled the office, followed by the putrid dust ball from fifty glorious years of Pentagon history. We knew we would be back . . . we thought. We had absolutely no idea what had happened. We had no knowledge of the World Trade Center attacks, which had taken place an hour earlier. Most of us wondered if the Pentagon renovation crew had hit a gas line. I worried that a crippled small plane had fallen on to the roof above. For years, I had noticed that the approach to Ronald Reagan Washington National Airport's western runway flew directly over "Ground Zero" (the famous center courtyard of the Pentagon . . . named in the Cold War as dark humor figuring that the Soviets would target the first nuclear weapon above that spot) and had feared an accident from "wind shear" or mechanical failure . . . but never purposely perpetrated in the name of God.

Charlene Ryan served as a customer liaison/computer specialist with the Requirements, Analysis and Design Branch of the Information Management Support Center (IMCEN). She submitted the following account of her experiences to the U.S. Army Center of Military History on 1 October 2001.

When the plane hit with a "wump" we looked around in shock, then I grabbed my purse and ran. Our sergeant major put our adrenaline into motion by shouting, "Get out, run, get out, go, go, go!" . . . We all ran. The air in the hall outside my office was instantly filled with smoke, debris, and flying glass from lights which blew out. I heard screams, coughs, cries for help, but couldn't tell where they were coming from. We were not far from an emergency exit door. We shoved it open and ran out. My office is on the first floor D-Ring, halfway between the fifth and sixth corridor. . . . The emergency doorway came out right at the left corner of the side that got hit. Outside there was burning plane wreckage close by; we had to dodge around it. There were police running toward us but still at a distance, calling to us to "Run, run, as fast as you can! There's another plane coming!"

Oh, Gawd! Move legs! One of us was bleeding. Something hit him in his head just above his forehead, and the blood was streaming down all over his face. We looked for something to put pressure on the wound—while running—someone in a suit and tie had a white handkerchief. Perfect. A white car with "Medic" on the door drove by. We hailed it, he stopped and helped him. Meanwhile, the rest of us moved on.

I walked along the road, one young lady was standing in front of me, shivering. "Something hit my car." The passenger side was shoved in. The window was shattered on the passenger door. A mass of twisted metal (green) lay on the roadway on fire. I bent down to look at it real close. Looked like a plane part. The girl was shivering from one end to the other. Police came and wrapped crime scene tape around her car and around the smoldering part. She was now on foot like the rest of us, wanted to know where we were going. Her arms were cut, and knee badly bruised. I hugged her, told her she survived, she's okay, and she can stop shaking now. I think it helped. We learned that she saw nothing coming. She was on her cell phone while driving along the highway, talking to her father (who is an American Airlines pilot), telling him she was passing the Pentagon at the moment, when she got hit. Eventually, she wanted to walk to her place of work—over the bridge to Georgetown. We left her at a cross road.

At that point, someone in uniform came screaming toward us (cell phone attached to his ear): "Everyone back to the building, we need everyone! We need all the help we can get." So, we ran back. Somewhere along the way, we met up with that yellow tape.

No one except military, medical, or police personnel. So, we ran away again. It was at this point I heard another explosion. Everyone was running every which way. We tried to flag down cars. "Help us get out of here!" We were shouting, running into the highway. One guy in a van stopped. Three or four of us climbed in, but there were boxes everywhere. I had to climb over them, I think I squashed one. Claritin. Penicillin. A drug man! He had his radio on, and that was when we learned that the plane that hit the Pentagon was a hijacked American Airlines from Dulles Airport. No sooner did we get going in this guy's van, but we got stuck in gridlock traffic. Stopped completely, I thanked him, said I preferred to be on my feet. He understood completely. We all got out, we all just wanted to get away as fast as we can.

I walked and ran for a couple hours or more, trying to get to an office building where I knew people. Our little group changed as one or two decided to change direction, and we picked up others who liked our idea better than their own. A couple just wanted to be with someone else. The Pentagon is pretty much alone among parking lots, highways, parkways, bridges, and the Potomac River. The closest civilization to us was the Pentagon Navy Annex. A couple from our group headed there. They knew people inside they could go to. I knew no one there, and it was right in line with planes coming from Dulles. The other buildings closest were south of the Pentagon, and we were on the north side of the building, and south was where my car was, so I thought a lot about going in that direction, but it was going to be impossible to navigate around harm. The easiest way from north to south of the building was the heliport walkway.

So, I headed north for Rosslyn, past the Newseum, to the Army JAG [Judge Advocate General] office, and brought everyone who wanted to come along with me. I assured them I knew where we could get help. This was an Army official Renovation Swing Space building and I knew a number of agencies there, including JAG. I was earlier talking with the warrant officer who works at JAG when she gasped, "The Trade Towers were just bombed, I gotta go." I hung up my phone just as many rushed to our conference room where the TV was, and CNN was on. The Trade Towers were in flames. I no sooner gasped over that situation when we got hit too.

Finally, about ten of us walked into the Rosslyn building, tenth floor, I headed the entourage with my suit coat tied around my waist and stated, "We are refugees from the Pentagon! We need a bathroom and water in that order, thank you!" The JAG office stepped to the plate and took very good care of us. Water, food, phones, money, rides, etc. Most of us had nothing with us, I had my purse but my cell phone was dead. One lady with me felt that she was ready for anything because she had her nitroglycerine. JAG's TV was on and it was then I learned that the Trade Towers had fallen, and a fourth plane crashed near Pittsburgh. I also got a full front view of the devastation to the Pentagon. I pointed on the TV to where I came out of the Pentagon and could only see billowing smoke and fire at an angle at the time. This was the first personal accounting of the event for these people, so they were all attentive and had questions that I couldn't answer.

It was only then that I became aware of the entire situation and the fear began to sink deep into my soul. While walking for hours we heard and saw fire engines, watched police shut down roads—set up that yellow tape, F–16s screaming overhead, helicopters everywhere. Seeing the larger picture on television was a shock.

One of our office rooms was ground zero (first floor E-Ring), now the gap in the building. We can only think the worst. But, New York is worse off right now. I feel lucky.

Neal Shelley was Deputy Director of the Information Management Support Center. He was interviewed by Pfc. Kelly Strand of the 46th Military History Detachment on 5 March 2002.

MR. SHELLEY: Well, the first thing that I see—I came out of the building through South Parking, out in that direction, out past the Metro—I saw a smoke cloud over the Pentagon. Now, we didn't even feel the hit where we were—

PFC. STRAND: You didn't feel it across the building?

MR. SHELLEY: Didn't feel it at all. In fact, our first notice was one of our guys came running into the room and yelled, "There's a bomb in the courtyard," which was a logical interpretation, I guess. And we thought there was something wrong with him because we hadn't felt anything, we hadn't heard anything, there were no alarms over here. Curiously, my wife had been in the dentist chair upstairs in the concourse. So, . . . we said, "Even if there's something wrong with him, we ought to get out of here," so we got everybody out. I went up and checked there [the concourse]. She had already evacuated the building. So I come out the door and the first thing I see is a black cloud. Now, it's kind of over in the area of my boss' office, but I don't know if there's a fire. I don't know anything yet at this point. And I guess the biggest memory or the most impact of memory was, after we got the people collected on our side of the building, I began to walk around the building to see if we could find more people.

And I got over near the Citgo station, where you had a direct line of sight of the whole—and at that point, I knew my boss was probably dead. And my boss was also probably my best friend. So at that point, we hadn't heard from him and at that point, that's when the whole thing hit. So that's probably the biggest memory that I have, is that moment of stepping there—there's a little knoll over there—stepping onto the knoll and looking over and realizing that we probably lost our front office.

Sheila Moody was in her second day as an accountant with Resource Services–Washington, Office of the Administrative Assistant to the Secretary

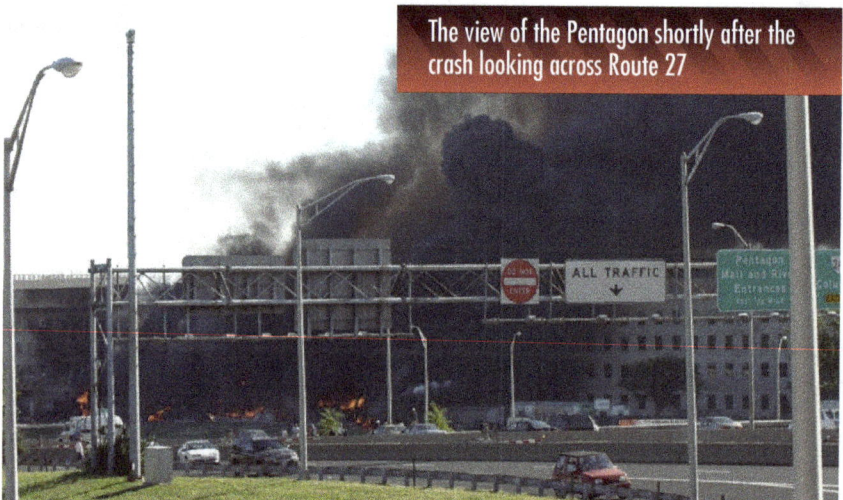

The view of the Pentagon shortly after the crash looking across Route 27

of the Army on 11 September 2001. She was interviewed by Frank Shirer of the U.S. Army Center of Military History at the Virginia Hospital Center on 13 September 2001.

MRS. MOODY: The plane crashed in between Corridors 3 and 5. My office was in Corridor 4, on the first floor. So I think, in the news reports, they said that it crashed on the side where the helipad was. That helipad was right outside my office window.

MR. SHIRER: Had you heard about the news of the attack on the World Trade Center in New York before the plane crashed?

MRS. MOODY: I had just heard it from a coworker, about ten seconds before the plane crashed into the Pentagon. It was another lady who started to work with me on Monday. She brought a radio to work with her that morning, Tuesday morning, and she had just heard. So she had come around to my desk to see if I had heard about it. I told her I hadn't heard because I didn't have a radio. And she was telling me that two planes had crashed into the World Trade Center and that they were talking about tightening up the security at the Pentagon. And then she walked away, and not ten seconds after she walked away from my desk, there was a whistling sound—you could hear the sound like a whistle. And then there was a rumble, and a large gush of air and a fireball that came into the office and just blew everything all over the place and knocked us over. It didn't knock me out; it didn't knock me down. It just kind of blew my chair back, and there were flames everywhere. I remember, I covered my face with my hands to shield my face from the flames, and the flames only lasted for a few seconds, maybe two seconds at the most. And then they kind of went out, but there were still things around us that were still on fire, and a lot of smoke and just darkness.

MR. SHIRER: Were you able to escape, although injured? Or were you trapped?

MRS. MOODY: I was trapped. I didn't have any injuries where I couldn't move. I was fortunate; I didn't have any broken bones or anything. I just had the burns. I had a jacket on, and my back was very hot, like it was burning. So I took my jacket off. Something ignited my jacket and my jacket was still on fire. So I took that off.

And then I started looking for a way to get out, and I couldn't find a way to get out. But I could see a window, a small window kind of at the top of the office, and I reached up to try to see if I could break the window. But it was too high and it was too hard. It's that tempered glass. So I couldn't break it, and I started looking around for something that I could maybe pick up, that I could throw up there or try to hit the window and try to break it out. Little did I know that the bomb [*sic*] had blown a hole out through that side of the building where the window was, so it was only a few feet away from there that there was an opening, but I wasn't aware of it at the time. I immediately started praying. And I heard a voice—I heard a fire extinguisher at first, and then I heard a voice of a man saying, "Is anybody there?" So I started calling back to him. I said, "Yes, we're here. We're here. We need some help." He said, "I can't see you," and I said, "I can't see you either." I said, "But keep coming. We're here. We're here." And then the smoke and the fumes started taking my breath away, and I couldn't really call out to him.

Sheila Moody's rescuer was S. Sgt. Christopher Braman, Office of the Administrative Assistant to the Secretary of the Army.

So I started clapping my hands, hoping that he could follow the sound of my hands clapping. And he started coming in that direction because I could hear the fire extinguisher bursts putting out the flames. And I was able to catch just a quick glimpse of his silhouette through the smoke. I guess maybe it was when he was squirting the fire extinguisher. He put out the fire that was between him and me, and I stepped over some of the debris and then he led me outside so I could get out. And when I got to him, I told him that I knew there was one other lady that sat in the cubicle behind me, that she was still in there and she needed help getting out. She was able to walk, but she was just really lost and kind of confused and didn't know which way to go. So he went back in after he got me outside and told me where I needed to go. He went back in and he got her out.

* * * *

MR. SHIRER: Could you describe the experience in the emergency room?

MRS. MOODY: The care in the emergency room was great. They took my name. They immediately wanted to get my name and phone number for my family so that they could contact my family and let them know that I was okay. Then they immediately started attending to wounds, cleaning off my hands and—because that's where most of my pain was, the burns that were to my hands—and just cleaning up my wounds and being very gentle and very caring, and they just took great care of me in the emergency room.

Janice A. Jackson was a contractor help desk technician in the Information Management Support Center at the Pentagon. Ms. Jackson was also an Army Reservist, serving as a sergeant with the 55th Maintenance and Materials Center at Fort Belvoir, Virginia. She was interviewed at Walter Reed Army Medical Center by Frank Shirer of the U.S. Army Center of Military History with Beau Whittington, assistant editor of the Walter Reed Army Hospital newspaper, The Stripe, *on 19 September 2001.*

MR. SHIRER: Where were you located in relation to the attack?

MRS. JACKSON: I was located in the D-Ring . . . less than a hundred feet away from where the incident actually took place.

MR. SHIRER: Thus you were in the section beyond where the E-Ring collapsed. Had you heard the news about the attack upon the World Trade Centers in New York that morning?

MRS. JACKSON: Yes, I did. We were sitting at our desks and what we were doing was looking on the Internet, on the CNN news, and we were looking at the actual pictures of where the attack took place.

MR. SHIRER: What was your reaction to the news of that attack?

MRS. JACKSON: Well, my reaction was—I was devastated. I'm like, "Oh, I can't believe this is really actually happening," you know? It was just really shocking.

MR. SHIRER: Please describe what happened upon the impact of the aircraft.

MRS. JACKSON: Well, like I said, we were sitting at our desks and we were looking at the computer. We were looking at the stuff that was on the Internet in reference to the attack in New York, and I'd say less than five minutes after that, was this loud explosion, you know? And it happened so quickly. The only thing that we actually saw was fire. There was this— it's like a fireball that just that just came through, and it just threw us all over the place. All I knew was that some heat was over my head, and I didn't realize that my hair was on fire until a coworker of mine, whose name is Stuart Fluke, he said, "J.J."—because that's what they call me at work—"your hair is on fire." So he took off his shirt and he put the fire out on my hair, and my hands had already got burned up from the flames just coming that way. And the next thing I heard was a baby crying, because the office that we were in—there were only seven of us in the office at the time—so there was no baby in that office. So what happened is it pushed us further down towards where the actual impact happened, because there was a baby down there at that time. Wherever we ended up at, there was a baby, and they were pulling the baby out, and I was trying to get across the rubble and stuff in there. And as I was going out, I said to one of my coworkers, "I can hardly breathe." And he was saying that he could hardly breathe either, because the smoke, it was so thick. It was really, really, really thick. It was really kind of hard to breathe. But we managed to kind of walk out, because it was looking like there wasn't any way out of there. But what we noticed is there was a big old large hole . . . in the far right corner. There was a big old hole in the wall, and some coworkers there, they were like, "Come this way. Come this way." So we managed to, you know, cross some of that debris and to climb over that way.

And on my way out, as I was walking out, there was a coworker of mine—her name is Racquel Kelly—I guess she spotted me, because she was down low, because she was stuck up under all that debris and all that rubble and stuff. It was stacked up on top of her. And she was saying, "J.J., please help me." And so what I did was I pulled her out. I managed to pull her out, because it was really stacked up on her and it was really heavy. And once I pulled her out, she was able to walk some on her own. And so we had to climb up all this other debris, up on where the hole was in the wall. We had to actually climb up a lot of stuff in order to get out of there. But we managed to get out. It was really stacked up really high.

MR. SHIRER: Now did that put you on the roof of the building or just into another section of—

MRS. JACKSON: It was right where the actual impact took place— where the helicopter was, right back there is where it put us at. . . .

MR. SHIRER: Now you said you were blown down the hall. The force of the blast blew you?

MRS. JACKSON: Yes, it just threw us all further down into another ring, because there was no way that we were still in our office, because in our office [there] were computers, computer systems, CPUs, and all that stuff. . . . There was nothing there anymore. The only thing you could see was debris, and, also, I think the second floor kind of like caved in, because I know something fell on my back. So that's how I got the burns on my back. . . .

MR. SHIRER: Once you got out of the building, what happened next?

MRS. JACKSON: When I got out of the building I was pretty blown away. I was hysterical. I was kind of out of control because my hands felt like they were still on fire here. My whole body felt like it was still on fire, so, I was doing a lot of crying and all that other stuff. And we walked—you know, they guided us out to the edge of the grass, because everybody was coming out, and the ambulance and everything. So they had us lie down and they were pouring some cold water on it, you know, to kind of cool it off, because it was just that bad. I'd say we had to wait there for about twenty minutes, because the traffic was so bad, it was all backed up, and the ambulances were trying to get in. So it took a while for the ambulances to get in. So what they did was they tried to pick the victims that were the worst wounded. I know we waited for about twenty minutes. And in between that, they came over and tried to console us. The chaplain came over and talked to us, read verses out of the bible and that stuff, to keep us in high spirits, because it was just horrifying.

* * * *

MR. SHIRER: Is there anything else that you want to add to this interview, ma'am?

MRS. JACKSON: Well, yes. As far as when I was in the building, when it first happened, I actually didn't believe it. Actually, the honest truth, I thought I was dreaming it. So it took a few minutes for it to actually set in and I actually felt my legs moving. That's when I actually felt that it was really happening. And what came across my mind was—because I'm also in the military. I'm in the Army Reserves. The thing that crossed my mind was two things: one, I knew I had two kids and I was going to get out, and the other thing that crossed my mind is the military always taught us, never give up. So those were the two things that strengthened me to get out of there. . . . But once I stepped out through that hole, that's when it hit me. Everything just hit.

Charles Young was a deputy sheriff in the Arlington County Sheriff's Office who arrived at the Pentagon shortly after the plane struck the building. He was interviewed by M. Sgt. Donna Majors and Capt. George Dover, 46th Military History Detachment, on 23 May 2002.

MR. YOUNG: And at some point, we came across someone hanging their hands out the window. And we ended up pulling out, I want to say, five people. The first person that got pulled out was a gentleman who—actually we were hanging onto [my partner's] feet because the windows sit up kind of high on the Pentagon, and we were holding onto him. And he actually had to reach down and grab this guy. His hands were burned. [My partner] Art didn't want to grab his hands because, I mean, there was skin hanging off, and the guy's eyes were burnt, burnt out. And the only thing he could grab onto was the guy's suit. So he grabbed it. And, of course, his suit was burnt. I guess it had burned into his skin. So when he grabbed it the guy started screaming, but, you know, there was nothing we could do.

We just had to get the guy out. So he grabbed him and pulled him out.

He and someone else took him over to Washington Boulevard where all the fire trucks and everything, EMS, was pulling up. And then the next person to come out I believe was a female. And we grabbed her and took her out. And she wasn't—I don't recall her being burnt or anything, but she was—I don't know if she was even alive. So we ended up, me and someone else, I don't know who, took her and took her over there too. And I think we took out at least another female. And I'm not sure if someone else came out. But someone told me we had pulled out five people. I mean, it happened so fast, you know, it was just, it was just, "Just do it." And then we went back and we started looking for more people and we couldn't find anyone else. . . .

I could smell the JP–5, which I remember from the Marine Corps being on a helicopter assault ship. I remember—actually, Art told me . . . when we were looking for people after we pulled these people out, that the glass . . . was melting, and it was actually falling down. And he said somebody grabbed me and grabbed me from the back because this is what I was wearing, this uniform. They grabbed me from the back and said, "We need to go" because that stuff kept falling down. And it never occurred to me because, you know, I guess I was so focused on looking for people that it didn't bother me. And there were flames, I mean, well past where we were, over left and up. I remember just smelling, just smelling that stuff, you know, just the smell of all that stuff burning was, you know—and it didn't seem real, honestly. When we first got out of [our] vehicle and we started running I thought we were in a Tom Clancy movie, I really did. And then it brought me back to DESERT STORM. I was sitting there going, "You know, this is"—and I didn't get involved really too much, nothing more than taking prisoners out there. But being in that kind of frame of mind then it brought me back.

M. SGT. MAJORS: We've talked to so many people that were victims of the Pentagon, only a couple that had been injured as badly as the ones you've described. But one thing that they all say is . . . "I don't know who pulled me out, but I wish I knew who pulled me out."

MR. YOUNG: We do, too.

Col. Mark Perrin was Deputy Director of the Army Quadrennial Defense Review Office. He was interviewed at the Pentagon by Sfc. Dennis Lapic of the 305th Military History Detachment on 1 November 2001.

COL. PERRIN: 11 September started out to be a very chaotic day. It promised to be a chaotic day—because it was the day that the first draft of the QDR [Quadrennial Defense Review] report was to be released to the services, and the services had already been given a heads-up that we had about twenty-four hours to receive that first draft, to review it in detail, and to provide comments back to the Office of the Secretary of Defense. . . . So, I had told my folks on Monday evening, the 10th of September, to plan on a very chaotic and long day as we reviewed the first draft of the QDR report. Now [Brig.] General [Hubert L.] Hartsell, [Director, Army QDR Office] was . . . actually on leave during this time period. So I was in charge. And I had the group here in the office ready to receive the QDR report and do the first review. In fact, the morning of 11 September began with an early-morning meeting, with Major General John Wood of Army DCSOPS, to review what we believed to be coming out of the QDR report and put together a game plan to review that report for the rest of the day. The meeting started about 7:30. It broke up about nine o'clock, because General Wood was to meet with the Secretary of the Army at about 9:00, and I walked down the hallway with a number of people who came out of that meeting as we discussed our game plan for the day. Actually got back to my office, downstairs in 1Delta536, at the Pentagon, at about 9:30 in the morning, and when I walked in, everybody was gathered around the office television watching CNN, and watching the World Trade Towers on fire. They explained to me that commercial airliners had hit the towers. It was obvious that it was on purpose, and it was just really, really a shock for all of us in the office to kind of watch what was happening. Coming out of the meeting with General Wood though, I had a tasker that was due by noon, and so I grabbed one of my action officers, Major Dave Irvin, and brought him back into my office to discuss the tasker that needed to be done. Just as we began to lean over my conference table within my office, we felt a tremendous pressure. It was like a tremendous concussion, a thud. It wasn't a great—it wasn't a great loud sound, but a sound of a loud thud. And, immediately we were both knocked to the ground, the lights went out, debris came falling from the ceiling. All the walls within my office came down, were blown down on top of us. And Major Irvin, who was closest to the conference table, immediately crawled underneath the table and I followed him. We weren't sure what exactly happened to us. My first thought, as I expressed to Major Irvin, was that it must have been a bomb.

But the walls had come down on us. The ceiling had come down on us. The lights had gone out. I smelled a very unique stench like burning wires and some smoke. We heard something from the ceiling above us come crashing down and hit the safe as well as the conference table on top of us. Still to this day, I really don't know what that was, whether it was the suspension of the ceiling, whether it was light fixtures, whether it was ducting for the air conditioner. I am really not exactly sure what happened. All I know is we were able to get underneath the conference table before that came down on top of us. We laid under the conference table for what seemed to be a minute or so, until all of the debris had stopped falling on top of us. We could hear it stop falling. We crawled out. We backed out from underneath the table and realized that we were pretty well covered with the walls and debris that had fallen down on top of us. So we picked our way out under the table and moved the debris together until we got to the area that used to be my office door frame. We could see because there was a little bit of light that was coming through a wall just outside my doorway, which had not been totally blown down. But the top part of the wall had been blown off. And I could see some light coming through over the top of the wall from the helipad exit, or entrance area from the Pentagon in Corridor 5. It was apparent that all those walls had blown down, as well. . . .

I could hear people next door, my people—Bill Delaney, John Schotzko—next door talking to themselves, calling to themselves. I could hear the secretary screaming bloody murder—I mean just at the top of her lungs. I could hear Colonel Rocky Ebener, Lieutenant Colonel Rocky Ebener, calling out to his office mate, Darryl Oliver, to find out if he was okay. And I could hear voices. One of the officers in the office was a Special Forces–trained Army Reservist, Lieutenant Colonel Sean Kelly, and I don't know where Sean came from but he came out of the darkness. He heard Dave Irvin and I talking to each other. I began calling out names, to see if people were okay, and Sean appeared out of the darkness and he

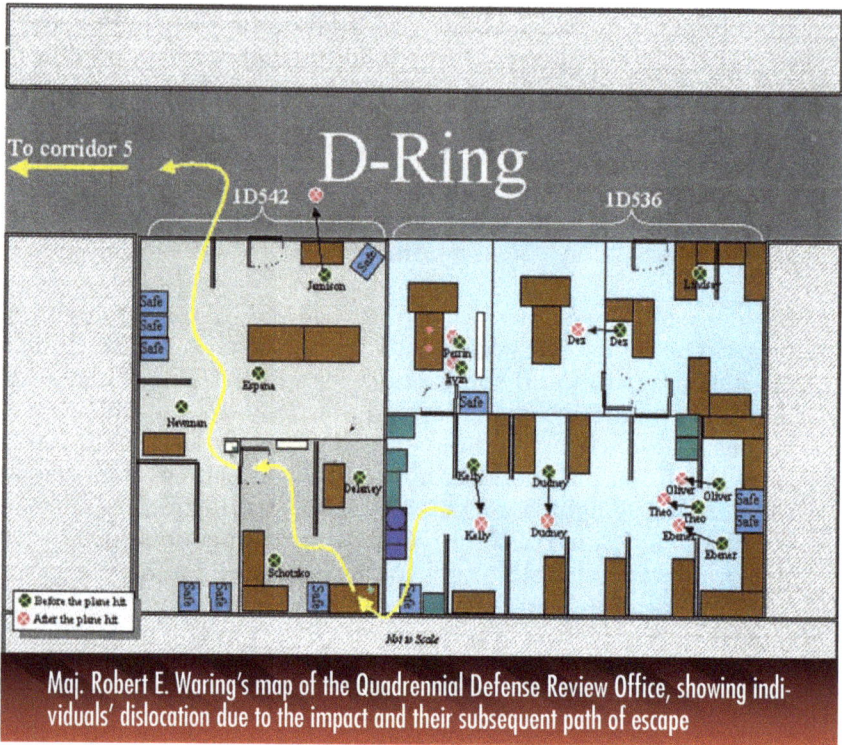

Maj. Robert E. Waring's map of the Quadrennial Defense Review Office, showing individuals' dislocation due to the impact and their subsequent path of escape

said, "Sir, while you were gone to your meeting this morning, here is who I know was in the office and out of the office." I already had a good idea of who was going to be out of the office that morning, but Sean was able to confirm for me who was actually in the office, gathered around the TV at the time that all this began to occur, that the attack happened.

So what we did, kind of collectively, was count noses and start screaming for people within the office. You know, "Colonel Ebener, are you here? Are you okay?" And he answered, "Yes." "Captain Oliver, Colonel Dudney, Colonel Delaney, Major Schotzko, Des, are you okay?" "Sergeant Lindsay, are you okay?" By the time we finished counting off the noses we realized that everybody who had been within our office was responding, was apparently okay. Some people had sustained debris wounds, just—just hit by debris, but were coherent, and were really remarkably calm. What turned into total chaos at the point of impact really returned to order pretty quickly. It was not something that anybody specifically did to return that to order; it was, I think, just a matter of military training, and people realizing that others needed help. So they stopped panicking, stopped being in their dazed state, and began to really focus on trying to help somebody else. I think it was Lieutenant Colonel Larry Dudney and Sergeant First Class Lindsay that made it to Ms. [Desiree] Duckett first, and were able to . . . calm her and prevent her from screaming any further. Because she had been blown through the wall behind her, into the General's office. Actually through the wall. Her office, her actual desk and chair were now located in the General's—what was the General's office, because his walls had been blown down.

I could hear Lieutenant Colonel Delaney and Major Schotzko, and by this time I heard Major Waring, who had gone to the Pentagon Library to do some research, and was in the Pentagon Library when the impact hit . . . and made his way back toward the office. Major Waring realized that the Pentagon helipad exit was the quickest way out. He came back to the office. I could hear he and Colonel Delaney talking about, "We need to get out this way. It is the closest way to get out." And it was over the wall because all the debris had us basically blocked into the office. So, what we did was started yelling to people to come toward us, toward our way, and we began putting people over the wall. Now at the base of the wall there was a five-drawer safe, our water cooler, which had been overturned, that we set back up again as a base, just turned it back up, and there was a filing cabinet. So between the filing cabinet, the water cooler, and the safe, people were able to crawl up and assist others up and over the break in the wall. And then Colonel Delaney and Major Schotzko were on the other end—and Major Waring— were on the other end of the wall, standing on desks helping people down to the floor so they could get out the door. There were a couple of people who were dazed beyond their ability to escape on their own. And the first one was Ms. Duckett. I mean she was—she was still hysterical, but she was not screaming at this point. She got to the wall by the aid of Sergeant Lindsay and Lieutenant Colonel Dudney, and she physically did not have the strength to help herself up and over the wall. So Captain Darryl Oliver jumped down, basically put her on his back, crawled back up over on top of the safe and assisted her in getting across the wall. Then he came back. And we had a janitor in our area that morning, as well, our normal janitor who came in every morning. His name was Theo. Theo was speech impaired and hearing impaired, as most of the janitors are here in the Pentagon, they are disabled people and do a really great job. . . .

Between, I think, Colonel Dudney and Captain Oliver, they got Theo to get up off the floor and to move toward the wall. When he got there, with their assistance, he was still totally basically confused and kind of fell back down on the floor—like he really didn't want to go, he just wanted to be left alone. The problem was though he was blocking the only exit. And by this time smoke was beginning to fill in the room pretty quickly. The odors were getting worse. The fumes were getting worse. The smoke was getting worse. And it was getting—it was just—it was taking away our life, what life we had. And so Captain Oliver again jumped down, grabbed Theo—who is not a small person—and also kind of threw him on his back, hustled back up the safe and got Theo over the wall, as well. And then he went ahead, Captain Oliver, and evacuated the building with Theo to make sure he got out.

About this time, people from outside of our office, within the Delta ring area, heard our screams, heard our commotion, heard Ms. Duckett's screams, and began moving toward us. There were people from the Information Management Center that came through. There were people from the chief's initiatives group, Chief of Staff of the Army's Initiatives Group, who came through. There were people from the Army Audio Visual Training Facility, across the hall from us, that came through our area, to get up over our wall and out to safety. Again because the majority of the D-Ring was totally blocked by debris. The person I remember the most—and actually stopped and talked to very briefly—was Lieutenant Colonel Bob Snyder . . . [from the] Chief of Staff of the Army's Initiatives Group, who came through, with his uniform still smoking, both of his hands and arms were burned badly, the skin on his arms had rolled up just like it was a sardine can. His face looked to be okay. But his uniform—his shirt and pants were still kind of smoking. We were able to get him up and out over the wall pretty quickly, and get him up in the triage area. There were, I would estimate, four to six other people that I don't know names of, but I did recognize faces as they came through, I had seen them in our Delta ring area, and they came through and got out over our wall. . . .

At that point, I was already coughing. I was already choking from the smoke and the fumes within the office. I never felt any heat within our office, but there was a lot of smoke, a lot of fumes. And when I was satisfied that, one, all of my people were out, and, two, that nobody else was going to respond to me in there, I went ahead and pulled myself up over the wall. And I got a hand from Major Schotzko and Major Waring.

They helped me to the floor on the other side. At that point, we kind of all left the area at the same time. As I went into the fifth corridor, I walked backwards more in toward the Pentagon, to look down the D-Ring, just to make sure that there was nobody that we could help in the D-Ring. And the D-Ring had been totally destroyed. There was debris laying all over the D-Ring. I could not see down even to where our former office door is located.

Maj. David Irvin was an action officer in the Army Quadrennial Defense Review Office. He was interviewed at his Pentagon office by M. Sgt. Donna Majors of the 46th Military History Detachment on 1 November 2001.

MAJ. IRVIN: Well, I had come in in the morning, and I had done PT [physical training] around six-thirty or so, and come back into the office about eight o'clock. Things were going kind of slow. We were waiting for a draft of the final QDR report to come out so we could react to it and start looking at input for it. Colonel Perrin had gone off to some meetings. We were standing in the front office where we had a TV working playing CNN. And some folks were talking about an aircraft, or something that hit one of the Trade Center Towers, and we were watching the planes and the smoke coming out that. And we discussed whether it was a

Lt. Col. "Rocky" Ebener, *left,* and Maj. David Irvin, *center,* were in the Army Quadrennial Defense Review Office in 1D536 when the plane struck. Maj. Stephen Waring, *right,* was in the Pentagon Library and returned to help his colleagues evacuate.

We didn't—at that point we didn't know what size the plane was. Whether it was an airliner, or whether it was a privately owned plane. We saw a second explosion while we were standing there. . . . It was at that point we realized that the towers were being struck by terrorists. That, you know, this—two towers being hit was too much for any kind of accident. So this was some kind of terrorist strike, or attack.

And Colonel Perrin came in. I showed him—I drew his attention to what was going on in the screen. There was nothing we could do about it there. So he had some information he brought back. He asked me to come back into his office so we could talk about a tasker. . . . He was giving me some last-minute instructions close to the door of his office when I heard a loud, I guess, whooshing noise, a movement of air, and a kind of a background roar. We saw the wall starting to come in toward us, and his chalk board, dry chalk board, I remember putting my right arm to try and block the board because it didn't fly at us immediately. It seemed like it was moving very slowly. And then the force of it knocked me on the ground. The next thing I remember is I'm lying on my back, there is debris starting to fall, and I think—and I hear a loud—a loud noise, you know, crashing, bang, and I—he has a conference table in there. So I pulled a chair away, and he mentioned, "Let's get under the table." We crawled in under there. We heard another explosion. It seemed like it was coming from the—towards the center of the building where we were lying. Debris continued to fall. I remember making a comment as the dust was filling my mouth that I hope this wasn't all asbestos coming down on top of us.

Eventually, a quiet overcame the explosions and the crashing stopped, and we heard people starting to speak outside the office area there. . . . I heard Lieutenant Colonel Kelly stand up and say, "I guess this means we don't have to give our briefing this afternoon." And then I heard Colonel Ebener saying we need to get out of here, smoke is starting to come in. That's when Colonel Perrin turned to me and said, "Let's get out of here." We crawled out from underneath the table. There was a slight glow, so it wasn't pitch black. There was a slight glow from some monitors that were still running. When we crawled out from underneath the desk, nothing looked familiar. There was no door, just walls collapsed in around us. We didn't know where to go. We just heard voices to our front. So he said let's make our way out of here, and we started moving dry wall and other pieces of material and throwing them to the side.

I remember looking to the right and seeing a hole in what used to be his one wall and seeing smoke come in through there. I could smell the smoke and the fire. I could see a little bit of light coming in through that hole in the wall also. It seemed like very quickly we were through the wall, and we could see the rest of the office. It was then that people started coming through from our left. They were moving from our left, and out to an exit over to the right that somebody had found.

I saw a girl I remember from IMCEN. She came in, she was crying, and she hugged, I think, Colonel Perrin, and then moved on out of our office area. Another guy came through and I saw blood coming down his face, and his swollen nose—or swollen part of over his nose. I don't know who that was, but apparently people were coming from other offices that were down the hall and getting out through our area. Colonel Perrin moved out. . . . Lieutenant Colonel Kelly was coming through. He was coming from the area of my desk, and I was thinking that I needed to get my keys and my cell phone so I could contact family and eventually get home. And I asked him if there was anything left back there and if I could get back to our office area. He said we could give it a try.

I clambered back over material and I came down—I jumped off, I guess, the pile of dry wall and desk where I thought my desk was . . . I knew where my leather briefcase was, which had the cell phone and some other stuff in it. And I grabbed those and threw them over my shoulder and then got back up on the—I guess the dry wall and desk, and walked back towards the exit. There was somebody standing there [who] told me to climb up over the water cooler, and then go to the right, and climb back over the wall, which I did. . . . Once you got over the wall, you couldn't see where the ground was or where there was open area, and he helped guide me down with his hands and I landed on the floor. And then I could see daylight to the right . . . and I went back out in the hallway.

It was unrecognizable. All the ceiling tiles were down. Lights were kind of hanging haphazardly. There were wires all over the place, and, of course, rubble all over the floors. But, there, it was fairly light because the doors were open exiting the building. And so I went out our hall, and then took a left down the fifth corridor, and went out the building, which exits right near the helipad. And there was a uniformed officer there, a woman, pointing us over to the right, which is where we normally went on our fire drills. So I went over to that area and started locating people from our office.

M. SGT. MAJORS: Is that the most scared you have ever been?

MAJ. IRVIN: No, I don't think so. At the time I was very calm. I was not scared. I didn't know—you know, because at the time I thought it was probably just one bomb. It was in, it was over. I was very calm and collected. I was more scared as we joined litter teams and went back to try and get in the Pentagon because at that point you knew the danger you were going into if you went back in the building. And then in addition to that, they announced that there was a plane unaccounted for. A highjacked plane unaccounted for, and they thought it might be coming back to the Pentagon. So, I was more afraid after the initial explosion. I had gone out[side], and then I knew what I was getting into in having to stand there. . . .

Capt. Darrell Oliver was the Executive Officer to the Director of the Army Quadrennial Defense Review Office. He was interviewed in his Pentagon office by Sfc. Dennis Lapic of the 305th Military History Detachment on 31 October 2001.

CAPT. OLIVER: On the 11th, the day of the attack, my normal routine. I got in about 5:30, conducted PT. I got into the office . . . to see other office mates gathered around the television. And as I passed through the immediate office someone said that the World Trade Center was on fire. And I thought nothing of it. I thought, "Well, it's a fire and the fire department will put it out. It's nothing really significant." So I went to my desk. And I overheard my office mates a few minutes later say, well, it was an airplane. And I thought then . . . something is wrong, an airplane hitting the World Trade Center. And a few seconds later they said—the office workers said, "There's another airplane; it hit the second tower." And immediately we thought it was a terrorist attack. . . .

The janitor came into the office, as he normally does every morning. And the janitor has a hearing impairment. And every morning I would get up and greet him and we would converse. And as I got up to greet him that morning the blast occurred.

And everyone said they heard a sound. I did not hear a sound. I saw a flash of light because I suffered a head trauma—a head injury. I don't know if [it was] the safe next to my desk—the drawer, the safe drawer—or the falling debris, but a large object hit me on the left side of the head right above the eye and knocked me out. . . . I was unconscious for a few minutes, but I thought—my initial impression was—"They've hit us, too." And my next thought was, "I haven't taught my daughters everything that I want to teach them in life." Because I thought we were goners. I thought that we would not survive because we were on the first floor. And here in the Pentagon there are four floors above you. I mean, the blast—it wasn't like DESERT STORM. In DESERT STORM we received attacks—in fact, a SCUD hit within a few miles of our location in DESERT STORM. But we had early warnings. We had alarms. We had sirens. Sometimes we would receive grids to where the SCUD's impact was expected. And we could plot it on the map to see if we were in the impact area, and we could immediately evacuate the impact area. Here, there were no alarms, there was no alert, there were no sirens. The smoke alarm did not go off. Nothing went off.

I was literally and physically blind-sided, being knocked out with no warning. . . . It was almost as if everything was in slow motion, as if time had stopped. And for a few minutes, the debris was falling, and the walls just collapsed. The ceiling tiles and everything around us just caved in. And a few minutes later it stopped. And I thought to myself, "I've been given a second chance," you know? Because I thought I was—I thought we were—I didn't think we were going to get out of there.

And immediately I heard my desk mate next to me. Lieutenant Colonel Ebener called me and said, "D, are you okay?" And I acknowledged, "Yes, I'm okay." But I was still dazed and had—I could not see. My vision was blurred in my left eye. And when he called my name I started hearing others in the office sounding off, as if it was a roll call. Colonel Kelly was in the office at that time. He was calling names. Colonel Perrin was calm. There was a sense of calm in the office. It was as if we were responding to an attack in training. You know, as soldiers have trained around the world—every day soldiers train how to respond to an attack. You immediately get accountability, account for your injuries, account for your ammunition, account for your equipment.

We immediately started accountability, calling out each other's names, responding, asking if anyone was hurt, anyone was injured. The officers in that office were previous commanders. We have all commanded previously and have all been responsible for hundreds of soldiers, hundreds of troops. So it was remarkably calm in the office. The only abnormal occurrence was the secretary, Ms. Duckett. Understandably she was frantic. . . . And the janitor. The janitor has—he has his hearing impairment and he also has a speech impairment. And he was moaning loudly.

* * * *

But as I got up to my feet, my immediate thought was we got to get out of here. You know, we've got four walls [*sic* floors] above us. You know, the walls are going to come down at any time. And everyone kept reiterating, "Remain calm, remain calm. Everyone is okay. We're going to get out of here."

As I climbed up on top of the fallen walls, the debris, I saw Colonel Kelly at the top of the debris. The debris was so high that he was almost in a prone position and his head was only a few inches from the ceiling. And I climbed up beside the wall and got on the top of the debris with Colonel Kelly, and the side rail on the wall is what we were walking on. The wall is at a forty-five-degree angle. Our office wall has a chair rail, which is about two or three inches. We were walking on the chair rail of the wall trying to get to the top of the debris. As I got to the top, Colonel Kelly, who is a Special Forces officer, had a little Mag light—a small one-inch Mag light on his bag that he always carries with him. It was dark. And the only light we had was the light from his little Mag light that he had on his bag and one of the laptop computers—the screen was still on. But other than that light, that's all we had.

As I got to the top of the debris and saw Colonel Kelly at the top, believe it or not, throughout this tragedy there was still humor in the office. And Colonel Kelly remarks that, "D, at least I don't have to do that damn briefing today." Because he had a briefing he had to prepare for that day. And he and I chuckled about it for a few seconds and we started looking for a way out.

There was only one door to our office. We have no windows in our office. The inner offices of the Pentagon, as you know, some of them do not have windows. The door—there was no door. There was no way out. The only door that we had—it just wasn't there. It was just debris. The secretary in her outer office was blown into General Hartsell's office.

* * * *

Once Colonel Kelly, who was standing on top of the debris of the walls, identified a way out, Colonel Larry Dudney was on the other side. They found a way over the wall and down to the other side of their office. And Colonel Kelly started calling, "Come this way, come this way, just follow my voice, follow my voice." As I got to Colonel Kelly's location and I went—initially I went over to the wall to find where the voice was coming and, you know, to find the path out. And once I saw the way out, I still heard— all the time as this was going on—the secretary and the janitor . . . and you just weren't sure if they were injured, if they could walk or anything. I went back down the wall. And Colonel Perrin had gotten the secretary. He and Sergeant First Class Lindsay, who is [the] NCOIC [noncommissioned officer in charge] of our office, had pulled the secretary out from underneath of the debris and got her to my location . . . the point to go over the wall. And I kept telling her, "Des, it's going to be okay. I'm not going to leave you here. I'm going to get you out of here. Just calm down."

And again, humor comes into play. She says, "Hell, no, it's not okay. I'm not all right. I mean, it's not going to be okay, don't tell me that." It was as if she was angry. She was angry, which is not her personality. She was angry. I think she was angry that this had happened to her—not so much as if she wasn't going to get out of there, but she was angry. . . .

I didn't have time to debate with Desiree, so I said, "Hey, just get on my back." So I threw her on my back. I took her and threw her on my back and scaled the wall and there were two walls at 45-degree angles—the walls [had] just collapsed.

SFC. LAPIC: Forming a tepee.

CAPT. OLIVER: Forming a tepee. But in between that it was a hollow area, and in between the hollow area was the floor. But there was—I think it was a water cooler in between that, and it was shaky. But I knew if I could step on that water cooler and over the next wall, I could get out of there. . . . So I climbed up, climbed up the wall with her on my back. And I went over the first wall and stepped on the water cooler. And I didn't know if it was going to hold both our weight, but I just had to try. And I stepped on that water cooler and got over to the next wall. And once I got to the next wall, Lieutenant Colonel Dudney was on the other side of that wall, and I passed her off to him, Lieutenant Colonel Dudney, and he showed her the way out.

And all the time I was helping her over the wall, I kept hearing the janitor in the background, moaning. And Lieutenant Colonel Ebener, who was on the other side with the janitor, other side of the wall, was trying to calm him down. I went back over the wall, I went back to get the janitor. I thought if it worked for the secretary, it would work for him, too. I went back over the wall. And by this time the room was filling with smoke. I mean, people were coughing. Initially there was no smoke. But by the time I got back over the wall, the room was filling up with smoke. . . . And we knew we didn't have much time to get out of there. And Lieutenant Colonel Ebener kept saying, "Hey, guys, watch out for the wires." Because we were about three inches from the top of the wall, from the concrete floor, the floor of—

SFC. LAPIC: Above the suspended ceiling? Are all the wires?

CAPT. OLIVER: Exactly—the cement structure. And the wires were hanging because the lights were gone and there were naked wires hanging. And Colonel Ebener kept saying, "Guys, do not touch the wires. They're still hot. They're still hot."

So I went back down and the janitor was there. . . . And so I got him up and I said, "If it worked for her, it could work for him, too." So he was a little bit heavier than she is, but I placed him on my back and I got him over the wall. . . . I stepped on the cooler and got him over to the other side, and the others helped him out, helped him down and showed him the way out.

And as I looked back to go back over the wall, to see if I could help, Colonel Perrin said, "D, I think that's everybody. Just, you go and I'm behind you.". . . And Colonel Ebener and Major Dave Irvin were the other two—so then I went out behind those two. But the whole time, the last thing that I heard Colonel Perrin say before

I went over the wall for the final time was, "Is that everybody, is that everybody?" The whole time we just kept accounting for everybody. As we went out to the helipad and assembled outside at the helipad . . . we did another accountability. . . .

No cell phones were working. The network was down. After we got accountability, Colonel Perrin's first thought was, we got to notify the spouses because they're going to see this on television. We got to notify the spouses, let them know that we're okay. [Colonel Perrin] dispatched Colonel Kelly to his apartment there in Crystal City, which was within walking distance, to call on the landline from the phone, the telephone, call the roster, let the parents—let the spouses know that we're okay.

Once Colonel Kelly took off, we assembled and we started volunteering for litter teams to go back to pull out others. And it was amazing. I mean, the DPS—the Defense Protective Service guys—would say, "Hey, I need twenty volunteers," "I need ten volunteers," and a hundred people would volunteer.

[Maj.] General [Thomas F.] Metz, who is the deputy director, the vice director of the J–8 and Lieutenant General [Bruce] Carson, who is the J–8, who were on the other side of the building—on the other side of the Pentagon, away from the attack—were there on site helping and assisting before—I mean, before we even got out to the helipad. It was amazing. These guys ran from the other side of the Pentagon. General Metz was out there with no shirt on. He had given his shirt to someone. And it was amazing the cooperation. . . . And [it was] across the services.

* * * *

When we got out, we started volunteering for litter bearers. And [Brig.] General [William G.] Webster [Jr.] and I were on a team together. General Webster is the deputy director for training on the Army Staff. General Webster and I were on one team—we just paired up. And we were waiting for the firemen to let us go back in.

But then the fire was still going and it was too hot. The building was unstable in that area. And then the decision was made that the firemen would bring the individuals out. They weren't going to let us go in. They were going to bring the individuals out and then we could take them to the triage area. So our litter team, we received maybe—I think it was the first few casualties that came out—injured that came out. We received this one lady who was injured. She was a civilian lady and both her arms were—the skin on both her arms was gone. She had no skin on her arms. It was as if you had dirt on your arm, where if you brushed that dirt off, the dirt would fall off, that's the way her skin was. If you touched her, her skin would fall off. But we had to get her on the litter. As we put her on the litter—we had latex gloves on—I mean, her skin was coming off in our hands. But we got her on and we got her to the triage area, which was right there immediately by the helipad, where the ambulances were.

But then we got notified that, no, there's another plane inbound, we've got to move further. We've got to move further. So we had to take her over to a second triage area. And then the decision was made to get her underneath—and others—to get the injured in a tunnel, under a bridge. So we got her over to the bridge. And we waited there for a few minutes to see if the second plane was inbound. And about maybe ten to fifteen minutes later we saw an F–16 scrambling overhead and we knew that things were going to be okay, that there wasn't another plane inbound. And then we started going through the process of taking care of the injured and started forming teams with the medical personnel.

And we came back to the helipad. And they started asking for logisticians, quartermaster officers. And Major Irvin, Dave Irvin, and I were there and both being logisticians, we raised our hands. And they said, "You guys are in charge of the morgue." And we thought, "We don't know—we've never done grave registration. But if that's what we're tasked with, we're going to do it." So we started collecting the body bags and the gloves and the masks and started forming teams, with the chaplains, to start forming the morgue. And throughout that time, we moved from several locations. The authorities were unsure where they wanted the morgue. There was confusion about who was in charge, so we moved a couple times. And for hours, the firemen they just couldn't put the fire out and the fire just continued to burn. So we waited to get the okay to go in, you know, get the okay to collect up remains. And that time never came. So the FBI made the decision that if there was anyone in there to bring out, they probably would not be living, so they were just going to leave the remains in the building. So there was no need for the morgue team.

Some of the other individuals—Lieutenant Colonel Ebener and some of the others in our office—had been dispatched around to the courtyard of the Pentagon to work on bringing out remains. Lieutenant Colonel Dudney and Lieutenant Colonel Ebener were on that side. And after the morgue team disbanded, we went inside to the courtyard to see if we could further assist and join those teams inside. And the fire was still going and the decision was made by the FBI that, no, we're not going to—if there were any remains to be brought out, medical personnel would bring them out. . . .

And it must have been about eight-thirty, nine o'clock that night before we left. And I was still a little—a little dazed, it seemed like, from the injuries. But there were four nurses that had hitchhiked up here from Fort Belvoir, believe it or not, to assist. And they needed a ride back to Fort Belvoir. Their cars were there. They just caught the first thing in this direction to get here, to assist. And I live two miles from Fort Belvoir. I gave them rides back to Fort Belvoir . . . I got back to Fort Belvoir, was a little woozy but did not—I didn't think I required immediate medical attention, compared to others who were severely burned. And I dropped the nurses off and I went home.

And the next morning I went into the emergency room to be examined. And the doctor, he conducted eye exams and treated me for a head trauma and did a CAT scan. And luckily there were no bones broken. I still had a small irritation right below my eye. Most of that is gone now. Occasionally I'll still feel it, as if a nerve or something twitches, but other than that, I'm fine.

Capt. Lincoln Leibner worked in the communications office of the Office of the Secretary of Defense. He was interviewed in the Pentagon on 23 January 2002 by Stephen Lofgren of the U.S. Army Center of Military History.

MR. LOFGREN: So, were you here that day?

CAPT. LEIBNER: I was not supposed to be here. I was supposed to come in at ten o'clock at night for an evening shift. I had worked a swing shift the night before, [so] I was at home reading the newspaper. I have a very, very small TV in my study—I don't even watch TV because I'm a freak—but I was reading the newspaper. I never would have turned it on. A friend called me and asked me, "What was going on? What was going on?" The first tower had been hit. I remember I, Mr. Voice of Reason, I told her that the Empire State Building had been hit during the forties by a bomber and, you know, it happens, it's unfortunate. She was saying it was terrorism, it was terrorism.

I actually went upstairs to watch TV, literally I was in my boxer shorts and a T-shirt and I was watching the TV, talking to her on the phone saying the exact same thing; "It's unfortunate. I have no idea how they will put the fire out." But I was watching and that's when I saw the second plane hit. I knew exactly what had happened at that point. . . . I hung up the phone with her. I told her I was going into work. I called the shift. In fact that lieutenant that's sitting there now, Navy lieutenant, she was on and I told her I was coming in and she said fine. So, within—I mean, I've tried to do the math. I live downtown Washington, D.C. So, somehow, within, I guess it's thirty minutes from the time the second tower hit, I changed, shaved, put on my uniform, showered—obviously not in that order—and drove in. I can't attest to all traffic laws being followed but I made it to South Parking where I always park. There wasn't a spot that day so I started doing the Mall of America search. Of all the places, I ended up in lane one, South Parking, which obviously is the southern-most lane. I got out of the truck. Started running towards the building. I was running, not at full speed, but I was jogging, I was going to try to work my way [over], I never go in that entrance. I got to the very end of the lane, which is perpendicular to that corner of the building, when I heard jet engines. I assumed it was a flyover, a military flyover at Arlington Cemetery, which equated to what I was hearing. I grew up in Arlington so I know the flight paths very well, and it was wrong. And I turned my head slightly to see where the noise was coming and I saw the jetliner clear the ridge right by the Navy Annex coming down Columbia Pike.

From that moment on, I—one of the most remarkable things to me was that . . . I was completely lucid, completely understanding of the situation. I can't explain it. I never lost [it], never freaked. I watched the plane go in. As I was to later report to the secretary . . . a plane came in full throttle, wheels up, a controlled flight. . . . [I]t was flown into the building. . . . I was standing—I paced it off later—at that point probably 100 yards to the point of impact.

What I saw, again I could see actually through the windows of the airplane as it came past. It was that close. I knew what was happening. I remember being a little concerned at the time that other planes were also inbound because at this point I'd seen two planes, you know, hit the World Trade Center on TV and then the plane here.

Very loud noise, like no noise I've ever heard. I have heard artillery. I've heard rock concerts. I mean, I've heard every noise, you know, it was obviously the loudest noise I've ever heard in my life. . . . I stopped for a moment, obviously. There was no particular debris field, but there was in addition to the concussion, the noise, there was a very strong percussion of air movement. No blast, no particular fireball. People have said they saw a fireball. I did not. I ran towards the building. I cleared—there's a little chain link fence there. A little chain fence. I cleared that. There were some construction workers running past me. They were saying, yelling to get away from the building. I obviously come up to the building—at this point now the building is not on fire. . . .

MR. LOFGREN: Do you think one of the reasons you might have been particularly lucid was that you knew what was happening?

CAPT. LEIBNER: Oh, certainly. And through it all one of the incongruities . . . I'm not in my BDUs, I'm not in a theater of war. I was very aware. Just hyper aware. There wasn't a question in my mind what had just happened. Also of note on the scene was that there was no debris field per se. The grass was scorched. There were a couple cars that were on fire right down there. The limb of a tree was on fire at first, but the plane itself had disappeared into the building. There was not—it was not a plane crash situation . . . the plane had penetrated the building as certainly as a model airplane into a birthday cake. The building had not caved in yet, so it was still standing. Everything was looking essentially as it did, minus a rather large hole and blacked-out windows. I approached the building. There was a door that was completely opened; it was off the hinges, blackened. I went into the building and immediately heard people inside. Immediately came upon one woman who was badly burned but standing, walking towards the door. Got her out. I mean, she was walking so I placed my hand under her arm . . . the only place I could touch her. She was—skin was falling off her fingers, her arms. . . . And with the exception of her blouse which was still intact and the wrist watch, her dress was very badly burned and her stockings were still in part on her and off her depending on what was burned and what wasn't. But she was standing and she also was cognizant of that she was walking and that she was burned. Every single person we found in the building subsequently did not know what happened. It was a weird time to tell them a plane hit the building. I guess they were all watching CNN as well. I walked her out of the building and there was a DPS [Defense Protective Service] agent that pulled his cruiser up on the grass and I asked her if she could keep walking. She said she could and she walked towards the cruiser. I went back in the building and that's when I noticed how bad the smoke was. I felt, subsequently, completely stupid because I know we tell every single third-grader to get down on your hands and knees and walk, but I didn't. Again you could hear people in the building even though it was pitch black inside. They said they could see me. That was one of the freakiest moment, when I heard like teams of voices saying, "We can see you," and I couldn't see anybody. And I couldn't see anybody. Just could not, so I'd call out. . . .

There was a shaft of light from where the door was and I could hear people, but I couldn't see anything. There were two people to my immediate right inside the doorway that were trapped. The plane had entered above us, so the ceilings and all the building material that go into the ceilings of a building had fallen down and left a layer over desk chairs. There were two women there. They were basically tripping over each other. . . . They couldn't get out. So that was not hard, moved a section of paneling with some chicken wire—I don't know what it was, building material—and they stood right up and got out. I walked out of the building with them and—I couldn't breathe. I walked over to the fire truck. There was a crash engine right by the heliport, and the fireman—the back end of the fire truck was on fire, but there was a fireman inside trying to move the vehicle—salvage it, keep it—and the other firemen were telling him to get out because the backside was on fire and I guess the axle had broken or whatever. Helped them with, there were a couple of fire extinguishers. . . . Went back in the cab of the vehicle, tried to get the air masks because I wanted to go back in the building. One of the more remarkable things through all this is time. I always try to reconstruct time after the event and I can't figure how long I was.

I couldn't get—there was one air mask, air tank, whatever, behind the driver's seat and I could not get that off and then for whatever reason it's the *one* day I don't have my pocket knife on me. I don't think I've spent a day without my pocket knife in fifteen years and also a day I don't have my dog tags on me. I wear those routinely anyway and people always make fun of me. This would have been a good day to have them. I went on the passenger side of the cab inside the fire truck and was able to get the air tank off but there was not a mask that went with it. I talked to one of the fireman, we had words. He said it doesn't work without the—I remember all these conversations now because they were heated. I was kind of, I was angry at the fireman because there were a couple of them that were—that didn't seem to be doing a lot at the time. I look back on them, of course, they just had a plane fly into them so I don't fault them, but they were, I guess, pretty well stunned. At this point, I went back in the building, same door, same place, again trying to find other people, because I could hear the voices, and was essentially overcome by smoke. I could still hear people.

MR. LOFGREN: How far could you get into the building?

CAPT. LEIBNER: [*Gestures*] Maybe from here to that door. Not that far. Honestly, ten yards.

MR. LOFGREN: Was smoke actually coming back out now?

CAPT. LEIBNER: No, it was—you couldn't see and it hurt to breathe and I will admit to whatever fear I ever felt was that—it becomes a game with how far you're willing to leave the door. It's like spelunking or maybe, I've never, I've seen only in the movies where people go scuba diving underneath the ice. The idea of leaving your exit. So, I don't know how brave I was to go further. I was never scared particularly, throughout; to me everything was a variable. I can handle the smoke. I can handle the fire. I knew where the door was. I got scared after the fact when we were sitting on the grass. I had an air mask on me and then the building caved in. I must admit I never had considered that as a possibility. Anyway, I did leave the building at that point and walked outside. At this point now the building was basically in fire, in earnest. The cars had started to cook off. In the movies, everything explodes. There they were burning and when the gas tanks ignited they just spewed, they didn't explode. They just vented off their gas. . . . There was one person in the window, had come to the window trying to get out. This was all on the ground floor. I was able to get around to another broken window. I crawled up through the window, which was about chest high,

Maryann Ramos, a physician's assistant with the Pentagon's Civilian Employees Health Services, with Capt. Lincoln Leibner on the grass outside the Pentagon

chin high. Pulled myself up through there and worked my way back around. And I say work my way because, again, there's an amount of debris inside the building that had caved in, I mean the ceilings had caved in. Worked my way around and there was like a line of people trying to get out.

Some were hurt badly. Others weren't hurt at all. At this point there were some people who had come to the building and . . . I got into the building where some people were by the window and was able to grab people and lower them down to other people who were taking them out. Honestly, I never got anyone's name. One man was hurt. It was a man, a fifty-year-old, somewhere in that range, hurt very bad and something wrong with his leg, but also burned and totally in shock. Did not know what happened. There were like three or four women who were able to get down through the window that had crawled to that point. Heard people and they kept saying, "Don't leave us in here, don't leave us in here." We got them out and at this point, people were saying, "Get away from the building, get away from the building." And I lowered myself back out of the window and with a group of people walked away from the building.

MR. LOFGREN: Is this window in the area that collapsed?

CAPT. LEIBNER: Yes. I walked over to where they had set up basically a triage area right by [Route] 110—is that it? I don't know. . . . At this point there was an ambulance—great effort, general officers and privates carrying stretchers. Can't say enough for people at that point.

I couldn't walk because I had a lot of smoke in my chest there, so I got down on a knee. Someone brought me over an air mask and that's when we were sitting there on the grass, that's when the building came down, I think, at that point. Again, very loud.

I remember—I was in the grass there with people in various states of injury—that the Secretary [of Defense] had come down with his security detail. Had come down to inspect the site. . . . We were in the grass there and they were treating people and that's when the second moment I got scared. Somebody came over and said a second plane was inbound. I must admit I've never been in an artillery barrage. I don't know what that's like, but a very, very vulnerable feeling at that moment. I've never understood panic. I could sense it. . . . I tried to help people into an ambulance or a couple ambulances that were there. . . . It took about eight of us to get [one person] over the guardrail and into an ambulance. . . . They put me in an ambulance. I looked very bad for the wear. I did not need to be evacuated. I had burns on my hands and some cuts and a lot of blood on my shirt but it was other people's blood, I imagine. Passing people down through the window, I guess I got pretty [messy], so they thought I was hurt badly and I wasn't. I got put into an ambulance at this point and there were four patients in the ambulance, two paramedics, and a driver, so we were a little tight back there. Now that was kind of a neat moment . . . we set off for—the dispatcher told us to go to the George Washington Hospital. We got about, I don't know [*laughs*], twenty yards down the road, which at this point is packed with cars with sirens going. People were not moving out of the way and then the banter back and forth with the paramedics and the driver was, "Go anywhere you want. Just go, go, go." So the driver said, "We're going to try for Arlington Hospital." . . . We eventually made it to Arlington Hospital. Went right up through Rosslyn. I mean, it was, we hit three cars on the way. Yeah, it was a good little piece of driving there and I, I remember I'd love to see those guys in court. Because people were not getting out—

MR. LOFGREN: Cars were not getting out of the way so they hit them?

CAPT. LEIBNER: Yeah. Got to Arlington Hospital. . . . Arlington Hospital was doing a great job. They obviously cleared—I was seeing everyone say, "Cancel all appointments," that day, and they were bringing in everybody they could. I wandered out of my treatment room because they kept me in there. They wanted me to stay put and I went to the lobby because I wanted to watch the TV in the waiting room and that's when someone told me that the State Department had been hit and the Capitol. That was, that was probably the lowest moment. Again, I was fine. I wanted to get a call out to my father at that point, and I couldn't do it. . . . There was a pay phone, which I used. . . .

[Captain Leibner found a ride back to the Pentagon.]

I came back into the building. A DPS agent stopped me and I told them, I don't know, I told them "I work with the Secretary of Defense, I have to go back to work." And again, I must admit the theater looking back—no one's going to say anything to me, I'm covered in blood. . . . I came back into the building and there were two DPS agents going past on one of the carts, the electric carts and I thumbed them down and got a ride to the Secretary's office. . . . I got off by the Secretary's office, I ran back to where you saw me in Cables, came into work. Wanted to let them know I was okay. The guys in cables were fantastic. They were up and running. Obviously many calls. Sat down with Colonel Sweeney. . . . I didn't know it, the Secretary and the Vice Chairman were in the conference room . . . and I didn't realize at this point there was still sketchy information about what had hit the Pentagon. I got brought in to brief the Secretary. Again standing as close as we are right now, the Secretary asked me, after I told him what I saw, Was I sure? Was I certain? And, again, I was shocked that he was incredulous, but looking back, when he had seen the building, I don't think it had caved in. They thought maybe it was a Learjet or a private jet or a bomb. . . . I remember telling, "American Airlines," and . . . I said it was powered in. It was flown in; no one grabbed the stick at the last moment and pushed it down or anything. It was full throttle. . . . It was the first time I'd ever spoken with him. . . . I got brought back to Colonel Sweeney's office at that point, and he gave me a cup of coffee and he told me to go home. I asked permission to stay just because I didn't want to go home. So, I went to work. I stayed until about nine o'clock at night. 9:30. I got taken in to [V.] Admiral [Edmund P.] Giambastani [Jr.]'s office. He's the Military Assistant to the Sec Def . . . and he told me to go home. . . . I got to my car and at that point . . . it was dark out with the exception of Atlanta burning. I mean the whole building; the roof was in flames. It was clearly burning, orange. I can obviously see inside the car, the entire interior of the car was illuminated by the flames and as surreal as it was I got in the car and drove home. . . .

MR. LOFGREN: Okay, so we're sitting down and somebody from the Center of Military History is writing a book about this ten years from now. What thing would you want to make sure was in the account—a fact, an anecdote, an observation?

CAPT. LEIBNER: . . . Every single person that I pulled out of there was a civilian. . . . Obviously it's the Pentagon. It is the Headquarters of the United State Military. Every single person I pulled out physically was a civilian female, with the exception of one guy. I'm just saying, to me that was very difficult. . . . And it's a statement about the United States; how safe we are. That we don't know terrorism. That we don't know attacks. Other countries live with this. . . . I wish I did not see what I saw. A lot of people said, "All right, you know you're lucky you saw it or you're lucky that you were there." I would have preferred not to have been there.

Lt. Col. Victor M. Correa was a Reserve component personnel analyst with the Office of the Deputy Chief of Staff for Personnel. He was interviewed by Sfc. Dennis Lapic of the 305th Military History Detachment on 7 November 2001.

SFC. LAPIC: So, how did your day start off on the 11th?

LT. COL. CORREA: Walked in the office. Basically, turned the computer on, read through the e-mails and all that. And then outlined what I wanted to do for that day, which was basically the Reserve component's numbers, get the spreadsheets out, get the reports out. . . . Sitting in my cubicle when rumors started going around that the World Towers were attacked by an aircraft. . . . Major John Jessup looked at me and said, "You know, sir, we're as vulnerable as the World Towers. If they wanted to, they could hit us right now." Or something to those lines. And he hadn't finished saying that when the airplane attacked the Pentagon. First thing that I recall is, I got up off the floor. I was not at the same area that I [had been] when I stood up. I'm assuming that the blast threw me. I can't tell you if it was in the air or if it was rolling. I was on the floor and as I looked up, saw a ball of fire come over the head. This is happening within seconds. The windows that were in B-Ring, saw them go out and come in. . . . Like the pressure, the blast made the windows go out. And thank God that they invested, I heard, twenty-one thousand dollars in each window. So, that's what was their job was, not to shatter and spread debris and become projectiles. So, it did work. The roof started coming down, some of it. . . . The fire alarm system goes off and it said, "Fire has been detected in your area, please evacuate." The water sprinklers started coming down. As soon as the ball of fire retreats a cloud of smoke just dropped immediately. And I'm talking—I can't tell you if it was one second or half a second, but that's what I was able to [grasp] in that short period of time. It was all—like it was all together. I was already on my feet. And Mr. Moon that sat two cubicles away from me was on the floor crawling, half stunned or dazed. And I picked him up and threw him or led him. He says I threw him to where John Jessup was, so he could show him the way out. A civilian lady came out half dazed, so I took her and led her also to John. And then, he pointed her to the right direction. Because of the smoke and, you couldn't see, I started screaming. First of all, the folks that I saw around me, I told them, "Get out. Get out. Get out."

SFC. LAPIC: And which way did you tell them to go?

LT. COL. CORREA: Towards this exit, 2C450. Because the majority of them were to my right. And I turned to my right, and the cloud had dropped very low. So, I started screaming, "If you can hear my voice, listen to me. Focus on my voice. Come towards this way. There's a way out here. I can help you." And started yelling as loud as I could because I could not go into the smoke, or I could, but I couldn't go far because it was so thick and you really couldn't see, hardly see anything in front of you. And, I don't know how long I did that. But, a couple of seconds [later], more people started walking out of that. At that time, I felt that I had cleared the area of the folks that could make it out. I ran towards the exit and I looked to my right and there, there was a person that was badly burned, badly injured. So, between the four of us, myself, Major John Jessup, Captain Lance Gibbons, and Colonel [Karl] Knoblauch, we picked him up and we carried him to the A-Ring and dropped him. Left him there because there was a group of paramedics there. When I did that, I thought, "Okay. He's already taken care of. He's with a medic. They know what to do." And I looked and saw a lot of smoke filling the A-Ring, going towards the A-Ring. And I noticed that the fire doors had closed. And I knew there were still some folks out there. So, at the first fire door that I came to, which was on the A corridor, the A-Ring, I pushed it open and then I went to our corridor. And that fire door had closed, was closed. So, I went and, I don't know if I did it by myself, I don't know if there were other folks with me, I'm not sure. To this day, nobody has commented that they helped me or anything. I just opened it, and when I opened it, more people started coming out. . . .

I don't think they knew how to [open the door] because of the smoke, and I would assume that the smoke had already gone to probably ground level. They were just faced with this wall. And all they were looking for was an exit. So, I know that when I opened it, some folks were behind me, so they held it open. And then, I went in with some other folks. We were like bees. We knew there were folks that needed help. So, we started yelling some more. We took off our shirts off. . . . We soaked them in some water fountains that were nearby and put them around us, so, to help us try to breathe and block some of the smoke away. And again, we started screaming and we started going as far as we could to help folks come out. And we did that. From there, I remember ending up in the first floor towards the B-Ring.

SFC. LAPIC: How did you get there?

LT. COL. CORREA: Following another group of folks that were trying to help. We could not enter to where we wanted to go . . . the E-Ring, because of the fire and the smoke and the heat. I didn't see any fire at that time, just a lot of heat, a lot of smoke. And we couldn't—we thought that maybe we could find a stairwell that would get us behind the E-Ring and go up that way. So, we made the attempt. . . . And then when we looked there, we saw some huge gaps in the wall. I think that's where the aircraft had gone through [C-Ring into A-E Drive]. There were some folks that needed help. So, I think it was at that time that I helped them move a big dumpster towards a window so folks could climb down from a second floor, down to the dumpster to get out. Once I saw that was taken care of, I followed the other group and tried to get through other ways we could. . . .

Then, at that time, they were telling us that we needed to evacuate because there was another, a second aircraft incoming. And we were forcefully told to leave because of the second aircraft. We knew there were some folks back there and still wanted to attempt to try to get back there, but we just couldn't. Went to the Center Court. And again, we were told we had to leave the area. So, [we] went to the North Parking lot. . . . As I was walking, trying to find my section of folks that worked with me, people were coming up to me and asking me if I was okay. And I said, "Sure. I'm okay." And about the third or fourth person, I said, "Why do you ask?" And they said, "You've got blood all over you." And I said, "Blood? What do you mean?" And when I looked, there were blood stains with some other stuff on my shirt.

Lt. Col. Thomas Cleary III was the Chief of the Program Budget Analysis Branch in the Office of the Deputy Chief of Staff for Personnel. He was interviewed at his Pentagon office by Capt. George Dover of the 46th Military History Detachment on 1 February 2002.

LT. COL. CLEARY: I'm not sure exactly what I was doing when the plane hit. It knocked me to the floor, and all of the ceiling fell, lights swung down. I wasn't hit by any of that. . . . I can't quite remember whether it happened [then] or when I went back in, [but] I got wet. The sprinklers around me went off. The sprinklers around most everybody else didn't go off.

So I was knocked to the ground. I got up and went around the cubicle to look at a lady that worked for me. And I said to her, "Get out of here now," because somebody was saying, "Get down." I was thinking, "You don't want to get down. This is no place to get down. Glass is coming. You want to get the heck out of here." Number one, I had no idea it was a plane. Until I got outside I was thinking, "How the hell did they get a truck over the railing to get that close?" I honestly was thinking "Oklahoma City." It didn't connect in my mind. Two planes have flown in the World Trade Center. I didn't think there was another plane out there. It just—I had not made that cognitive leap that, "Oh, yeah, there is more of them out there." I thought it was a coordinated attack. And as I told people to get out, make sure they get out, my biggest concern was this is the first of a number of more explosions. . . . I thought this was the first of a couple of more that were going to hit us. That's what I was expecting. It didn't happen obviously. But, you know, that's what it was like around me.

Now you've got the people out. And, obviously, believe it or not, it was a very, for the most part, very controlled exit. . . . We got people out to the fourth corridor, and we saw everybody leave; and then, myself, Colonel [Roy] Wallace, and Colonel [Gerald] Barrett, went back in because we wanted to see everybody else had gotten out, that everybody was okay.

We went back in. I can't remember how far we went back in. This is where it gets fuzzy. I don't know if I went to an area where the sprinklers were working or not, because I'm the only one—if you saw my shirt, you could see where the smoke was and the water came out. And it looked like little, you know, little splotches of dirt. . . . But, anyway, we went out, and came back in, and we went in, and we yelled for somebody. "Is there anybody out there? Is everybody okay?" Something like that.

It was the eeriest, dead silence I have ever heard in my life. I mean that's what really struck me. And I guess that's because of the fire, and then oxygen is being sucked out of the air because there is no sound. It was almost like a vacuum.

And so, we waited for awhile, tried to penetrate a little deeper but you couldn't, because the smoke was just—smoke, it was a rolling current of smoke coming our way. So after a couple of minutes of trying to find out if anybody is—you know, we just didn't hear anything, not a sound, not a peep, just us. And we looked at each other and said, "Okay. There's nobody left here." Went out in the hallway, and that's when Lieutenant Colonel Brian Birdwell came stumbling down the hallway. And we picked him up. . . . he was severely burned. He's one of the last people to be released out of the burn unit in Washington Hospital. He was burned on his back, and most of the back of his body. . . .

You know, unfortunately for him, he was lying on his back, and we carried him on his back, and we didn't know that. Well, we saw his flesh come off. And, you know, it was pretty gruesome, but we carried him. We picked him up, carried him, and we tried to get out through the fourth corridor. This was the new wedge, and they had these fire doors that had come down. You have the fire door and you can't get through. It's like, "Holy s——t. This isn't good." So we cut through the B-Ring, and somebody had been—somebody from DMPM [Directorate of Military Personnel Management] or somewhere else knew that there was an exit from the B-Ring down up into the A-Ring. So, honestly, I had no idea. I thought, "How are we going to get out of here?" Guys were carrying Birdwell, and there are a couple of us trying to figure out how to get out of there. Come to find out later on that it was real easy. You could have just lifted the fire door, and it would have lifted up by itself, which we didn't know. . . .

So we made our way out to the A-Ring, and moved down to the fifth corridor, down by Redskins cafeteria, where we—somehow a medic showed up with a carrying board and we put Birdwell on there; and then, poor guy, he went into shock at that time. But they had started cutting stuff off of him and they evacuated him out.

What we did at that time, Wallace, myself, and a number of other people to include Colonel Karl Knoblauch, we tried to go back down the fifth corridor to get back into the DCSPER [Deputy Chief of Staff for Personnel] area, because Knoblauch said, "I have some people back there." He definitely knew he had people back there. So we tried to go down the C- and D-Rings to penetrate back into the area to try to get back in but we couldn't. The first thing you encounter was the smoke, I mean, completely dark smoke that was just overwhelming, in terms of trying to—you just couldn't breathe.

It's really sort of weird. You can breathe up until you hit it, and then the second you walk in you can't breathe. And that was a lesson to me that smoke kills you, just like that. It really, really does. Because you also start to panic and your blood pressure just shoots up because you can't breathe. And you back out, you get calmed own; you go back in, and then all of a sudden your body distinctly reacts to what is going on. So we kept trying to go in. We had taken our shirts off. We had T-shirts. We wet the T-shirts, wrapped them around our head.

That didn't do anything. You don't know what you don't know. But you needed obviously better equipment to try to get in there. By putting a T-shirt around your mouth with water in it, probably made it harder to breathe whatever oxygen you were trying to get into your throat. So we tried a number of times to break through the smoke to get to where we thought people were. And, at one point in time, I remember I got down to one door that was pretty bent and you could feel heat, significant heat on—there was clearly a fire on the other side—and really couldn't stay there very long.

And we even tried to crawl; you know the drill. You crawl on the floor, and everything else. The smoke was uniform from the top—from the bottom of the floor to the ceiling. There was no layering of smoke. . . . So we tried that for about fifteen or twenty minutes and didn't have any success, unfortunately, so we went back out and we looked at Colonel Wallace. . . . Colonel Wallace said to us, "Go try to get accountability [of] people."

We had no plan of where they were supposed to go. So it's sort of—it's just wandering, went out the fifth corridor, out to the North Parking, where you saw hundreds of people that were being pushed to the far side of Boundary Channel, next to the little channel by the harbor there, the little tiny harbor for Lady Bird Johnson Park. We saw all of those people. So we walked out there, and we walked through all of those people, walked over Lady Bird Johnson Park trying to just find our people. We had no success and we thought, "Well, we can't get back in the Pentagon. No one is there."

So . . . Colonel Barrett and I were going to go and try to get down to the Metro because we heard the Metro was at least running. So we got down by the river entrance to the Pentagon, and there was a call that went out to help—to have some people just bring in stretchers into the Center Court.

Barrett and I said, "Well, you know, we want to get back in there." We were right—right there where people were potentially killed. We didn't know what was going on, so we just wanted to get back in there and help. So we went back into the center courtyard. . . . From there we were paired off. There were groups of people that obviously—military/civilian, all different, you know, male/female, all different bunches of people just standing around put off into teams trying to, you know, just be of assistance somehow to get in to help people. I would say there are about a hundred people at least in there. And it's sort of funny because every time I planned [something], these calls [would] come out: "Okay. There is another plane." By then I had figured out it was a plane because we heard it on the news. . . . We were paired off and set up four-man teams. It was Colonel Barrett, myself, an Army major, and this Air Force NCO [noncommissioned officer]. We were sort of paired together. And they would pick us up and move us around the courtyard as they heard air threats coming in. It was sort of entertaining. "Okay. Everybody move over to this side." So, I mean, a whole blob of people would move over there and do whatever.

Now while we were in [the courtyard] . . . obviously people were frantic to get a hold of their relatives and their loved ones. So what people would do was once somebody would get through on their cell phone, once they did and talked to their family, they would just take the cell phone and hand them out to everybody else, have that person on the other end take the person's name, get the phone number and say, "Call, please let her know I'm okay." My wife got a call from somebody from Indiana, which was pretty cool. But somebody took the number and said, "I can't make that many phone calls. The lines are dead or whatever." They called Indiana. Indiana called back to my wife, which I thought was pretty cool. . . .

Firemen and the rescue guys started to stream into the center of the courtyard, so we were all sort of just standing around. Because, obviously, we didn't have the gear, the equipment to go in and try to rescue anybody. It quickly became apparent that we'd be recovering people or bodies.

So we are all standing around, and all of these fire guys were coming in. It was a beautiful, pretty warm day. These were the guys who were dehydrated. So a call came out for somebody to start filling—they broke open all of the machines, and water bottles, and started filling up because there is a little cafeteria in the courtyard. So Barrett and I just went over there and started filling up water bottles, emptying water bottles, and you know just keep busy, do something to contribute to what was going on, did that for about an hour.

I think around two o'clock, finally, somebody said, "We cannot do anything from this side." They moved everybody, and everything else, back outside. We walked through the first or second corridor. I can't remember which. There is an exit that goes out into the Pentagon parking lot on the South Parking [side]. Went out there, came around, all of us, and we were going to go . . ., to be stretcher bearers, or something like that. And it's interesting because I walked out, and then I knew we passed right by the lamp post that the plane had hit. It was just sitting there lying on the ground.

We went over there and we sort of milled about for about another half an hour, when I think it was [Lt.] General [John A.] Van Alstyne, an Army three star, said, "You guys, everybody here, I appreciate your help." With the Old Guard [3d U.S. Infantry] starting to stream in. . . . And, obviously, those guys were going to go in because they had helmets, and the gear to be able to go in there and do stuff. And we're clearly just a bunch of majors, captains, lieutenant colonels, and colonels, and civilians standing around in class Bs trying to do something. Well, he said, "I appreciate your help but go home to your family." So, that was essentially the word, and then we walked down to the Metro, got on Metro, and got on home.

Lt. Col. Brian D. Birdwell was the Executive Officer to the Deputy Assistant Chief of Staff for Installation Management. He was interviewed by Frank Shirer of the U.S. Army Center of Military History on 7 March 2002.

MR. SHIRER: What was on your schedule for the day on the morning of 11th of September?

LT. COL. BIRDWELL: There was nothing scheduled. For me there was nothing scheduled. Ms. [Janet C.] Menig [Deputy Assistant Chief of Installation Management] and Major General [Robert L.] Van Antwerp were across the street, at the Doubletree [Hotel], from the Pentagon, at the Garrison Commander's Conference. . . . So that's why only myself and the two ladies in our office were actually in the office at that point.

MR. SHIRER: Had you heard about the World Trade Center that morning, sir?

LT. COL. BIRDWELL: I had heard about it and, in fact, at the time we heard of the first one, we went into Ms. Menig's office and turned on her TV that she has on one of the network news channels and we watched the second plane hit the second tower live on TV.

MR. SHIRER: Where was your office located?

LT. COL. BIRDWELL: 2E486.

MR. SHIRER: That's the second floor of the E-Ring of the Pentagon.

LT. COL. BIRDWELL: Right, that's correct. Ms. Menig's office, her far wall bordered [Lt.] General [Timothy J.] Maude's office.

MR. SHIRER: And this was in the newly renovated wedge?

LT. COL. BIRDWELL: Right, that's correct.

* * * *

MR. SHIRER: What happened? You went to the restroom. Where was the restroom?

LT. COL. BIRDWELL: The restroom was in the fourth corridor, as you exit the doorway threshold from our office area into the E-Ring you'd turn right, walk through the path of the airplane, get to Corridor 4, turn left and then the restroom was about where the B-Ring would have been before the renovation. Then when I was done with the restroom I came out, walked back toward the E-Ring, took about five or six steps, that was when . . . the impact occurred. Of course, it blew just all kinds of stuff. So had I been any later going to the restroom I would have been walking across the path at the time of impact. Or had I been earlier I would have been walking past the point of impact to get back to my office. So I think that's pretty close to where I was.

* * * *

I remember it all, I never was unconscious during this until I actually get to Georgetown [University Hospital]. . . . At the time of impact, I had just stepped out of the restroom, turned right to go toward the E-Ring to make my way to [my office]. Four, five, maybe six steps out of the restroom, I hear the sound of a very loud explosion. In my number of years in the artillery community

I hadn't heard anything that loud. . . . I thought "bomb"—and why I thought bomb I have no idea why—even though I had watched what was going on at the World Trade Center with planes—in a nanosecond from the time I thought bomb then immediately I went from light and knowing my path—the A-Ring behind me, the E-Ring to my front—I went to, I was on my back struggling to get on my feet.

It was complete darkness and fire. I struggled for what seemed like an eternity, but, given my burns on my arms, it was enough time to have the third-degree burns but not too much time that would have caused the burns to be so severe as to cause amputation. So I don't know how long that would equate to—it would be a guess on my part because it seemed like forever—but a minute to two minutes that I'm struggling to get to my feet, determine where I am and then get to safety.

In that struggle you've got to—I want you to try to picture with me what this is like. The best way to describe it is an earthly hell and I don't mean that just because of the fire—I've been a Christian since I was ten—so it's like a hallway and then in just mere moments it's pitch black, smoke. I can taste fuel on my mouth or at least the vapor of it. It's complete darkness, I'm on fire. The only light around me is fire. I have no orientation as to the direction I need to travel and I know I'm in a really bad situation because I've got bad burns and I've got very little time to make my way out of the building or make my way to safety within the building.

So as I'm struggling with those physical aspects I'm struggling with emotion as well of—the physical pain of the burns but the emotion of the abject panic in my heart that I cannot find my way out of the building. That, of course, leads to the realization that I was dying at that moment. When people tell you that their life flashes before them in that moment, it's not your life that flashes before you in the sense of the tape of your life of your history flashes before you. It's really more things that are dearest to you that flash before you. I made the realization that that morning was the last morning that I would say goodbye to Mel or see Matthew [Melanie Birdwell, his wife; Matthew, his son]. And at that moment I cried out for my God: "Jesus I'm coming to see you."

Shortly thereafter, exhausted from the struggle, I did what military folks aren't trained to do and that's I gave up. And from a physical perspective it happened, but from a faith perspective—I had a friend of mine I was telling this story to who visited me in the hospital. He said, "Brian, you didn't give up, you just stopped trying to save yourself and let God take over." At which point I had collapsed to the floor still having no orientation to where I was. I knew I was in the fourth corridor, don't get me wrong. The part of the building I was in had not collapsed yet and I don't think it ever collapsed according to the engineer who's doing the study for the redesign of the wedges. But I collapsed to the floor and had no orientation as to what way is the A-Ring, what way is the E-Ring. If I do make it to the E-Ring—if I make it to a wall, is it the E-Ring wall or is it the corridor floor wall? I had no idea. But as I'm lying there on the floor waiting for whatever that experience is of the soul leaving the body, my eyes still closed, I'm breathing but it's choking me and stuff like that and the taste of fuel is very much on my lips. I can feel liquid going down my face and it takes me a bit of time to realize that's water. I had 60 to 65 percent of my body burned and a good chunk of that is on the backs of my lower legs, my back. The third-degree burns are all on my arms and one very small portion of my back right calf; the remainder of my burns are all second-degree burns. So it's 40 percent third degree, 20 to 25 percent second degree, equaling to 60 to 65 percent of my body that's been burned. I had flash burns on my face.

So it takes me a bit of time to realize it is water. I don't feel it on my back or on my legs, only going down my face. Because I'm lying close to the floor and the sprinkler system having engaged I'm now able to [know] one, I'm not on fire, and two, I can see down the corridor floor some light close to me. But I can see further down the corridor floor so I now have directional orientation as to the direction I need to go toward the A-Ring. Then of course, third, it's not my last day on earth as I thought was the case just moments prior.

Because of the concussion my inner ear is still way out of whack and I do not rise to my feet and calmly walk to the corridor. I struggle to get to my feet and I'm stumbling as I'm going down the hallway. Now, Colonel Wallace . . . says that he and some other gentlemen out of DCSPER in the new wedge had come out of the B-Ring and they said that they saw me walk out of the smoke and saw how badly I was burned. I came towards them. I fell before they got to me and then they picked me up and carried me through the B-Ring to where what used to be Redskins' snack bar and the Korean War Memorial hallway meet in that foyer area or whatever where you can take the stairs outside to the courtyard.

That area was being used as a triage center. They carried me to that site. I asked [Lt. Col.] Bill McKennon, who's a friend of mine. I knew Bill, we had gone to Leavenworth that school year '99 to 2000 and had some classes together, and then our lockers in the POAC [Pentagon Officers' Athletic Club] were pretty close to each other and on those occasions where we had to do PT in the morning or afternoon that we'd see each other, we'd sometimes do PT together. So Bill and I knew each other. I know him and what he looked like and I was telling Bill to call Mel. Bill had to look at my uniform nametag to see my name to tell who I was, that's how badly my face was burned and then all the crud that was all over me from the pieces of the building that had gone to ash and other stuff like that.

The areas of my body that were not burned were for the most part my thighs around the entire circumference of my thighs, my frontal torso area and my feet. When I was laid down on the floor, I was beginning to shake. I knew the onset of shock was coming just by how I was shaking so badly. At this point I'm still feeling some pain but my body's mechanisms were dealing with that for the most part. I was really more concerned at making sure that Mel knew I was alive and I was telling anybody who would listen her name and phone number, "Tell Mel I'm alive. I'm hurt but I'm alive."

Very shortly thereafter after, I'd been laid down on a blanket or something was placed underneath my feet. I don't remember the colonel's name but he was out of the Air Force Flight Detachment . . . he came down and was asking me questions about if I had any—was there anything else wrong with you, Brian, besides the burns that I could see. I said "I don't think so. I don't feel any punctures, I don't feel any flying debris injuries or anything like that." It was just predominantly the burns.

Shortly thereafter he took my shoes off—I was wearing my leather shoes that morning. He took my shoes off and placed an IV line into my feet, I think it was my right foot, and started to provide me liquids and morphine because the good colonel had brought his Go bag with him. . . . So the doctor talks to me, they're cutting parts of my pants off. My shirt was pretty much left intact. I'm soaking wet from having collapsed under the sprinkler system. They say I smell like fuel and they're concerned that my wetness is from fuel. I told them that I had collapsed and [was] pretty confident it was under the sprinkler system and not fuel from the fire, that they smelled the vapor but it's not the liquid itself because otherwise I would have been a complete blaze. If what on me was wet had been actual fuel at the moment of my burns I would have just been completely engulfed and water would not have put that fire out.

So shortly after, the little golf-cart-type things that they used as ambulances inside the building, one got to me. . . . It got to that site and there were about four or five people I think around but they placed me on the body board first and got me outside first through North Parking toward the DiLorenzo TRICARE Clinic. Through those doors was how I got from the second floor down to the first floor and then out of the building out to North Parking. So I knew that at that point and time with those people there I was the most badly injured of those people around. They got me out through the POAC exit to the building. I was taken down to where you can catch a cab at North Parking just west of the parade field there that they use for diplomatic or other military ceremonies associated with diplomatic visits.

I was taken off of the ambulance but was on one of those rolling gurneys that roll you onto an ambulance and take you off of it to get you in emergency or other services. I was lying there out in the daylight and there are people yelling there's another plane coming, there's another plane inbound, get away from the building. So at that point the Air Force tech sergeant, Sergeant [Jill] Hyson—who was with me from the time of evacuation out of the building and then she got in the vehicle that eventually carried me to the hospital—she's with me and another lady, Natalie Ogletree, who had been praying with me and for me through the time that I was placed at the triage site to the time I'm out in North Parking. They moved my stretcher, gurney, from the sidewalk area where you could have pizza dropped off or whatever coming into the North Parking facility.

As the Defense Protective folks were saying move away from the building as far as possible, they pulled me across the street and onto the grass area that overlooks the marina that's part of the inlet of the Potomac right there, the marina area. I don't have any idea how far we went. I think we got very close to Ladybird Johnson Park, that wooden boardwalk that crosses over to that park if y'all are familiar with it. We were over there in some capacity. But I remember my face is facing up. Thank goodness Natalie was there—I think it was Natalie or somebody else—that had an umbrella and was able to shield my eyes from the sun because it's really hot out there. . . .

It became readily apparent that an ambulance was not going to be forthcoming on the north side of the building. At that point I do not recall the lady's name who was asking people . . . [for] a large enough vehicle [for me]. I had one person with a Ford Explorer try to get me in. I would not fit because I'm on the body board and the body board would be sticking out of the back of the Explorer. . . .

Captain [Calvin] Wineland, when he was approached, he said, "Sure, I'd be happy to take you." I don't remember what they had in the back of his Excursion or vehicle, but it was chucked out onto the grass. They brought the car up to me where I was, took me on the body board off the gurney, put me in the back of the truck. Sergeant Hyson . . . she's the medic, and then Major John K. Collison who is out of the ACSIM [Assistant Chief of Staff for Installation Management] Plans and Operations Division, he came over. Because I had all the ladies around me, they couldn't pick me up and get me in, so he and a couple of other folks came over because they could see they were trying to get this person that's hurt into the back of the vehicle. Of course I'm barefoot because my shoes are off and that is where the medics and the doctor at the triage site had placed my toe tag that said what the nature of my injuries were, what medical items they had provided me, the morphine or otherwise, and it had my name on there. And as John's helping me get put in there he looks at the toe tag—he didn't recognize me—and it says Lieutenant Colonel Brian Birdwell, and then John gets in the vehicle, he says, "Oh my gosh, that's Colonel Birdwell." So he gets in and I'm lying in the back of this Excursion. John is on my left, Sergeant Hyson is on my right, and my head is towards Captain Wineland driving.

After what could only be described as a very wild ride over sidewalks, other things to get around traffic. I don't know the exact path we took to get there. Again, I'm just looking at the top of the upholstery in the car, but we did go across Key Bridge to get to Georgetown University Hospital. That happens to be where Sergeant Hyson works part-time as a civilian medic. And that's the only hospital she knew how to get to, that's where we went. I got to Georgetown and we came up and pulled into the emergency room area. I don't know that the hospital ever got a call saying I was coming. I think it was just knowing what had happened, all the local hospitals were, "Okay, we're going to start getting mass casualties, let's get ready for it."

So when I got to Georgetown I was the first person there. I also was the only person they saw so I had the full attention of the medical staff there. They took me on the body board and put me onto the gurney with it, rolled me into the emergency room. John went in with me, I had asked him to. When they got me in there, there were all kinds of activities going on. There are only three things I concentrated on a lot when I went in there. One, Dr. Williams, the attending physician—this is the Lord's hand in this—he had spent a year of residency under Dr. [Marion] Jordan over at Washington Hospital Burn Unit. So from a medical perspective of being familiar with burns, I was in the best emergency room care available. And Dr. Williams told me, "Brian, you're very badly injured but we're going to clean you up and get you ready for the best medical care available and I'll be back in just a moment." And I said okay.

At that point I'm still in charge of my faculties and you're going to understand why here in just a moment. I asked John, he was standing off to my left still, that I wanted him to take the ring off my finger. It took several layers of skin. I shouldn't say it took skin, it was more like wax. It was like melted wax. It wasn't like taking a ring off a finger. But it didn't hurt; I sat there and watched him take my ring off, give that to Mel, and tell her that I love her.

Just having gone through all this still I still knew that God was sovereign and that maybe my whole purpose in arriving to the hospital alive was so that people that I encountered from the time of the explosion to the time of my possible death in the emergency room would be a witness for what God can do. So what I was doing was making peace with Mel so that in the event that after anesthesia was applied if I never woke up again I knew that John Collison would tell her that and hand her my ring.

So after John took my ring off I asked him to make sure that—I want to talk to the hospital chaplain. The lady that—I don't recall the exact faith, I don't care. She's Christian, that's all that mattered to me. I'm not Catholic and I wasn't really worried about last rites but something that would be in that same vein. I asked the chaplain to say one final prayer because of course through this whole process Natalie had been praying with me and John and Sergeant Hyson had been taking care of me and I was praying as well on my own. But just in case the Lord was going to take me after I was under anesthesia—he knows what he was doing, but I just wanted to let him know that okay, Lord, it's okay with me. But that I was at peace with Mel and that whatever his will for my life was that that would occur. And then afterwards the chaplain said, "Christ is with you" and I said, "He sure is." And that's when I looked at Dr. Williams and said, "Okay, let's get on with it." Then shortly thereafter I was conked out. . . .

And then just a real brief summary, I spent the next twenty-six days in intensive care on a respirator going through a number of débridements and then on October 4th I went from intensive care to step-down care, where you step down to a lower level of intensity care. And I spent the next eight-something weeks there, got released from the hospital December 5th, I came home for good on December 14th. Between the 5th and the 14th I stayed at the hospital's hotel except for that one Saturday night and then that weekend. Then I've had two follow-ups in January and February, still going to physical therapy three times a week and I expect about a year from now I'll have a final cosmetic surgery of some kind to correct some of the facial scarring and my ears. And then on my neck I have what looks like a hanging scar.

And I probably have a few other surgeries between now and that cosmetic surgery to correct some orthopedic problems and some things, what's called adhesion of the skin to the muscle in both my wrists. And [I] continue to let people know what God has done for me and I think the Army's been good to me as well through this whole process.

Melanie Birdwell, *wife of Lt. Col. Brian D. Birdwell, was interviewed at her home by M. Sgt. Donna Majors of the 46th Military History Detachment on 7 March 2002.*

MRS. BIRDWELL: I home school. Matt and I were doing history that morning, and a friend had called and said, "The World Trade Center has been hit by a plane." So we turned the TV on and watched that for just a few minutes and then turned it off and went back to doing school, which is really very odd for us. Generally, we would have just been absorbed in it, but we just—just felt like I needed to turn the TV off and did that.

And we went back to doing school, and then one of my neighbors called probably a half-hour or so later and said, "Do you have your TV on?" I said, "No." She said, "Well, the Pentagon has been hit." So I hung up with her, turned the TV on, and immediately they're showing the helipad. And I knew that Brian's office overlooked the helipad, so Matt and I just sat down, and we prayed, prayed that Brian was out getting somebody a tuna sandwich, anything not to be in his office at his desk. Matt was trying to reassure me, "No, mom. Dad's office is on the other side of the building. It's not by the helipad." And I was like, "Okay, honey. I hope that you're right."

I called a friend and asked her to come and be with me, and she came over just as I got the call from the wife—or the husband of a lady who had been leaving the building, the Pentagon, when it was hit. And as she left her office she saw Brian lying on the floor being triaged. And so she went over to him and stayed with him and prayed with him until they took him outside the building to get him to an ambulance. . . . Her husband is the one that called me and said, you know, "I don't know anything except that he's on his way to Georgetown Hospital, and he's alive." So we did cartwheels. We were very excited. I called Georgetown and talked to the emergency room doctor there. Brian was there already. They'd already initially evaluated him and said, "He's got a very serious inhalation injury. He's got some severe burns," and that I need to get there as quickly as I could.

So I ran outside to ask my neighbor who had called me if her husband was home to see if he could drive me—because he's active duty also—drive me to Georgetown because I didn't know how to get to Georgetown, and I knew I was not in a condition to be driving either. So he wasn't home yet, and I turned to come back thinking, "Now what am I going to do?"

I turned to look at the opposite end of the sidewalk, and there's a sergeant major that lives at the end of the sidewalk, never met him before, had only lived there, like, a month. And he's standing outside his truck talking on his cell phone. So I go running up to him. I'm like, "This is who I am. This is what's happened." I explained to him, I said, "Can you take me to Georgetown?" He said, "I don't know where Georgetown is, but yes, I will take you."

So he ran in and changed his clothes, and I came home and got my tennis shoes, and off we went. It took us about two hours to get to the Key Bridge, and, when we got there, it was closed. So I got out, and I started just running across the bridge, and I ran for probably a mile and a half and was able to flag down a D.C. police officer to take me the rest of the way.

I got to Georgetown, and one of the nurses who had initially been treating Brian was there waiting for me, one of the doctors, and they walked with me the whole time to prepare me for what I was going to see and said, "The first thing you need to know is your husband told us at least fifty times `Tell my wife I love her.' You're not going to recognize him. He's extremely swollen. He's swollen past recognition in some cases. He's very, very badly burned. We've done some debridement on him to get the immediate burns off of him. We're in the process of getting permission from the FAA to open airspace to medevac him to the Washington Hospital Center to the burn unit."

They just prepared me all the way up there. So I got there and put gloves on and the mask, and everything, because it was a very sterile environment, and went in, and they were right. I mean, I knew it was Brian, but he was—his head was so swollen it was almost the same size as his shoulders. It was just—you know, he's skinny, skinny anyway, I mean, he's just a teeny tiny little thing. He was as white as a piece of paper. He was so white because they've had to take all the burned skin off of him, and he was bandaged. He had already been sedated, so he didn't know I was there. And it was—oh, it was just like the most horrific baseball-bat-to-the-stomach moment I've ever had in my life. It was just—oh, it was horrible, but he was alive, and I was thankful for that.

We waited about probably an hour and finally got permission to medevac him to Washington Hospital Center. So the Georgetown security folks drove me over to Washington Hospital, and they medevaced Brian over, and he was there for twelve weeks and a day.

M. SGT. MAJORS: Was his condition critical—

MRS. BIRDWELL: Critical, yeah. Extremely critical, yeah.

M. SGT. MAJORS: So even, you know, when you called and they said, "Get there right away," I'm sure it was—there's an extreme possibility he might not make it?

MRS. BIRDWELL: Oh, very much so. Yeah. Yeah.

M. SGT. MAJORS: Did you realize that at the time?

MRS. BIRDWELL: No. I had no clue. That's one of the blessings in all of this is God did not allow me. He allowed me the gift of ignorance to not really understand how critical Brian was through a lot of this, because I don't think I could have handled knowing exactly how close to death he was.

The night it happened, eleven o'clock that night, I get a fax from Walter Reed telling me that I have to medically retire Brian because his death is imminent in seventy-two hours. Well, this is the first time anyone said this to me. Yeah, this is the first time anyone said to me that his death was imminent. And so, you know, I'm not the—I'm not, like, a very medically smart person, so at this point I said, "Okay. Who said his death is imminent?" And they said, "Well, it was Dr. Jordan."

And I said, "Okay. Well, I don't know who Dr. Jordan is, but I want to talk to Dr. Jordan." And so Dr. Jordan, thankfully, was just coming out of surgery and was able to talk to me. He said, "You know, that's not information that we've given them. We don't say that death is imminent ever unless we know for sure." He said, "I don't think Brian's going to die." He said, "He is very critical, but I do not think he's going to die. I think he's going to live." And one of the other surgeons, I was talking with him, and he said, . . . "I think his chances are sixty/forty, sixty-five/thirty-five." And to me, at that point, you know, it felt like great odds. I mean, in retrospect, okay, they probably weren't the greatest odds, but they were working for me then. He said, "You need to get on the phone and ask the tough questions." Well, I didn't have a clue what questions I needed to ask.

So I just sat down and I prayed about it, and I just knew, knowing Brian, because he is a soldier to his soul, that if I were to medically retire him—because I knew in my heart he was going to live—if I were to medically retire him, I was going to have to go in his room three weeks later or two weeks later when he was better and say, "I medically retired you." And I didn't want to face him and do that. So I said, "You know what? I don't care what the financial benefits are. It's not worth it to me to medically retire him. He's going to be fine, and we're not going to do this." So we proceeded from there, and we did not do that. . . .

His boss, General [Robert L.] Van Antwerp [Jr.], is the most awesome godly man, and I am so thankful that God gave him to me through this because I—many times I've cried on his shoulders.

The day—the night it happened, three in the morning, the Surgeon General was walking through the burn unit and I was in there with Brian, and he said, "What can we do to help you?" And I said, "I need an active-duty person here to hold my hand," because this was right after the medical retirement thing.

You know, they're throwing all these numbers at me, and I'm, like, "I don't understand this. I am not in a position mentally to comprehend what you're saying to me." And so I said, "I need an active-duty person to hold my hand." Ten o'clock the next morning there's an O-6 from ACSIM standing there, and he stood there with me and held my hand for weeks.

I mean, to this day if I need something I can call Dave Rhodan and say, "This is what I need." Unbelievable support. On the 12th, his other boss, Jan Menig, she's an SES [senior executive service], calls me: "What do you need?" I said, "I need mousse, and I need deodorant." She's there with this huge bag of goodies stuff. They were at the hospital every day. If they weren't at the hospital, they were calling me several times a day to make sure everything was okay. They were incredible, incredible through all of this.

Brenda Hirschi was Chief of the Military Personnel Division in the Army Budget Office, Office of the Assistant Secretary of the Army for Financial

Management. She was interviewed at Jefferson Plaza II in Crystal City, Arlington, Virginia, by Stephen Lofgren of the U.S. Army Center of Military History on 12 October 2001. Also present was June Kronholz of the Wall Street Journal.

MS. HIRSCHI: On that day—on the 11th of September—I had two jobs. I had two offices. . . . I was on the third floor in the seventh corridor, A-Ring, until about 9:30, and about 9:30 I went into my second office, which was 2D461. And I had a staffing action that I needed to talk to one of my staff about. As I was going down the hall about 9:30 that morning, I looked up and I saw [Lt.] General [Timothy J.] Maude [the Deputy Chief of Staff for Personnel] coming up the corridor and as he went into the men's room, I went into the women's room. And that—I was probably one of the last people to see General Maude. . . .

Fortunately, I had two people recently retire, and three of my staff were on leave that day. I hadn't been down there yet, so I didn't know that some people had not come in that day. . . . Normally, there are eight or nine within that office. But on this particular day, I didn't know that everyone had not come in that day. So I went into the office. As I was going in the door, one of my staff, Dave Jacobini, said, "Brenda, have you heard about the World Trade Center?" And I had heard somebody mention it, but there were so many things to do that day that I just really wasn't focusing on it. I thought, you know, it was a little commuter plane that had accidently hit the World Trade Center. And he says, "You know, I'm going to go over now to another office to watch CNN to see if I can catch some news on this," and that was really quite fortunate, because the area . . . where his desk was . . . was not there after the crash.

So I went in, put my bags down, and then I had the staffing action that I needed to talk to Joan about. Joan was one of my staff, and as I was standing there, we're getting very close to 9:38. As I was standing there waiting to talk with Joan—I was waiting for her to get off the telephone, and all of this is kind of like slow motion now. A cable service technician walked into the office and he's got a little ladder in his hands. He walks in and he goes over to the side and he's working up in the ceiling. And Joan's on the telephone and she says to her husband, "You know, Ronnie, that could have been the Pentagon." And the instant she said that, the explosion occurred, and it literally knocked the senses out of you. You cannot even fathom how it—how it shook you, you know, it's just—every fiber of your being was being shaken, and everything is, everything is very unstable. The lights came down. The cables came down. The ceiling tiles all just fell all around us. And then when—I mean, it was like—I think there was some time there—I mean, probably seconds, that I can't—I mean, I couldn't think at all. I was just frozen in place and numb. And when I looked up, I couldn't see anywhere. We had these lights that were supposed to come on, but I don't believe they came on. It was just—it was just surreal, because there's stuff still just floating down. Stuff just coming down. And you could see shapes, but you couldn't see—that's what you could see, you could see the shapes of stuff.

The cable technician came out. He comes out and Joan stood up and we're like, you know, what do we do now? And all of a sudden, there's like a flash and you could see the fireball up there. You could see the flames, because I mean there's nothing up there now. We were really, really, really blessed because in that particular area there was a huge bay. But before we had moved over there, I had insisted that for my work section, that we have walls around us, and that's why, you know, we didn't get burned, because those walls were up there. They provided enough protection for us.

So, I believe I was the first person out the door. I was the nearest. And I went out to go out as I would normally go— and you've got to remember, we had just moved in there in June, the end of June, first of July. I was working two jobs. So I hadn't been down in that area that much, and I knew of one way to get in. So I went over to the door and the door wouldn't work. You couldn't get out that door, and so—there were other people over there, too, trying to get out. You just can't fathom the absolute terror that you can't get out, you know? You can't get through that door. So the cable technician—I don't think he said anything, but we knew that he knew where to go. It was like, Joan and I grabbed—at some point, early on—Joan and I grabbed each other's hands and we didn't stop holding each other's hand for two hours, or maybe even more than that. And we knew that if we followed this guy that we could get out of there. So he took us and he followed along these cables, and he took us up a way that I hadn't been. And we came over— you know, you've still got to remember, you can't see anything. You can see forms, but you can't see anything, and there's just debris and stuff everywhere and fires going. And so he took us over, and there's an area there, that people were just huddled up, and not everybody could go through this door. There's a door there, because—what I didn't know then—see, I didn't know what was going on—but I've later learned that there was this firewall that came down. So all of us were there . . . and you've got to have a particular access [card] to get in this other door. And Colonel Mark Lewis was there, and Colonel Mark Lewis could get us in. So he took us in there, and then we were able to get out into the A corridor.

I never saw the cable technician again. Joan never saw him again. I know he had on a blue T-shirt. But nobody's ever seen him again. Nobody knows who I'm talking about.

So anyway, Joan and I got out and . . . we're just in this mass of people. We're just like in a group reacting, and we end up out in the center courtyard. See, at first, I thought Jim, one of my other staff, was there in the office. I thought he was in there, and Joan assured me, no, Jim had not come in that day. And we knew that Dave was somewhere watching TV, so, you know, we looked for a couple minutes out in the courtyard for Dave and we couldn't find Dave. And so we're standing out there trying to figure out what we should do next, and somebody near us said, "You know, there's a second plane that's hit the World Trade Center." And then somebody else said, "And there's another plane that's coming to hit the Pentagon." See, I didn't, until that moment, put it together, that we were being attacked by these planes—that the terrorist attack involved planes. I didn't even make the connection until that point.

And then, when that happened, when we heard those two pieces of information, Joan and I looked at each other and we said, "The last place we want to be here is in this courtyard." So she and I ran, like you can't believe, and we got out of there and we came over into Crystal City. Joan lives over here in Crystal City, so we came over. We had nothing. We had no keys, no money. We got nothing with us. We came over to her apartment building and she asked for her key. So we went up to her apartment on the 14th floor, and we had just gotten in there, and they came around and they told us they were afraid that there's another terrorist attack coming and we needed to evacuate the building. So here we are, we're running again, like the devil, running again. We get downstairs in the lobby and then they start, "Well, what are we going to do with you now?"

What do we do at this point? Then the apartment management said, "You know, you're not safe outside, either, if you're not safe in here." So this woman came up and she told us, she said, "You can come up to my apartment," because we needed to use the restroom. She says, "You can come to my apartment." She was on the fourth floor. So we went up there and we stayed at her apartment about two hours.

Now remember, Joan was on the phone talking to her husband and the last thing that he hears is this crash and the screams, so her husband is frantically looking for her. So Joan's husband had been searching for her. He had gone out, you know, on a bike and he was looking all around, and so he was so thankful to find her.

Then about twelve o'clock I asked them—I said, "Can I borrow a bike?" And I borrowed their bike and rode the bike home. So that's how it happened. And all the way home—which is Mount Vernon—I was thinking, "You know, I haven't eaten nearly enough ice cream. I'm going to stop denying myself. [*Laughing*] Life is short. I must eat more ice cream."

Maj. David J. King Jr. was Facilities Manager of the Office of the Deputy Chief of Staff for Programs (DCSPRO). He was interviewed at the Pentagon by Capt. George Dover of the 46th Military History Detachment on 22 January 2002.

CAPT. DOVER: Let's talk about the attacks. When did you become aware of the attacks on the World Trade Center?

MAJ. KING: I guess it was about nine o'clock, somewhere around there I'd been walking through the building or out in the center area, and I heard that the first tower had been hit by an airplane. I came back in, and a friend of mine working in Nigeria had just sent me an e-mail, and I sent him [one] back, and said, well, one of the towers of the World Trade Center—a plane crashed into it. At the time, no one considered that that was a terrorist act. I was thinking, you know, some guy in a Cessna had a heart attack and crashed into it. I walked down the hall to another office that had a TV, and was watching the TV when the second airplane crashed into it, and the camera angle was such that you could see the second airplane hitting the second tower. And I told the guy I was with, "This is a terrorist act. This wasn't some accident." Went back down to my office. It just happened the guy from Nigeria wrote back and said, "What's going on? We don't get any news." And I saved a copy of the e-mail. I typed back to him: "Second plane crash, terrorist act. I hear on the news President Bush is returning from Florida. This place is so unprepared for terrorist activity, they should just release everybody in the D.C. area and let them go home. Of course, I'm not going to ride the Metro because that's a target waiting to happen." And I sent that. At the same time, I was on the phone to my wife saying, "No, turn the TV on," which she never watches in the morning. "Hey, go turn the TV on, watch the World Trade Center attack." She turned it on. I hung up. And about two minutes later is when the Pentagon got hit. . . .

I was in 1 Delta 518—if you look at the chart of where the plane hit, it's on the left edge of where the plane entered. . . . The damage that it inflicted on the Pentagon came into the office, [but] my first thought when it happened—and why I didn't think of an airplane, since I just saw two airplanes crash into other buildings—was a truck bomb. . . . [My office was] on the outer portion of the D-Ring, so the E-Ring is right over the wall from me. When the plane struck, the entire wall behind me that goes into the E-Ring was knocked askew, the top knocked out toward the E-Ring. I think something hit low on the wall and caused it to jar out, so there was an opening in the top. I didn't notice that at first. What I did notice, the whole office erupting in flame. I was spared from getting hit with any fuel because . . . next to me was a huge column and a safe, so where my desk was here, the fuel splashed away. I was standing there. I don't remember a large noise. I do remember thinking, "Why is my head not ringing and why is all this—why is this place in rubble?" You know, I was thinking of a truck bomb.

CAPT. DOVER: Describe what you heard. What did you hear?

MAJ. KING: I don't remember hearing a crash. All I just remember is the whole place erupting in flames. I don't remember a large crash or anything. And that was—I remember standing there: "Why isn't my head ringing?" Because an explosion would definitely ring my bell. And, "Why is this place in rubble? Why is there all this flame?" I immediately moved across the room. I

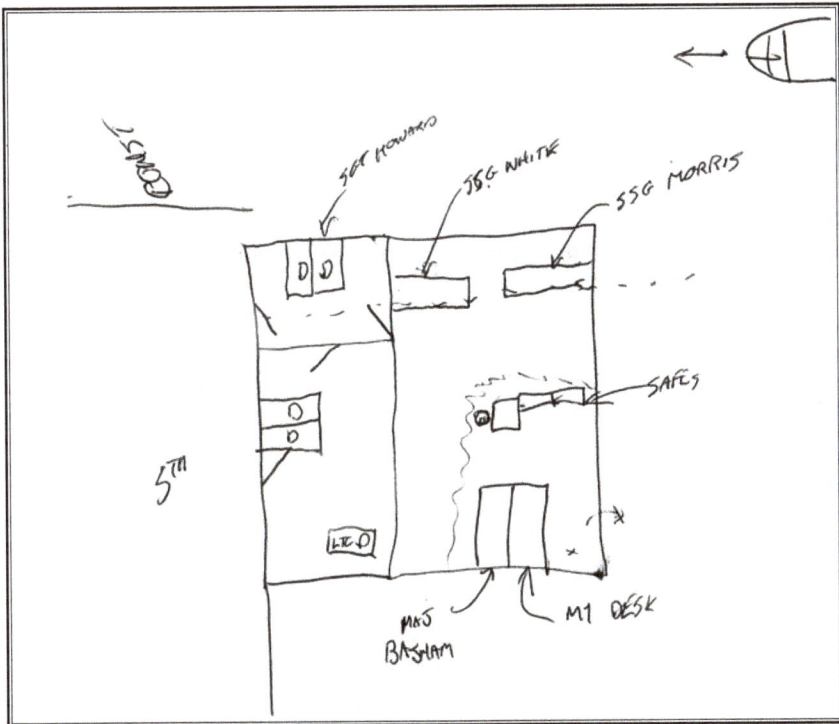

Map of Maj. David J. King Jr.'s area that he sketched during the interview

can draw a picture of the place for you. I moved across the room to a desk.

CAPT. DOVER: So the flames came across your office, or—

MAJ. KING: Right. I'll draw this, this being the fifth corridor. Now, these doors were all open. These were two desks that—this was Lieutenant Colonel [Jerry] Dickerson. He was buried out in Arkansas.

CAPT. DOVER: So he was one of the casualties?

MAJ. KING: Right. . . . These desks had been abandoned. This had been abandoned. This desk belonged to Sergeant Howard, who had ten minutes prior been called upstairs to sit in the general's office, so she wasn't present. There were two desks here, this one

belonging to Staff Sergeant [Maudlyn A.] White, who was killed.
. . . And this belonging to Staff Sergeant Morris, who did not show
to work, he was not scheduled to come to work 'til 11:00. . . .

CAPT. DOVER: How many casualties were there from this office?

MAJ. KING: Three—[two] dead and me. These were safes here,
my desk, and Major Basham's desk was here. He was on leave.
. . . Roughly, the edge of debris and everything was right along
here. Flame was all through here, and all out into this area and
down the hallway. . . . Right along here, along that, over her
desk, from the ceiling, were just tables and debris. I don't know
what all. When I initially got hit, when it initially hit, I was right
here. I immediately, after realizing that, you know, looked over,
and I could see her desk covered. I mean, at that point, I was
untouched. I ran over and started to bash through all the tables
and everything, trying to get to her, and that's how I got burns
on my arms, because I—

CAPT. DOVER: Now, this was—

MAJ. KING: Staff Sergeant White. I was attempting to get to her
because she had been sitting at her desk. . . . I'd just looked
into Lieutenant Colonel Dickerson's office just a few minutes
before, and he was talking to a civilian in there, a contractor
or a civilian worker so, I'm not sure who it was, but he was
sitting at his desk. I was going to talk to him about something
. . . but they were in a conversation, so I walked back to my
corner. Boom, it got hit. I ran over, attempted to get to Staff
Sergeant White, was unable to get to her. I stepped out into
here and looked in towards Colonel Dickerson's desk. This
whole area, the whole room was just flames. I couldn't even
see his desk across the way.

CAPT. DOVER: Did you encounter flames getting to her desk?

MAJ. KING: I did. This whole area was in flames. It was in flames. . . .

I stepped in the hall, thinking, "Well, I can get into the door
here." When I stepped in the hall, that thought immediately
left me, because I was thinking, "Well, this isn't an escape
route," because the entire hall was just a river of flame. I
couldn't even see down the hall. I didn't know how far the
flames went. I mean, at that point, getting Sergeant White was

not an option, getting Colonel Dickerson wasn't an option, and running down the hall wasn't an option. I didn't know how far the flames went. So I went back to my little corner. I remember walking back there, stopping in front of the water cooler that was here, thinking, "Okay, fire. What are you supposed to do? Oh, get on the floor and breathe," and I looked down, and the whole carpet was on fire. So I said, "Okay, I can't do that," and I stepped back into my corner, and beat my polyester pants out that had started to melt to my leg. At that point, both my arms and hands were burnt. I remember looking down at the desk and seeing a picture of my family, and saying, "I got to get the hell out of here," and I looked around and saw the hole opening behind me in the wall, and crawled up over the wall and dropped into the E-Ring.

At the same time I did that, I noted the people in the room next door, who were part of the computer contractors, they were doing the same thing, and we all gathered up and somebody over at the hole where the airplane came in shouted, "Hey, we can get out over here." Again, we still didn't—I didn't know it was an airplane or anything. I just—this huge hole, lots of black smoke. The entire E-Ring area looked—it was just dark. There were pockets of fire. They kind of looked Orwellian. You know, you see the movies of the future where everything is destroyed, and just flames? This whole group, we moved out the hole where the plane had entered. And after, I ran into [Lt.] Colonel [William] Delaney, who worked for QDR [Quadrennial Defense Review Office], who was in an office farther down the hall, and he had a cell phone. . . . He later said when I came walking out of the big, black ball of smoke, he said I was covered in white dust, my arms were stuck out in front of me with my skin hanging off. He said I looked like a ghost. . . .

But I ran into Colonel Delaney, and I saw he had a cell phone, and I said, "Sir, call my wife and call my mother and tell them I'm okay. My parents still live in Montgomery County [Maryland]. My wife is down in North Carolina." And he said, "Okay, what are their phone numbers?" And he wrote them down on a card, and he had a magic marker. Then he grabbed my shirt. I still had my Army—the mint green shirt on. He wrote the phone numbers on my shirt, across my right side. And I said, "Okay, while you're at it, write, "O Positive, no meds, no allergies." So he wrote all that on my shirt, because still at this time, I wasn't feeling any pain. I don't know if I was already in shock or my body had just shut down—it burnt away any nerves that would be sending pain to me.

I went over. He had one person injured in his group that had sliced her knee. He—we—everybody moved to our triage area they were establishing over by the guard rails, by the road. I do remember, coming out, that the fire truck was on fire, and I thought that was humorous, because here's our brand new fire truck in flames. Moved over to the triage area. He sat the civilian next to me to keep an eye—so he'd know where all the people were. He was trying to get a count of people from that corridor who worked for DCSPRO [Deputy Chief of Staff for Programs]. I informed him that Sergeant Howard had been sent upstairs, Colonel Dickerson and Sergeant White were still in the office, as far as I knew, and as far as I could determine, both of them had been killed, and nobody else had been in the office at the time. So he noted that.

I sat on the guard rail. Two individuals from a media center across the hall made their escape. I basically knew them from saying "Hi" in the hallway. They both sat on either side of me. They cut away my pants, my shirt, my shoes. They were continuing to bring people out, and at that—I was thinking, "I'm not as badly damaged as they are." . . .

CAPT. DOVER: Do you remember those people, their names, from the media center?

MAJ. KING: Carl and Dave. . . . I ran into these folks up at the awards ceremony. . . . And they explained to me, I had been sitting there, they were continuing to bring people out of the Pentagon, and I remember them bringing [out injured civilians]. . . . I'm thinking, . . . "They're burned. They're in a lot worse shape than me." And they kept saying, "Get down on the stretcher," and I was [saying], "No, they need help more than me." That's what they said I kept saying, "No, they need help, they need help more than me." And finally, I started thinking, "I'm going to start hurting pretty soon." I remember yelling at the medic, "Hey, sarge, you need to jack me up or something, because I'm going to go into shock pretty soon." He turned around and he said, "Where did you come from? How long have you been here?" And Dave and

Carl told him, "He's been here the whole time." He said, "You need to get on a stretcher now." Got me on a stretcher. An ambulance pulled up, and I was on the first ambulance that left there, and I went to the Washington Hospital Center. . . . I remember on the way there the EMT [emergency medical technician] guy was saying, "Oh, there are reports that they hit the mall, there are reports they hit here and there," and as the ambulance is driving through D.C., and I'm looking out the back window, I could see pillars of smoke, and I'm thinking, "Wow, this is a well-coordinated hit." But it was all the smoke from the Pentagon that was coming up, and I was just seeing it from different angles, but I was thinking D.C. got hit three or four times.

Got to Washington Hospital Center. From there, I was able to make a phone call to the folks. . . . I don't remember everything, except they took me up to put me in one of the tubs, cleaned all the skin off and everything. . . . When they wheeled me out of there, or before they did, a nurse told me later that I was coherent enough to tell them, "Hey, you took my pants. My wallet's in my pants." So she had to go back and dig through the garbage to get my wallet out. When they pushed me out of the room with the tub, my cousin was standing there, who I haven't seen in like three years. He lives down in Adams Morgan near the Washington Hospital Center

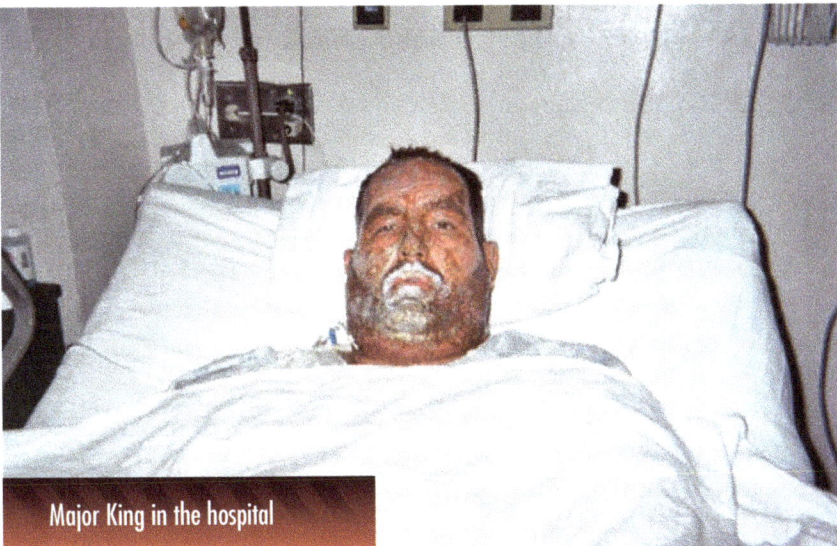

Major King in the hospital

King with his sons on Military Appreciation Day in May 2011. Major King retired from the U.S. Army in 2008.

and heard my name on the radio and drove over there. So I remember seeing him. He went down to the room that they put me in with me. My folks showed up. Evidently my head was swelled up like a basketball, because of the water retention that rushed to my head, and it kind of freaked my mother out a little bit. But I basically spent the next five weeks in the hospital and had four separate operations to get the grafts on my hands and arms.

CAPT. DOVER: So you had second and third—

MAJ. KING: Third-degree burns. . . . My entire left arm, from fingertips on up to above my elbow was grafted. My right arm, it's about half of it, from my fingertips up to my elbow, was grafted, and they took the grafts from my thighs and my ribcage. My head received a severe sunburn. . . . My legs were, the pants melted to it. They weren't as severe as the burns on my arms and hands. . . .

CAPT. DOVER: Is there anything else you'd like to add at this time?

MAJ. KING: Just that the medical service I received at Washington Hospital Center was outstanding. They've got the best burn doctor in the country, and I'm not just saying it because he worked on me. He's the president of the National Burn Doctor

Association. We're fortunate he was there. The nursing staff was outstanding. The rehabilitation staff, at the time, I thought was very brutal, but was outstanding. They knew that they had to push us. The support we received—President Bush came to visit real soon after that. The Secretary of the Army came. [Chief of Staff of the Army] General [Eric K.] Shinseki, [Vice Chief of Staff of the Army] General [John M.] Keane, the head from Walter Reed, the Surgeon General of the Army came several times to see us. The support we got from every sector of the military—the "Hey, guys, what do you need?"—was outstanding. But I can't praise the Hospital Center enough for what they do. They had ten people show up there, which is—I mean, all at once—which is not a fun thing. They're lucky it was only that many. One of them died. Seven of them remained up on intensive care for weeks. Two of us were sent down to the rehab floor immediately because we had less than 25 percent of our body burned. And, you know, the way they patched the people back together and saved them is—I can't say enough positive things about them.

Maj. Gen. Peter W. Chiarelli *was the Director of Operations, Readiness and Mobilization, Office of the Deputy Chief of Staff for Operations and Plans. He was interviewed in his Pentagon office by Frank Shirer of the U.S. Army Center of Military History on 5 February 2002.*

MAJ. GEN. CHIARELLI: I was in my office at nine o'clock in the morning when I was first alerted to the fact that an aircraft had hit the World Trade Center. . . . I was getting ready to go to a meeting, pretty intense on getting through some e-mail, so that I had pretty well a clean slate before I began that morning round of meetings.

I'd only been in the job for just a little bit over a month and had planned to do an exercise for the crisis action team, the CAT. . . . In some of my pre-briefings, in learning about the job, it was briefed to me that really the Crisis Action Team had not stood up, except for an exercise, in about ten years in any great role. It really kind of went back to DESERT STORM. Not to say that it hadn't been up before—it had been up as early as the millennium, when Major General [Richard A.]

Cody had a command cell up for a period of time, working the Y2K piece on the first of January 2000 and the day before and a couple of days after. But as far as being up for any great period of time in support of a crisis situation, it had been quite a while. And it was kind of evident to me, having been in operations for a while, that folks weren't necessarily—SOPs [standard operating procedures] weren't necessarily as sharp as they needed to be, and the TOC [tactical operations center] needed to be taken out, so to speak. It needed to be given a shakedown, a little bit of an exercise. And I had planned to stand up the CAT on a no-notice exercise, that I had my folks design for me, on the 17th of September. But I missed it by a couple of days.

But I was in the office, clearly working to try to get through some e-mails, to make sure that I had a clean slate going into the morning's round of meetings, when Kathy, Ms. Condon [Special Assistant for Military Support in the Office of the Secretary of the Army], came down, and I believe was going to escort me. ... The red switch rang and it was General Burns from FORSCOM [U.S. Army Forces Command], the DCSOPS [Deputy Chief of Staff for Operations and Plans] of FORSCOM. He called and he said, "Pete, have you seen on CNN that something's run into the World Trade Center?" Now, I always have CNN on. I glanced up, looked—I had had it on mute because I was kind of in a hurry. I was concentrating on getting my work done. I looked up and saw the live reporting taking place, showing something had, in fact, run into the World Trade Center. I said goodbye to General Burns and took the TV off mute, just about when Kathy walked in. We listened to the initial reports. I remember some of the initial reports were, I believe on CNN, that, well, it could have been a plane. No one saw a plane. People thought it was a rocket, thought it was something that could have occurred. Then the idea was that it was a small plane. And it was really kind of confused right around 9:00 in the morning. At that time, it became a little more clear, if I remember right, that we had a really serious situation at the World Trade Center. And I called for [Lt. Col.] Kevin Stramara, my Chief of Operations, [DAMO-]ODO, and he has responsibility for the CAT, called him in. He came in and I said, "Kevin, we need to look at standing up the CAT because I believe we've got ourselves a possibility of a mass casualty."

I've got to go back in time a little bit. One of the in-briefings that I received, one of the things that we were working on was a new mass casualty SOP for the Army. I've got an organization down here called the PCC, and PCC stands for Personnel Contingency Cell. . . . Basically that's the G–1 representation and PERSCOM [U.S. Army Personnel Command] representation down here in the Army Operations Center. They had been directed, I believe, by the chief to put together a new SOP. And about a week prior to that time, Robby Robinson [Raymond C. V. Robinson, Chief, Operations Division, Directorate of Plans, Resources, and Operations, Office of the Deputy Chief of Staff for Personnel], who was a key and critical guy who worked with me in the aftermath of 11 September, along with two of his officers, came in to brief me on their new SOP for mass casualty, in the event that we had to handle another kind of Gander-like [plane crash disaster] operation. As part of that briefing, we decided to integrate a scenario like that into my first CAT exercise. . . . The real amazing thing of that SOP is that the scenario was an aircraft crashing into the World Trade Center. . . . We had all made a decision that we were going to kill two birds with one stone. I needed a driver for my exercise I wanted to run down here. He had an SOP that he was working. We decided that we would use a scenario similar to that to kind of drive this exercise.

Well, woe be it, on 11 September, of course, the first plane ran into the World Trade Center. As things started to kind of unravel, it became clear it was an aircraft. It was unclear at that point whether or not it was a terrorist action. I mean, deep down inside, everyone suspected that, but when Kevin came in—and this is just a few minutes after—we stared and looked at the TV. I told him, "Kevin, it's time to activate the CAT. Get it set up." He turned to walk out and as he turned, I remember, that's when we saw the second aircraft go into the second tower. And both of us responded in the same way and that was, "My God, they got that on tape." And when I talk to people, a lot of people thought that. They thought that what they were really seeing at that particular point in time was the first aircraft crashing in, when in reality we saw that aircraft come around and circle and crash into the second tower of the World Trade Center. Once we realized that that was the case, there was no doubt—and I remember looking at Kevin and saying, "Kevin, who has responsibility for this building?" And he looked at me and said, "Responsibility?" I said, "My God, if there are other aircraft up there that have been hijacked or if there are other aircraft getting ready to do this, this building has got to be a target." And he said, "I don't know. I will check, but first I'll stand up the CAT."

MR. SHIRER: And "this building" being the Pentagon itself?

MAJ. GEN. CHIARELLI: This building being the Pentagon itself. At that moment, I got a call from the Chief of Staff of the Army. The Chief was, in fact, TDY. He was attending a conference, I believe, in Singapore. He had heard about the first aircraft that had gone in, he called me, asked me to give him a SITREP [situation report]. All I could tell him, basically, was what I had seen on TV. I didn't have any time to leave the room, to go to the CAT, to check with the Intel folks. We were really early in the crisis. At that moment, as I was talking to him, I had a couple of folks from my ATOIC [Antiterrorism Operations Intelligence Cell] . . . come in to indicate to me that there were additional hijackers. As I was telling the chief we'd had a second aircraft, they handed me a note that there were additional hijackers, and if I remember right, in their note or in their—I don't know if it was in the note or whispering in my ear—they told me one of the aircraft was suspected to be heading for Washington, D.C. The chief asked me a question. I indicated to him I really had no other information except that there was a possibility of another aircraft. He immediately—having a lot of operations experience—realized that I had a lot to do other than to talk to him in Singapore, and he said, "Pete, it sounds like you really got a lot going on back there. You need to do that. I'll call you later." Because now the information was coming in fast and furious.

General Shinseki and I had a special relationship because I was his G–3 when he was the division commander, 1st Cavalry Division, so we worked with each other at least in training situations and similar kinds of high-stress environments. I think we knew each other very well. He knew me and he knew that we had a lot that—I mean, I indicated to him that there were other aircraft. He immediately knew that there was little he could do from Singapore, that he would call me later, and for that, I'll be forever appreciative, to have that occur, because there were other things to do.

We then went out on the CAT floor. The leadership of the Army started to show up and at least started to call down. I think one of the very first people to get down here was [Maj.] General [Philip R.] Kensinger [Jr.]. He was the ADCSOPS [Assistant Deputy Chief of Staff for Operations and Plans], the assistant G–3. He had left his office, I believe, when the first aircraft hit, and when he got word that it was an aircraft—possibly it could have been just after the second aircraft—to come down here to see what we were doing as far as standing up the CAT. Because the DCSOPS of the Army was also TDY. In fact, he was on leave, if I'm not mistaken. He was on leave in the Caribbean. I think he was in Jamaica—[Lt.] General [Larry R.] Ellis. . . . [General Kensinger's] office was the one that received the most damage in the G–3 area. That's where his secretary and his aide died, that morning, but he had left his office. He has very little left of anything. All he's got is his colors from one of the units he commanded. In fact, the only thing he really has left, after going through the personal effects, is the emblem of his unit. All the rest of the flag and the satin and everything, burned away. It's quite a touching piece to see, the embroidered emblem of a unit with everything else burned away. The fire stopped when it hit the emblem.

But he came downstairs. I went out onto the CAT floor, asked again who could provide any kind of defense for the building. It was at that time the Intel folks came back in and told me that they had credible information that one of the aircraft was headed for D.C., and it was right about then that we heard the noise and the building had been hit. The third aircraft impacted, and it impacted on the building. The effects down here were nothing but a muffled noise, at first. Additional folks coming downstairs. Initial reports of damage upstairs. Initial reports of a fire took place. I was getting additional reports from my Intel guys, telling me that we had the possibility of a minimum of four aircraft that were hijacked, a possibility—at one time, I think we were as high as seven. There were reports of one coming in from Europe, that one was flashing the international distress signal. . . . There was a report of another aircraft out of Los Angeles, and we had one out in the Pacific. I think we were up as high as seven at one time.

Just about that time, the Vice Chief of Staff of the Army [General John M. Keane], who was the senior man, arrived in the balcony. . . . The CAT floor, with all the workers and everyone who mans the operations cell of the Title 10 headquarters, is down on a floor on its own, and, up above it, one floor up, sits a balcony that overlooks that floor, and in that balcony are rows of seats that are glassed in. The glass is such and the balcony is such that you can yell as loud as you want down on the CAT floor and they don't hear a thing you're saying upstairs. All communications is done by a hand mike that we have and that balcony is miked. They look straight forward onto four gigantic screens that are up above all the computer workstations . . . where we prepare the briefing or any kind of other graphics that we want to show them at that time.

We had people starting to wander in. We had gone through a telephonic alert. We have a machine called a dialogic machine that automatically goes out and calls people to come on down. We had done a dialogic test to see how good our alert rosters were, the week before, and made some corrections. That was kind of the ramp-up for my exercise I was going to run. The dialogic machine is nothing other than an automatic machine, a phone machine, that automatically calls you up and gives you a recorded message, a prerecorded message, that tells you to report immediately to wherever it might be. In this instance it was to report to the CAT floor. . . .

People were starting to filter in down on the CAT floor. Some of my folks who had been here for a while, some of the civilians, were kind of directing people to where they needed to go, helping them turn on computers, get things cranked up, start talking to folks. Calls started to come in from FORSCOM, wanting to know what our status was. I knew the building had been hit. The Vice showed up in the building. He asked for a SITREP of what I knew. I was able to tell him basically what had occurred at the World Trade Center. We were able to tell him that the building had been hit—he knew the building had been hit—and that there were other aircraft in the air. Around that time we got two additional reports. I think at the height of our reporting, we had three unaccounted-for aircraft. We had an explosion on Capitol Hill that was reported to us. We had an explosion at the State Department that was reported to us, neither of which proved to be true. There were a number of false reports that we got. Then we got word of the crash of the aircraft in Pennsylvania. I got word that the Air Force was flexing to put a CAP [Combat Air Patrol] up, over Washington, D.C. We even got a report of an explosion outside the White House. That was one of the very last reports we got.

And then the Sec Army [Secretary of the Army, Thomas E. White] came down. Things were starting to get real confusing now, because it's one thing to have all this occurring but it's another thing to have your CP hit and, in reality, in a way, it was like our command post had been hit. We were going through all this and, at the same time, the building had been hit. The Sec

Army came down to the AOC. We got early reports of the extent of the fire. We got word that the Joint Staff was evacuating. . . . At this time, the balcony started to fill with senior leadership. I think more than would have normally come down, came down, quite frankly, because a large portion of the Army portion of the building had been destroyed. People had been forced out of their space. They were looking for someplace to go.

I remember [Lt.] General [John M.] Pickler was out of the building. He was the DAS [Director of the Army Staff] at the time. As we were trying to account for people and figure out where all the key leadership were, he was one of the early people we were trying to find, to find out where he was, worried that he had been hurt in the attack. I remember getting a phone call from him later on in the day, that he was fine, and he was with a bunch of other folks we were looking for, outside the building, trying to evaluate whether or not to try to get back in the building.

When the Secretary of the Army came down, we gave him as many reports as we possibly could. People were intent on watching CNN. We were standing up the CAT cell, trying to get a feel for exactly where the building had been hit. That became clearer and clearer, and we realized early on that we had a real problem that we were going to have to attack as soon as we can. That was the accountability for the command. It's one thing to do in a unit, where you have alert rosters and a predominance of military folks who are used to being on an alert roster and being accounted for. It's a totally different thing when you realize that not only does this building have a lot of military folks, it has as many, if not more, civilian folks, part of the DA [Department of the Army] staff, DA directorate. It's a very mobile building with people moving around. People have meetings, they're in different parts of the building. It was a very, very daunting task. It proved to totally occupy my time for the first thirty-six to seventy-two hours of the crisis.

At one time, we got word that we were going to exercise a relocation plan of some key leaders to a place called Site R. I had the NCO who ran that program, and I had been briefed on that. I think about two weeks before, I got an hour briefing on the relocation and continuity of operations plan—COOP. The NCO came down and was down on the CAT floor standing next to me. Just an *unbelievable* NCO, one of the finest I've ever served with. He understood this plan inside and out, and immediately started whispering in my ear, when I needed it, the details of the continuity of operations—where buses would be to pick up people should we have to leave the building, where we would go. And at one time we got word that a specific stage of the COOP exercise had been ordered. And at this time, the Secretary of the Army was up with the Vice. We informed the Secretary that it was time for him to leave. He indicated he was not leaving. He was staying in the building. We knew by the regulation that he had no choice. The NCO looked at me and said, "Sir, he has no choice at this time. This has been directed, and he must immediately proceed and leave here. This is bigger than him. This is continuity of the government of the United States." I remember looking at him and saying, "Are you sure of this?" And he said, "Yes, I'm sure. Sir, you need to go up and tell him that he needs to get up and go." And I remember—I had been in the job for less than a month, and having heard just a few minutes ago that there was a CAP over the building, I was about to leave my desk, walk upstairs to the balcony, walk down to the Secretary of the Army, and basically order him out of the building, along with my NCO—I was thinking, "My God, when is somebody going to wake me up. When is this horrible, horrible dream going to end!" But it didn't end, as we all know. I left with the good sergeant. . . . We went upstairs and I basically leaned over between the Vice and the Secretary of the Army, who were sitting next to each other, and so informed the Secretary that he had no choice. He was bound to do this. We had gotten word that this portion of the implementation plan was in effect and that he must proceed directly to a specified place in the building where he would get in a helicopter and leave. He said, "Well, how do I get there?" I said, "The sergeant will lead." Sure enough, he said, "All right," and off he goes.

Only to find out later on, like most reports go—this was the phenomena of the first report, something I know very, very well, but it was one of those where you couldn't take a chance, where we had verified the information and were told yes— we found out that it wasn't required for him to leave at that particular point in time, because the level of evacuation did not reach his level. It was, in reality, a splitting of some key and critical people in the national command authority to go to a different site, but it was not a requirement, and the person who had told us had misspoke over the phone, only to find out that we kicked the Secretary of the Army out of the building to get into a helicopter to fly to a location, when he, in fact, really didn't have to. At that time, I wondered if I was going to have my job because I knew he would not be pleased. But when he got back, it was kind of a joke at the time, but at the same time he did come back, about four hours later—was not happy that he had had to leave, but totally understood what had occurred. And I think he had been with the Dep Sec Def [Deputy Secretary of Defense], who had been on the same helicopter that he was on.

Once we understood that there were four aircraft and only four aircraft—we were still tracking the one over the Atlantic, tracking one that we thought was coming from the Los Angeles area—once we got through all those pieces, we kind of settled down into a mode of trying to determine what had happened in the building. At the same time, I was starting to get calls from Capitol Hill, and the [Sergeant at Arms of the U.S. Senate], a major general, retired, M[ilitary] P[olice] Corps, [Alfonso E. Lenhardt] . . . having his connections with the Army and having a whole bunch of folks up on Capitol Hill, in the form of congressmen and senators, who were very, very concerned and did not know what the hell was going on, thought we knew everything down here. He called down and asked us to get somebody who could brief him and get him a secure phone he could use so he could talk. . . . He started to call down here, repeatedly asking for assistance, assistance which we rendered later on in the day.

The Vice directed that what we needed to start doing immediately was try to get accountability of the command, and we started the entire process that went on through that night and into the next day or two. In addition, we began actions to try to get General Ellis back from where he was, and General Shinseki back from where he was. General Shinseki created some problems for us because, of course, by this time all air space had been shut down. We knew he was going to have to fly from the west coast of the United States all the way to Washington, D.C. But we were able to arrange that without too many problems, and I went out to pick him up at the airport the next night, along with some other folks, to give him a report on where we were and the accountability of who we thought we had missing. Our initial count, as we started to work our way through that, started at somewhere in the vicinity of over two hundred folks. I believe by the time I went home to change into BDUs about three o'clock in the morning, we had that number down to about thirty-six folks, but then the number grew back up again. It grew back up the next day when one of the civilian agencies, that we thought had been rolled up under another agency—we got some bad reporting from an almost total civilian agency—came and told us that they had some additional people, so that drove our final number. I tell you that now because that created some angst, in that we thought we were down around thirty and I believe we ended up in the vicinity of about eighty folks, in total. God, I thought I'd never forget that number exactly, but I have over the last five months.

One of the things that we attempted to try and immediately establish was a call-in line. As confusing as everything was, we wanted to get a feel for people who had not shown up back home, in hopes that that would help us to determine who was missing, if in fact we had gotten some bogus reports. . . . Our concern was a call-in line would also give us an opportunity to bounce statistics, or thoughts that people had about people being missing, against our list, to try to justify, so that we could get it down to the exact number. We worked really, really hard to establish that, to set up the ten lines and do that, initially down here, and then we wanted to move it out to PERSCOM—I think we finally got it set up at PERSCOM, a 1-800 number—got it set up at 10:00 to 11:00 at night on the night of September 11th. We started receiving calls from folks who felt that they had loved ones or friends that were missing. And we started to justify and to work all those.

I remember there was one young man who was down here working for like three days straight, a sergeant who didn't go home. . . . But we got a tip that he was missing. His family called in and said he was missing, only to find out that he was literally down here and had been down here for seventy-two hours. His only sin was that he failed to call home, which we chewed him out for, but at the same time it was kind of funny. He was only down here working his tail off and making sure things got done, and never called home. I also remember in the middle of events, my son called in on the line down here, wanted to know if I was okay. I'm answering the phone on the CAT floor—"General Chiarelli"—only to find out it was my son who said, "Dad, are you okay?" because I, too, had forgotten to call home, at about the eight-hour mark. But accounting for people and those things, that's basically what we were doing the first day.

The flames inside the building

Col. Mark Volk was Chief of the Strategic Leadership Division in the Strategy, Plan and Policy Directorate, Office of the Deputy Chief of Staff for Operations and Plans. He was interviewed in his Pentagon office by Stephen Lofgren of the U.S. Army Center of Military History on 1 May 2002.

COL. VOLK: We were in 3D415. Pretty much directly behind [Maj.] General [John R.] Wood's office in the line of—

MR. LOFGREN: From outside of the building.

COL. VOLK: Yes, that suite. In fact, just as a reference, my office was right at the midway point between the fourth and fifth corridor. There was an emergency stairwell right behind my office. So, our suite was from the fourth corridor to the midpoint of the fifth corridor in the D-Ring. My offices, where my folks were, were closer to that inner wall. So right at about the midway point between the fourth and fifth corridors.

MR. LOFGREN: Was Tuesday a normal day for you?

COL. VOLK: [Laughs] Up until that point. I have a total of twelve people working for—in my office, including me. Everybody was at work. It was a normal day for us, a normal pace, flow. We do a lot of discussions with, for example, foreign area officer trainees who are in a phase of their training called in-country training, where they're posted somewhere at one of the fifty-five overseas sites that we do, so we spend a lot of time talking with those people on the phone or coordinating with PERSCOM [U.S. Army Personnel Command] to get them into their training assignments. So, yes, it was a very normal day for us. . . .

I was sitting in my office . . . talking [and watching CNN] and something happened to catch my eye that was going on at the World Trade Center. So I turned up the volume just a few minutes before the second plane flew into the—so I had seen that happen. At that point—although I thought from the beginning that it was not an accident—that confirmed to me that we were really talking about a terrorist act, [and] I recognized that there were some implications for [the] future and given the overall directorate's responsibility for doing strategic planning for the Army, I hopped up, walked out of my office, back around out to the E-Ring, to let the folks know in our front office, General Wood and others, that something had occurred. So, I got their attention. Everybody then went to those televisions in the front office to watch what was going on. So, I then walked back, again, around the E-Ring and back to my office and was sitting there at the desk kind of watching what was going on with two other people in my office, two people that worked for me, when the plane impacted.

Because I had been watching everything on TV, it seemed like I immediately knew what it was. The force of the concussion was such that you knew it had to be big and having just seen two planes fly into the World Trade Center, I assumed that that's what it was.

MR. LOFGREN: Can you describe what it felt like?

COL. VOLK: I've lived through some very low-scale earthquakes, and that to me is kind of what it was like on a larger scale. Although my sense is that it was not a huge jolt. I was sitting in my chair and I got bustled around a little bit. The two people in my office lost their balance, but not violently. I mean, it didn't seem like it was a huge impact, but clearly you could feel it. The lights went out. Emergency lights came on and I could see at that point kind of an orange glow from flames.

My office is kind of strangely oriented because I did sit behind [*gestures*] that emergency stairwell. So I kind of—my door faced the back of the suite wall looking in towards the C-Ring. So it was a blank wall. I had to go out, turn right, turn right again along the cubicles, and then came out to the middle and then I would exit out this way to the fourth corridor. It was kind of a weird orientation. I couldn't see much. I couldn't see out into the office. I looked into kind of a blank wall, but I could see the flames. I could see the yellow glow of flames, so I knew that there had been some damage. . . .

So I immediately jumped up and yelled for people to evacuate, to move out, and began herding out the folks in my shop, although most of them were moving already. The sense that I had at that time was that—and this is the thought that I was having—the impact was such that I believed that I was not on kind of the center, where the plane had slid underneath us. I believed that it was probably more toward the fifth corridor than the fourth, just the way it felt and the way things looked as I walked out, and I'll tell you why I thought that in a second here.

As I came out, most of the folks in my office were up and were moving almost immediately. And so I got those people who were in my office moving and I began to clear my way down through cubicles to make sure that people were going out. The sense was that people were scared, but not panicked. They moved rapidly, but they weren't running, there wasn't screaming. It was, in my sense, very orderly. I was pretty amazed as I thought back after the fact at what had occurred.

As I came out and made those two quick right turns, as I told you, I could see flames now outside of our suite on both the C-Ring side, the windows out there, as well as the D-Ring side, ultimately realizing, after I knew what had happened, that fuel had washed over top of us, came up over the E-Ring, down into the area between the D- and E-Ring, up over the D-Ring, and down into the area between the D- and C-Ring. But there were, at that point, no flames in our suite. They were all external. Broken glass, ceiling tiles on the floor, some of the overhead lights hanging down, but not a whole lot of destruction. So at that point, again, I had a sense that we were not as close to the impact as we actually—

MR. LOFGREN: Was your air quality—

COL. VOLK: At that point, it was smoky, but not very bad. We were getting some of the black smoke from the burning fuel—but it had not yet started coming up very rapidly from the lower floors. Now, when I came out, again, when I came out my office suite, I have to come out one door, turn right, then almost immediately turn right again and walk to the center of the suite and then there was a fire door immediately to my right . . . and then the normal flow of traffic between all of the cubicles was out to my left, which went to the fourth corridor. When I got to that fire door, I felt it to see whether it was warm. It was warm, but not hot. So I popped that door, thinking that was a faster evacuation route and saw flames coming up the stairwell. Seeing that, and looking to my right and not seeing flames, other than outside of the suites on both sides there, my sense was we were, as you stand there kind of looking at the Pentagon, we were on the right edge of where the plane impacted, because when I looked down toward the fourth corridor, I didn't see any. There were no real flames and there was not a whole lot of damage down on that side. So that's why I kind of felt that we were off-center much more than we turned out to be.

We moved people out of the suite. I was the last one to go out. Again, it was very orderly, relatively calm, and I got out to the corridor, the fourth corridor, and, at that point, as I remember, if you looked in towards the A-Ring, the air quality was relatively clear and clean. As you looked immediately out towards the E-Ring, there was, at that point, smoke, dark smoke probably three-quarters of the way down from the ceiling and [it was] not possible to see all the way through to the E-Ring at that point. There were still people coming out off of the E-Ring. So I stood there with several other people and called to individuals to bring them through the smoke, called, "Come this way, stay down, keep moving," that type of stuff, just to clear them. Smoke, at that point, rapidly began to fill. It was in just a few minutes that smoke then was floor to ceiling and you couldn't see through it.

A woman who works in our Staff Action Control Office, Lee Gutwald . . . came up at that point. Her new offices were located right at the head of the fourth corridor on the E-Ring, third floor. She had been out of the office, in our old DCSOPS conference room over on the fifth-corridor side, actually closer to the sixth, conducting a class. So she was concerned at that point that she didn't know what the status of the people in her office was. She had not seen them, so she was concerned. She was adamant that she wanted to go out and check the office. So after the flow of traffic had stopped coming out, she and I, and a civilian contractor who works for us, ended up ducking through the smoke—and I had grabbed a fire extinguisher and headed back—went out into the E-Ring. There was another individual who went out with us and, to this day, I couldn't tell you who it was.

I went and looked—as I got out to the E-Ring, I could tell that the floor was partially buckled, but the air quality out there, there was some smoke, but very high up in the ceiling and I could pretty much stand and have fresh air. So it was very strange. I passed through almost a total floor-to-ceiling wall of smoke only to come out into the E-Ring and have relatively good air quality. Obviously, the windows had been blown out, and so there was airflow coming through them. I guess the smoke from the burning fuel was vented up through the inner stairways, and so that's why we had that area, that pocket of the smoke.

I looked into the office where Lee's folks worked. It was charred black. It was hot. I didn't step in very far, just inside the doorway. It was so hot that the heat almost wanted to force you back. But saw no one. So at that point then, we started to clear other offices just to make sure no one was left out there. Lee and [another person] . . . went down the E-Ring towards the third corridor and some of those offices there.

I was on that other side and that other individual, who I don't know who it was, was also on that side. We checked a couple offices and I was—at that point, the smoke was starting to get a little thick. I was kind of kneeling down and he was trying to open—he was banging on the door, as I remember, of General Kensinger's office, but could not get it open. At that point, there was another explosion. I've seen several pictures of that later explosion. I believe it was probably a fuel cook-off, a pocket of fuel that detonated, and that sent a huge ripple through the building. The floor waved, ceiling tiles dropped, but, again, at that point, still the third, fourth, and fifth floors were standing, although the third floor was buckled, but passable. At that point, my sense was, "This is dangerous now. I'm not really sure whether that was another plane or what it was, but we need to get out." So I yelled for everyone to get out and, again, herded people out in front of me. We then evacuated out. I stood there in the corridor for a little bit of time to make sure there was no one else coming behind us and then moved into the center courtyard, where we started to try to account for all of our people.

Spent quite a bit of time—I guess maybe we were in the center courtyard for five or ten minutes, until we were moved out initially into the South Parking and then consecutively. . . . It was very difficult because we kept getting moved because of concerns with security, another plane in the air, whatever. We'd get out into the South Parking and we'd be told, "You can't stand here, you have to move farther south." So we'd move. And then it was, "On the other side of 95 down by the mall." Then it was, "You can't stand here, you need to move farther." So we just got to a point where, talking with General Wood, basically, he had said, "Okay, send your people home, stand by your phones, get an accountability, let us know that you're good, and then stand by for orders."

Col. Marcus A. Kuiper was the Director of the Army Initiatives Group in the Office of the Deputy Chief of Staff for Operations and Plans. He was interviewed by Stephen Lofgren of the U.S. Army Center of Military History with Diana Grant of the Office of the Chief of Public Affairs and June Kronholz of the Wall Street Journal *on 30 October 2001.*

COL. KUIPER: So around, I guess it was 9:00 or something, I was back in my office [after briefing Major General Philip R. Kensinger Jr., the Assistant Deputy Chief of Staff for Operations and Plans (ADCSOPS)]. . . . I had a window to—kind of in between the two rings, Echo and Delta. No view. Just a view to the other building, but, you know, the gravel roof [below], and at least you can see outside. And I had a television. . . . So I was in the office, and I was talking with Ms. [Caridad] McDonald basically about her personal situation, about getting her promoted and professional development, that sort of thing.

What happened was one of my guys' wife called. She was watching TV at home or something and called up and said, "Hey, you've got to find a TV. You won't believe what's happened. We think terrorists have flown a plane into the World Trade Center." And so that was [Lt. Col.] Rob[ert J.] Ulses. His wife called. So Rob and someone else—I've forgotten who—there were only a couple televisions around. One was in my office, and since I was behind closed doors, they didn't disturb me. They literally went down the hallway, so they went from here down the hallway to the ADCSOPS office, and he had, basically, CNN hooked up through his computer, so you could watch CNN on his computer. So they went down there, and they were just watching it. They were going, "Whoa, look at that." So they watched it on CNN. So [during] one of the interesting, I guess you would call it subvignettes, was Rob Ulses' wife had called him and said, "Hey, you know, you won't believe what's happening." He had run down to go find a TV, and so, within fifteen minutes of impact, he had been standing basically at the point of impact watching TV, based on his wife being the person who said, "Hey, go find a TV." So an interesting substory there.

So they had watched it there, and they watched the replays of the first plane hitting the tower. And then they saw the second plane hit the tower, and so that's when they said, "Oh, boy, we better tell the boss." So they came back, went up the hallway, back to the office, knocked on the door, and said, "Hey, boss, you've got to know this." So we stopped the interview and turned on the TV. . . . I'm sitting here, the TV is about right here, and there's probably about six or seven folks gathered around the door here, and we're all watching the TV. So we're watching CNN, and we're watching them replay the second plane flying into the second tower, and basically, we're sitting there kind of watching it with our mouths open, like everybody else, and discussing it. And the thought was forming in my head—I was thinking, "Well, this is a very organized, prepared attack, and I wonder if they're done. I wonder if two planes is all there are?" And then I was thinking, "And the Pentagon would certainly be a good target." And about that time, we felt, you know, the impact. The room kind of shuddered, and I was sitting in a chair just like this, and it just kind of shook like that, and my immediate feeling was it was a plane. The thought that I had was, "Those bastards just flew a plane into the building." So I immediately thought plane. I did not immediately feel any particular danger. It felt like it was farther away than it was, I didn't have the sense of, "Oh, it was right here." I felt like it was somewhere over there.

What happened is we had the impact, it kind of shook, and then everybody who was standing here immediately dove on the floor. And like I said, I didn't have the sense of danger, so I'm sitting here like this, and the TV is here, and this is the window, behind me. But I see everybody diving for the floor. So I kind of looked . . . and the only thing—what you could see out my window was just a huge wall of flame. The whole thing was just a huge fireball with debris flying in it. And my immediate thought was it was the jet fuel, the aviation fuel, being thrown up onto us, which I think is what it was. So it was a huge wall of flame just engulfing the entire section. As it turned out later when I was able to get back into my office weeks later, it turns out my window was impacted. Large pieces of debris hit the window, and beyond the hand of God, what saved us in that regard was the safety glass, because huge chunks of plane, brick, whatever, did, in fact, hit that window, and it was, in fact, broken in three separate places. There was about a baseball-size hole, there was about a golf-ball-size hole, and there was a smaller hole, and you could see where things had just choked up against it, and it cracked. It shattered, but it didn't—I mean, it didn't shatter like come in. It cracked very severely, but the structural integrity retained. So looking back, it would have been very easy for the glass to come flying in and shred us because we were all standing there watching TV. It also would have been very easy for the flames just to come rolling in and barbecue us right behind that as well. So the fact that neither one of those happened is pretty amazing.

So everyone was on the floor. I looked back, saw nothing but flame. I knew that this whole section here was on fire because there's just nothing but flame everywhere. The temperature started to go up rapidly. The place started to fill with smoke, but not real fast. In other words, not so fast that it was just like, wow, like that. It was just like, "Hey, smoke's coming in and it's building up." . . . Somebody—I think it was [Lt. Col.] Sam[uel A.] Guthrie, who's my Deputy—made the comment of "Get in the doorway" or something because he was concerned that the thing would start collapsing. Amazingly it did not. The office did not collapse, and later we found out the plane had gone right in—originally my thought was I was afraid the ceiling would collapse, because I knew the fire was above us—I did not know the plane had gone right beneath us. In hindsight, it's amazing that our floor didn't collapse on us. But he yelled, "Get in the doorway," because he was thinking it was going to collapse on us.

But basically we got up. I never hit the floor. I was just in my chair already. I said, "Okay, let's go. Let's go. Everybody out." And it was a very orderly evacuation actually. I was very proud of the way people reacted. Nobody panicked. I was the only person really talking, and what I said was, "Okay, let's go. Let's everybody get out. Move with a purpose. Don't run." And that's basically what people did. People got up. A lot of the people were stunned. The people in the outer office, they didn't have the advantage of seeing the window and a lot of them hadn't been watching TV, and so a lot of people didn't know how to react. It was like, "What's going on?" And some people kind of freeze. And the other thing is people don't know—like we all left—like I lost my keys because they were sitting there on my desk—keys and wallets and things like that— people don't know, do I have enough time to grab my stuff or do I just get out? And basically I didn't let anybody, you know—I just, "Let's go, let's go." And so everybody got out.

Colonel Mark Volk—I mean, the way the office was set up, this is the big office room and this is our section here—his office was way back in this corner. So he came out, and I asked him, "Is everybody out?" and he said yes. So we swept out. We went out into the hallway, and out there there's probably about, I don't know, five or six of us standing around the hallway. . . . So there's a crowd here. . . . Looking this way [toward the E-Ring] you couldn't see hardly anything because the lights are out, so the power is off, and very thick smoke. So looking this way you can't see anything except smoke. Looking this way [toward the A-Ring], you do okay, because there's some light into the center courtyard here, penetrating down the hallway. So if you're looking this way, you can see okay. But looking this way you can't see anything.

So we came out here, and . . . I said, "Okay, I want to make sure that this room is clear." So I went back into the main room here, and basically I didn't go cubicle to cubicle, because I didn't, you know—I just didn't feel I had enough time to do that. But I wanted to make sure that no one was frozen or cowering or, you know, I just wanted to make sure. Okay. So what I essentially did was go into the center of the room . . . and basically just yell and say, "Okay, is anybody in here? Is anybody in here? We're leaving now. Everybody get out. We've got to clear this room." And I got no response. So I figured okay. And I was very pleased later when I got back in a couple weeks later. When the FBI goes in, what they do is they put it's almost like a tic-tac-toe thing on the side of the wall, and they put zero or one, and they write down if they found anybody. So what they do is they put zero on the left, they go through it once, and then when they go through it again and double-check it, they put another zero. So I was very pleased when I came back later that, on the outside, they had painted the kind of tic-tac-toe with double zero, which meant nobody in there. So it was, in fact, clear. And I worried about that because, like I say, I didn't check under every little—if someone had been unconscious or hiding under a desk and didn't answer me, I wouldn't have known. But I went in and yelled.

So then what I did is I came back out, and there's another very similar, almost identical type thing right next door. So I went out into the hallway, came back, and did the same thing in here. Just ran inside and yelled and said, "Hey, is anybody in here? Is anybody here? We've got to get out. Everyone's got to leave." And once again, no real response. Just a couple stragglers were getting out as I was going in, but that was cleared as well. And then I went down and I did this here as well, this one, same thing. Just went in and yelled and made sure nobody was there. . . .

Okay, and then I went back out in the corridor, and one of the people who works here in DCSOPS is Lee Gutwald, and she works with our SACO [staff action control officer] office, and her office was about here. She was not in it. She was teaching a class somewhere else in the building. . . . Two of her people were in that office, and she wanted to go hunt for them. She wanted to go into the smoke and go get them, and I would not let her. I held her back and said, "No, you're not going in there." Because, like I said, the smoke was extremely thick. You couldn't see and you couldn't breathe, either. There was no fire extinguisher and there was no breathing apparatus. And I tried stepping about two steps into the smoke and you just immediately lose your oxygen, and you can't breathe and you can't see, and you get disoriented. I said, "No way are you going in there." I said, "If you go in there, we're going to lose you, too." And she was very upset about her two people in there who, by the way, it turned out both did fine. They both survived. She found them out in the parking lot later. Now how they got out, I don't know. I think one of them was physically not in the room. They were on bathroom break, or somewhere, but they weren't there. And the other one, by pure chance, was kind of like in this far corner of the room, and the same kind of thing as us. Even though it was on fire and it was nasty, the thing did not collapse, and there was time to get out.

So all these people here—this is probably fifty people . . . maybe more—there was time for us to get out. So even though it was filling up with smoke, it's getting warm, it's kind of dark, but it's enough to see, and we had time to get out. So then . . . I told my folks to go down to the courtyard and assemble here, which is what they did. And there were about five of us standing around here and I'm kind of saying like, "Okay, what should I do now? How am I value added to the process?"

There were still people down in here. You could hear people moving around in the smoke. . . . I don't know how long it took me to run in those three rooms and yell and make sure nobody was in there. But then we were standing around the hallway. And when I came back, one of the first people that emerged then—some people could have emerged while I was gone—was [Maj.] General [John R.] Wood. . . . I guess his door had stuck, and they had to kick the door in to enable him to get out. . . . [Brig.] General [Karl W.] Eikenberry and the secretary and the people who got him out did not come out the way he came out. . . . He was smart because he used the wall to help guide him out. He was leaning against the wall, you know, kind of sideways, and then used that as a guide to come out. And when I first saw him, I thought he was burned badly because he was holding his face, and his skin was very red. But he was actually fine in terms of burns. He was okay. So he was coughing and hacking from the smoke, but he was not physically burned up. And somebody kind of grabbed him and helped him down this way to the courtyard.

Then we had two more guys come out, and it was more of a near thing for them. And they were struggling more. In other words, they came out, they were staggering, they were getting down to their hands and knees kind of thing—because you can't spend much time in here. As that smoke builds up and the oxygen goes away, you've only got so much time to be in there before you're done. So the next two guys that came out, they came out, they were still under their own power, still moving, but they were hacking up, and they were hacking and puking, when they came out. So then basically—I don't know—one or two more guys helped them out and got them down the hallway. And then it was just me and another guy standing here.

Then we still heard there was another guy in there, and I was tempted to go in and get him. But it was just like, you know, once you run in there, then you're just like he is—you know, you don't know where you are or what you're doing. And so what we're doing is we're yelling to him, "Over here, over here. Come towards the light." Because we're thinking he could see light, but we're looking into darkness, so we can't see him. So we're yelling to him, and we could hear him go down. He fell and went down hard. And we didn't know if he was going to get back up. We told him to stay down. We said, "Don't get back up. There's more air. Stay low, stay as low as you can. Crawl towards our voices. We're here, we're here, we're here." So what we did was we crawled into the smoke, I don't know, about ten feet or so. And it was a fairly close thing. I don't think he had much more distance. In other words, twenty feet and he probably wouldn't have made it because he was—and what's interesting about this is the difference between—like I said, twenty more feet, and I don't think he would have made it. And once he got to where we could see him and he could see us, we grabbed him and we pulled him out—we just pulled him and dragged him literally down here. He was sitting up and okay I'd say in five minutes. After he coughed and hacked and puked and got some fresh air, the recovery was just like, wow, he was okay. But he was just about suffocating and losing it, and he was very close to not being able to find us and probably dying right down there at the end of the corridor. . . .

So this whole thing, what I just described, is probably another five minutes. It's not a long time, from the time General Wood appeared to the time we dragged this last guy down the hallway. Because what we did was we dragged this last guy down the hallway, and the other guy stayed with him to make sure he was okay. And then I ran back down and I stood there, and I listened real hard, and I said, "Okay, is anybody in there?" I'm just standing there, "Okay, is anybody there?" And I heard nothing. What I was concerned about—probably the wrong things. I probably should have been concerned about the thing collapsing, but I wasn't. What I was concerned about was a fireball coming down the hallway because I had seen the massive fire, and so, you know, the other people in here probably did not know the degree to which the place was on fire. But I did because I had seen it out the window. So my concern was, I knew oxygen was depleting here . . . there's a lot of oxygen down this hallway. And I was thinking I don't know what's keeping the fire from this hallway, but if it burns through a door or something, I don't want to be standing in the middle of this hallway when the fire basically blows itself down here. I don't want to be standing here when that happens. So that was my concern as I stood there. I said, okay, I don't hear anybody else in there. I can't go in, but I can wait here a little bit. I don't know. Am I placing myself at risk? What are we doing? So anyway, I waited, I don't know, probably another minute or so. . . .

So at that time I came on down the hallway and came out into the center courtyard. . . . Interestingly, in the center courtyard, not very many casualties. There was one guy who I saw who was badly burnt, who had his clothes burned to him. He was lying in the grass right here, and there were a couple of people helping him. As a matter of fact, a third guy ran over and said, "Hey, I'm a paramedic," and they said, "Well, so are we." So he was getting plenty of attention. But they were trying to get water to put on him. And they were debating whether or not to try and take his clothes off because his clothes were really burned on to him.

There was a park bench sitting right here. The park bench is up this little alley or this little walkway. And sitting on the park bench were three women—actually, I guess there were two on the park bench and one on the ground—who obviously had also been someplace where it was pretty bad. There was one woman whose hair had been basically singed off. I mean, her hair was kind of grayish anyway, but you could tell that she's missing the top half of her hairdo, that her hair had like kind of melted down, closer to her head. And then there was another woman sitting next to her, kind of a heavyset lady. And she had obviously come out on her hands and knees because her hands were all red, and her nylons were burned into her knees. Her knees—she was a black lady, and her knees were all pink, because her nylons had burned into her skin. So it was like down a layer of skin. So they were both sitting there. The lady with the singed hair was just kind of stunned. She was just kind of like out of it, and the other lady was sobbing. She was really shaking, and she was really shaken up. And the other one, on the ground, didn't look to be a physical casualty—seemed to be more of a psychological casualty. Don't know what had happened and where she'd been, but she was pretty upset.

So I got out in the courtyard and once again counted noses on my people because I have about a dozen people working directly for me. We had two that were physically off-site at the time. Interestingly, another small vignette. One of my guys was on leave, and he's famous—we call it "Matthew's time"—he's famous for

The damaged section of the E-Ring collapsed around 10:15 a.m.

being late. He doesn't show up on time, and he was officially on leave that day. One of the things he does is he writes speeches for the DCSOPS and the ADCSOPS. So on that particular day, he was writing a speech for some event for the ADCSOPS, and he had talked to the ADCSOPS XO [executive officer] from home and said, "Okay, I'll come on in and we'll work on the speech." So he was on his way in, at the time, when the plane impacted. So if he had been on time, he would have been sitting in the ADCSOPS' office, which was obliterated. You know, the ADCSOPS' office is literally right in this part that collapsed. So it's right in what is now the hole. It's right there, point of impact. And the two people that were in there, the XO and the secretary, were both fatalities. So he would have been sitting there right next to the XO. The other guy who wasn't in the office was across the river reconning an event we were going to have at Fort McNair that got canceled. So he was across the river. He didn't see the impact, but he certainly saw the aftermath, you know, the smoke and the fire and all that kind of stuff.

Now we were in the courtyard. So we got accountability of all our folks. Like I said, probably I had been away from them for maybe ten minutes, not a great deal of time. And then we had a Marine three-star come out, and I'm not sure who he was. And he basically was having the same thought I was, you know, we've got two planes into the World Trade Center, what makes us think we're not going to get two planes in the Pentagon? And standing here in the middle of the courtyard may not be the best place to be. So basically a Marine three-star came out and told everybody, "Okay, I want everyone to go out to the parking lot." He says, "Everyone get out of—we're going to clear here and just keep anybody who's a casualty and the people who are qualified, medical people. Everyone else move out." So what we did was we tried to police up some of the folks who were, I guess you'd just call it, more mentally affected. I mean, there were some people who were very—like, "What's happening? What are we doing? Oh, my God." You know, that kind of thing. And I guess it's more understandable—because one of the things that was fortunate is we had a pretty good handle on what had happened. We knew it was plane. We knew where it hit. We kind of had a feel. Whereas, a lot of people didn't have a clue what was going on. But anyway, what we did was we tried to help herd folks and reassure them, "Hey, we're okay. We were there. We're fine. Let's all move to the parking lot." . . .

So that was the first time we got out in the parking lot, and we were able to . . . look over and you could see the big plume of black smoke coming out. So a huge crowd of folks gathered here. Probably stayed out there, I don't know, maybe twenty minutes or half an hour, and tried to determine, okay, what next? What's the plan here? And at that time, this is when they started to set things up here. First responders are showing up. They're laying people out in the grass. Medics are showing up, that kind of thing. . . . And the issue was we're trying to figure out who's in charge. We're trying to say, "Okay. Do you need extra bodies?" And basically the answer was no. They said, "We don't want more people—we've already got enough good Samaritans over here. We don't need more bodies. We just need to make room for the trained—for the fire department and the trained medical personnel. Let them do their job. They're arriving on the scene. They're doing okay. We don't need more people coming in."

So, okay. . . . And there was still concern about a second plane coming in. That report came in. . . . They said, "Oh, we might have a second plane coming in." So we said, "Okay, everybody get out of the parking lot and move over here." And it was very interesting, because Crystal City had pretty much evacuated too. So you've just got—the streets are full of people everywhere. The Metro has been shut down, so nobody can Metro, and everybody and their brother is trying to talk on a cell phone, and none of it works, because it's all jammed up. And so that's kind of what happened. . . . We went over. Actually, there are some apartments over here, and some folks actually invited us in. And we were able to see what was going on on TV, and we were able to call our wives and say, "Okay, we're alive. We're okay. We have a 100-percent accountability in the office," that kind of thing.

Then we hitched a ride with a lady who works for—I think it's Department of Justice or Department of Transportation. She was also trying to get out of Crystal City. It took us a good three hours to travel about a mile. It was frustrating because you could see [Interstate] 395 was totally open, absolutely no traffic, but you couldn't get to 395. And so it took us about, like I said, three hours, and once we got to 395, we were sailing and got out of here and went home.

* * * *

My wife—she was very calm through this, she did very well. . . . I have three daughters. She was successful in pulling two of them out of school before they heard the news. She got my elementary schooler and my junior high schooler out of—she was able to go there and scoop them up before they knew anything was going on. My high schooler, that was kind of messy. Because at the high school, basically what they did was, they announced there's been an attack at the Pentagon, anybody whose parents work there come to the front office. So she was fine until she got to the front office and then you've got like fifty kids, and people panicking and crying and fearing the worst, and no one knows anything. So [my wife] was not happy at all about how the school handled that one because we tried not to make this a memorable event for my kids.

Brig. Gen. Karl W. Eikenberry *was the Deputy Director for Strategy, Plans and Policy, Office of the Deputy Chief of Staff for Operations and Plans. He was interviewed by Frank Shirer and Stephen Lofgren of the U.S. Army Center of Military History on 6 February 2002.*

MR. SHIRER: What were you preparing to do on the morning of 11 September?

BRIG. GEN. EIKENBERRY: I had, that morning, a briefing that was provided to me by a Major Andy Mueller who is a staff officer in our war plans division. . . . Major Mueller had come in and presented me with about a one-hour briefing. . . . I was sitting in my office there on the E-Ring. I was not aware at the time—the briefing was being conducted, with just Andy and I, one on one with each other and the door closed—that the attacks on the World Trade Center had occurred. No one had opened the door to inform us of that.

Andy completed the briefing and I had just told him, "Good job," and he had begun to stand up when we had the aircraft strike the Pentagon. . . .

The shock of the aircraft hitting the outside wall of the Pentagon just outside of our office caused a considerable concussion. As I recall, I think I was thrown up against the wall and had no idea as to what that concussion had come from, not aware of the attack on the Trade Center at that point, not clear whether it was some internal building explosion, whether it was a terrorist bomb outside, certainly nowhere in my list of possibilities was an aircraft strike.

We looked outside of my window. We were both of us sitting against the wall looking out towards my window, which is perhaps twelve feet away, and could see the entire wall of the window, the entire glass covered with a ball of flame, and could immediately feel the heat coming through the glass. The glass was the mylar protective glass, and so it withstood the shock and withstood the heat stress.

We didn't hesitate to leave the office. As I was heading out of the office, our secretary sitting out there, Ms. Linda Moore . . . she was screaming and I ran up to her to get her moving, and she conveyed then that General Wood, our Director for Strategy, Plans and Policy, was behind his door in his office and the door had bolted shut. He was unable to get out. So I credit her with perhaps saving General Wood's life, because had she left immediately, I'm certain that I would have left that office area not checking for General Wood. You know, the nature of this kind of staff office is if you ask me at any one point in time who is outside there, I don't know, and so it was her that triggered to me that General Wood was behind that door, which enabled me then to kick the door open and get him out.

We then left and got into the E-Ring of the corridor and there was, by this point, a considerable amount of smoke that was starting to fill the E-Ring of the Pentagon, the large ring that our offices opened out into, and there was some flame that was starting to appear in the hallway.

General Wood and I first went to the left to try to use that as our escape route, and as we worked our way down, perhaps about twenty-five feet, someone in advance of us had opened one of the doors leading down the flights of steps—us being on the third floor—had opened up a doorway to, then proceeded down to the ground floor to get us an escape route out. But, as I looked, there was a huge amount, a dense amount of smoke pouring out of that door. If you opened it you could see some flames coming out, turned around and said it was too hot, and we turned around and went back. What was interesting is we were to find out later, none of us having any idea about where this—what was going on and where the best route was to escape. It was exploratory learning. So heat and smoke telling us that's as far as you should go in that direction, we turned around and went back. As we went back then, we were to go over two broken fractures in the floor on the third floor, both of them several feet high, and climbed up over those, climbed back down over another one, and eventually made it then to one of the corridors that leads towards the interior of the Pentagon, that would be corridor number four that we were heading back down. Now, when we looked later at the damage that occurred to the Pentagon, what we had discovered was that when we first made that move to the left, had we just gone about another ten more feet we were through the—we had broken out of the real problem area, but it was just that that one door that had been tried, in fact, did have huge—had a large amount of fuel down there and was burning upward, so that dissuaded us from going any further. Had we just run right past that thing on the third floor we were out of it.

So, those two break points that we ran back over, that eventually was to be the collapse zone at the Pentagon, which you saw on the television or in the event you drove by. So we made it past that, got down into the fourth corridor, I then remained at about the C-Ring, and held a position there while our people were getting evacuated out. I remained behind with several of our people, several of our officers, our Colonel Mark Volk distinguished himself by heading back to the E-Ring and doing as best he could continuing to search for people.

* * * *

[T]he biggest stumbling block was just the density of the smoke and the blackness, the darkness, then that was in the E-Ring. I tell you, at one point, I do have a very distinct memory of . . . wondering if I was going to make it out of there because I was sucking in a fairly good amount of smoke at that point.

MR. SHIRER: How far had it come down?

BRIG. GEN. EIKENBERRY: The smoke was down at probably four feet. In other words, from four feet off the ground, that's where the smoke level was very dense at that point in the hallway.

MR. SHIRER: That's pretty fast.

BRIG. GEN. EIKENBERRY: Yeah, it was pouring in quickly.

MR. SHIRER: So at this time you were crouching, you were crawling?

BRIG. GEN. EIKENBERRY: Unfortunately, no. I'll admit it, no, I was not. You know, big lesson learned, because, yes, I was crouching to the extent that—yes, I was crouching, I guess, somewhat, but would I have been better to get down on one knee and assess? Yeah, I sure would have. . . .

We heard a big rumbling about ten or fifteen minutes after these initial shocks had occurred in the side of the building, and I estimate now that . . . that rumbling that we heard—which led me and some of our fellow officers that were together at that point, to say, "It's probably time to leave"—that that rumbling was probably the collapse then occurring in the Pentagon itself. From there we proceeded to the interior courtyard of the Pentagon. . . . After about twenty minutes then we proceeded out to the South Parking area of the Pentagon, having difficulty trying to get a full accountability of our people. We were quickly to about a 90-percent count, but were having difficulties in getting some of the—bringing that 10 percent down to zero. . . . So, then we proceeded from South Parking, we were pushed by part of the security force then as it started to tighten up and more law enforcement took control, we were asked to move from the South Parking area further towards the site of the Pentagon City Mall. We waited there for about an hour, and probably got the unaccounted-for now down to perhaps about five people, and then a decision made that we weren't going to be going back into the office anytime soon. We made a decision made sometime around 12:30 to just release our people. . . .

Maj. Gen. John R. Wood was the Director of Directorate of Strategy, Plans and Policy (DAMO-SS), Office of the Deputy Chief of Staff for Operations and Plans (DCSOPS). He was interviewed by Stephen Lofgren of the U.S. Army Center of Military History on 1 March 2002.

MAJ. GEN. WOOD: I think we had just moved out of our historical spaces. I say, "historical," because we've been in there since the Pentagon was built, I believe. . . . We moved down into wedge 1, the new third-floor . . . 3 Echo 450, I think, was one of the numbers, something like that. . . . [We] had been in there about maybe two months at the most, in the new area. . . . We were— the whole area was essentially in the state of flux. . . . We were just kind of getting our rhythm back up. . . . What was going on at the time, interestingly, too, I think, was we're concluding most of the strategic studies that been ongoing since Secretary Rumsfeld had come in. There were a lot of ongoing meetings, almost on the hour, reviewing all of the new strategic planning documents. The QDR report was being concluded—the Quadrennial Defense

Close-up of the right side of the collapsed section

Review . . . and then we were also finishing up or working hard on what was called the Defense Planning Guidance for '03.

So, at about the moment in time when this attack happened, we were finishing a summer-long process of Quadrennial Defense Review meetings and then defense-planning guidance meetings. So, most of that material was stacked on my desk and we were perched on a point where we thought we had the strategy about right, having fought it hard with this incoming administration, who were frankly learning what they had inherited and frankly learning what it was to organize the department, and that was painful, but we had pretty well finished the process. I tee this up because it really was an interesting moment in time. September 11th was just about the moment where, at least, the incoming administration felt that they had—they had it about right. . . .

So the 11th of September dawned. As I recall that morning, we had the standard review of what we had written and submitted the night before, the day before on these strategic documents. I think there was a tank [a tank is a meeting of service representatives in the Joint Chiefs of Staff's area] that was being proposed that day and I was working on the preparation for that tank. And I had two meetings in front of me. . . . The next thing on my calendar was a meeting with a group of people who were preparing with me to go over to Congress to talk about an issue with Congressman

[Duncan D.] Hunter, who was asking questions about wheels versus tracks and why we were doing certain things with the interim brigade combat team. . . . So here we were that morning worried about the strategy and tactics in a new world that was being presented.

I had gone down—I had an early call that morning to go down and talk—to reinforce a pitch that was being given to the Secretary of the Army on Crusader and how Crusader fit a particular strategic need for our Army. I was down in the vicinity of the Secretary's office, the Secretary of the Army's office, Secretary White, talking to a number of programmers and material developers, and the aide to the Secretary of the Army came up to two of us, three of us standing there. . . . He said something to the effect, "Did you hear a plane hit the tower?" And we couldn't even understand what he was talking about. We had no idea at all what he was talking about. He explained that the World Trade Center had been hit by a plane. We really couldn't register that. It just—it just seemed like a horrible accident. So I walked down the hall. It turns out—I talked myself out of going into the meeting with the Secretary because things seemed to be moving towards reaction to the event. It didn't look like the meeting was going to occur.

I dropped into the DCSOPS office on the way down back to my office, and while I was in there I found out that the tower had been hit by a second airplane and saw it, actually the films on a TV there in the DCSOPS office, as we all stood there in shock and looked at it. And at that point the DCSOPS office was clearly working its way towards a crisis response and gathering information, and it seemed apparent to me I needed to get down and take stock of what was going on in my world down in the—with my people—and knowing that this was going to be an event that would kind of bring all the lights up in the crisis response center, the Army Operations Center. So I walked down the hall down to my office. I found my office staff, you know, obviously concerned. We had CNN on two of the TVs in there and we all were just essentially trying to make sense of what was going on and how this could have occurred. I think this is about 9:30. . . . I went into my office and sat down and the phone rang, or my secretary, Linda Moore, talked to me. She said, "Your daughter is on the phone." And—so I was sitting at my desk talking to my daughter, looking at the TV in front of me. It was across the office space there and it was just constant replay of the towers being attacked. My daughter was—this is my oldest daughter, who works in Maryland, and she had just heard from my other daughter who works up on Capitol Hill for [Congressman] Ike Skelton. They were very concerned and had called each other about what had happened.

My oldest daughter was very upset. So I spent about five minutes with her, calming her down and reassuring her and we were just comparing thoughts. She was particularly upset because my youngest had called her and expressed concern that I was personally at risk because her premonition was that the Pentagon was obviously a problem for a terrorist attack. The thought hadn't occurred to me frankly, but I calmed my oldest daughter down. And so I was in my office by myself. I calmed my daughter down, and I . . . told her I loved her and I said, "Well, listen, keep your head down," and I hung up the phone. And just as I hung up the phone and turned back to my desk, picked back up this strategic document, the QDR, to read it, this last copy of it to make sure that everything was what I wanted it to be, I just remember turning back around towards my desk, having hung up the phone from talking to my daughter about—probably a second after that—I heard an enormous—I heard it. I got blown out of my chair. I was—I heard a—it was a double concussion. There were two very discrete explosions right next to my head and they were—I mean, two separate in the sense that they were maybe, you know, maybe a millisecond between the two, but two very distinct, "Boom. Boom." Huge not—it didn't burst my eardrums, but it was clearly an explosion.

My first thought was as I got back up, was—for whatever reason I knew immediately we were under attack. It was not—there was no doubt in my mind that these, all these things were connected because I had been turning—I had been watching the towers burn in front of me. As soon as I heard that hit I just—I had absolute assurance that we were under attack, and my first thought then—I felt it was like an RPG [rocket-propelled grenade] round or someone had fired a LAW [light antitank weapon] at the building or something, because—and not only that, they fired it at my window, because it was right next to me. All of the—everything that wasn't nailed down on the walls had blown into the office, and there was glass all over the tables. But my office was fairly much intact except for all of the shattered things on the floor. So within my office space, it had been a terrible concussion, but there was no evident blast damage except what had fallen off the walls.

So obviously my first thought was to check—get out, check my people and, you know, see how everybody was, because I had no sense of the enormity of it at all because I was in this little enclosed space. As it turned out I was in a space on the E-Ring where the yellow windows in my office—I had thought it just had a tint, had been tinted to prevent maybe microwave intrusion or some other strange thing. It turns out they were blast windows, $10,000 each. They did not—although I remember from the corner of my eye when I got thrown out of my chair, I remember seeing them bulge. I remember the—it was like there was a bulge in the windows, but they were blast windows. And then the walls actually of that office space, the new office space had—the outer walls of the E-Ring—had Teflon inside the walls, and then I found out later that actually the frames of the windows and the walls themselves were all bolted together with steel. So I was living inside a fortified cocoon without knowing it, so that could take a certain level of blast.

I could hear screaming. I could hear confusion. I could hear commotion. . . . I fought my way through all the stuff that was down. I didn't fight my way, I just worked my way through all this as quickly as I could because there were flames outside my window that covered the—I was on the third floor and there was just violent fire outside my window that covered the entire top—I mean, it covered the windows from bottom to top. It was a raging fire. And that yellow tint—I remember the yellow tint of the fire caused by the yellow tint of the windows, but I knew it was a fuel fire because I could see the black tips of all the flames. I'd seen fuel fires before. It was a fuel fire. In my estimation that's sure what it looked like.

Well—so I get to the door of my office and the door doesn't open, there's no way to open it. There's—the door handle did not engage the latch. . . . So I was frantic, starting to get frantic, about getting out of that door because things were just adding up at a rapid rate. And I'd say it took me about, oh, not more than twenty seconds to kind of get up, sort myself out, and move my way to the door. So I'm starting to add this up. I've got big planes outside the window, things are falling now from the ceiling, and I can't get out the door. So I started pounding on the door and pulling on the handle. I might have called out, I don't recall, and obviously—so it's getting worse. Smoke is now in the office and it's starting to come down from the ceiling. The smoke is—it's kind of a gray-like smoke we had. It wasn't the black smoke, it was kind of a gray-like smoke and it's starting to fill the office up, and I'm starting to think through options about how to get through that door. I later learned I could have taken a chair and thrown it through the walls because they were plasterboard. I now know that. I now check walls out. I can get out of this office without going through that door, I guarantee you.

So I was looking up at the ceiling. I remember looking up at the ceiling and thinking I could go through the dropdown, drop ceiling, and probably—because I had seen workmen up there. I could probably get into that space and get out. So I was about ready—I was just about ready to get up on the conference table . . . to go through the ceiling, and the door exploded open. I mean, it literally burst open and I find General Eikenberry, who had kicked the door down—laid down and kicked the door down. And Linda's right behind him, my secretary, and, you know, it's this, "Are you okay?" Linda looked in absolute shock. I looked behind her and everybody is moving out of the office as quickly as possible, but at that moment there were a lot of faces staring in my door to make sure that I was okay. So I assured everybody I was fine, and quickly thanked those who had gotten me out, and ran out and we started counting people to make sure we could account for everybody.

I remember . . . General Eikenberry's secretary, I had never seen such a look of horror and shock in my life. She just—she was almost hyperventilating, just constantly screaming—not scream-ing, but she was absolutely stunned and upset. And [Lt.] Colonel [Bruce] Foreman, my XO, was reassuring her because all we wanted to do really was to count the people and get out of there. I don't remember a smoke alarm. I don't remember a fire alarm. I don't remember anything going on in the building that would have helped us get out of that building, and I told this to the engi-neers. We were just trying to make sense of what had happened.

But in general things were intact, except the smoke. There was a lot of smoke, and we knew that there was a fire, and we knew we had to get out of there. So we went out into the hallway and noticed that the wall across the way had—there was a lot of destruction on the wall across the hallway from our office space, but our side, the outermost side of the E-Ring had, at least where we stood, was fairly contiguous. We looked left out of my office, back towards the DCSOPS office, and in fact towards the old space that we had moved from, and there was very thick black smoke. Clearly, we thought, realized immediately that—because someone had gone down there and looked around and said, "This is not the way to go." So we went to the right out of our office. So we're standing in the hallway on the E-Ring looking back towards the fourth corridor, and that appeared to be the best place to go. So there was not as much smoke and we proceeded down that hallway.

The hallway itself was buckled, the floor of the hallway was—it was like going down a rough road and, you know, it was buckling. . . . As it turns out, that was the space that collapsed about fifteen minutes later. All of that area collapsed, fell in. What we didn't understand at the time was—as I was sitting in my office with my back to the wall . . . facing, sitting north—everything behind me and below me as it turned out, behind the wall to my back and below me, had been destroyed. The plane flew right under us. The plane actually hit about sixty feet between the second and third floor, right at the breakpoint of the second and third floor and down. We found out later that everybody below us and behind that wall died and only, frankly, because of those windows and the strength of the concussion down below us. . . . The engineers later told me that [this] was the closest space not destroyed, on this side of the building, to the impact of that plane.

So we moved down the hallway, kind of collecting people as we went, and made it down to the fourth corridor and there was—clearly the smoke was becoming a big problem, but we could still see and moved down—we all went to the left, down the fourth corridor and headed towards the A-Ring, towards the closest way out from our estimation. Probably about thirty people in the hallway at about that point, at least when I got there. And I would say I got to that hallway, I got to the fourth corridor to head into the A-Ring five minutes, six minutes—you know, about five to seven minutes after the plane hit. Having kind of worked our way down . . . a lot of shouting, and a lot of screaming, and a lot of reassuring, and a lot of "Everybody stay down," and . . . you could just see the emergency response and then the training going on. There was general calm to things in terms of steady action to get out. People accounting for people, reassuring—great shock, great uncertainty as to what was going on. . . .

So we all moved down the hallway and I was kind of taking reports from them as I went, "Do you have all your people? Have you accounted for all your people?" . . . So I was not

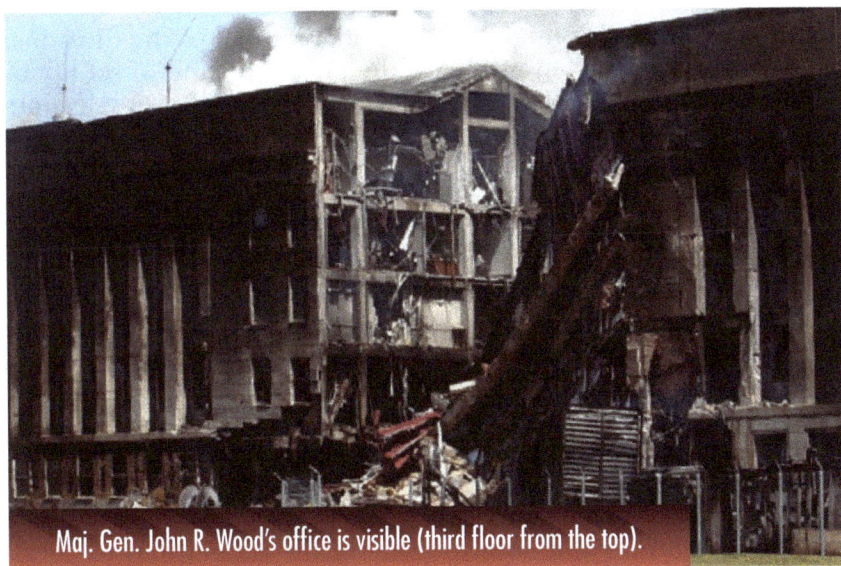

Maj. Gen. John R. Wood's office is visible (third floor from the top).

moving very fast because I was kind of taking reports as we moved down the fourth corridor in the hallway. . . . But it became pretty evident that we had to get out of there because the smoke was really building up. It was starting to get very thick and black and we were really, frankly, leaning over at the waist and starting to move down a little bit further as we had to kind of get below the smoke and move down that hallway, down the fourth hallway.

So we all ushered everyone down, like herding ducks, down the end of the hallway. I looked behind me. When I looked behind me, maybe two or three people left in that hallway doing the same thing I was, just looking in spaces and calling out. . . . So we got into the A-Ring and obviously we needed to get into the central courtyard of the Pentagon. It was a pretty large group of people going down the stairs, getting down to the courtyard. So we all moved into the courtyard. The scene in the courtyard was pandemonium. Pandemonium at our exit. There was—there was a calm on the other side of the building. There was not— it was just the difference between those who had been closest to the blast and those who really didn't understand what had happened. All they knew is they'd been told to evacuate the building, or for whatever reason they evacuated the building. We were leaving because of the smoke and the intensity of the shock that was on our specific area of the building.

I found, at that point, all of my leaders for all of the divisions, and so we assembled inside on the grass. We kind of set up an SS [directorate] collection point and I sent all of my leaders out to find all their people and get them to that point . . . and so that took about fifteen minutes. So we got everybody accounted for that we could. . . . Suddenly there was a Navy admiral that I knew from the joint world who came—he was running over to me and said, "We've got to get out of here and we've got to get out of here now." I don't know what he knew, but he was trying—he was a three star and he came over to me and found out that we had organized, if you would, kind of our quadrant of people. And you could just see the military chain shaping in front of our eyes. And he said, "Okay, I think we've got what we need. We've got to get out of here right away." It made sense to me.

So we told everyone to evacuate out the tunnel that—I think the tunnel was somewhere around, below first corridor, somewhere—it's the access tunnel that comes into the inner courtyard. So all of us moved outside the courtyard. At that point we walked, everybody was kind of—we had fallen in on a crowd that was again not really sure of what had happened, and we were still trying to make sense of it ourselves, but we kept keeping each other together. So we moved all the way into the South Parking, and we moved all the way through South Parking with this crowd of people to the bank . . . below [Interstate] 395.

We were sitting on that highway bank down there. We just did not—we were standing there, staring back over to the side of the Pentagon where the smoke was immense, and just initially some response people coming in. All of us trying to get to a cell phone, all of us trying to check in, and most of the cell phones worked at that point because people were calling to get—account for people. I was able to get a phone call through about that point to General Kensinger, who was the deputy DCSOPS. He was down in the Army Operations Center. I had called down there to tell him I was outside the building, and I was accounting for all the people I could from DCSOPS, and I was doing that as best I could outside the building with all the leaders I found, the director-level leaders I could find from my area in that part of the crowd. Probably, I don't know how to estimate a crowd, but there were probably two thousand or three thousand people in the area I was in.

We were suddenly told to move away from the building even further because of some suspected threat, plus we were kind of making it difficult in that area, where we were at the fringe of the South Parking lot, for the evacuation vehicles to move in and out. We moved out of the tunnel that goes under 395 and we were standing over by where the Drug Enforcement Agency is, DEA, this crowd of SS, all my people and some others, and suddenly they told us we had to move away from the DEA building—we didn't know it was the DEA building— because suddenly it was potentially at risk. So we were kind of being moved around and moved away by policeman, not many of them, but some had some sense of what was potentially going on.

The question on all our minds at that point, in my mind, was to get those last three or four people accounted for. I remember at about that point, as we were being shuttled away from the DEA building, I had not accounted for the planners, the joint planners, and I hadn't heard any report from them. And so I immediately went into, you know, energetically trying to find those people and was able to find one or two people who could connect me back to that, who had seen who and that sort of thing. We stood around by the shopping center across the way here for about another half an hour accounting for people, kind of making sense of what was going on. I remember . . . a civilian who works for me here, had his cell phone and finally got through I think to his sister, and we gave him a bunch of names to, you know, get on . . . the phone lines, and get some phone calls out to some of our relatives. And that's how my wife was notified that I was all right, through kind of a third party call back to her.

Well, we finally agreed—I was talking to Phil Kensinger again down in the AOC and there wasn't much else we could do. I would say this was about an hour and a half after the plane attack. . . . We were told we can't go back into the building. We were all standing out there without our berets, with no jackets, you know, without any of our personal effects. We were just kind of standing out there figuring, well, what more can we do? There was nothing more we could do, nothing except get to a phone and get to our families and remain accountable through our chain of command. So I released everybody. . . . I rode the subway home to King Street Metro. It wasn't very crowded. People didn't really understand what was going on, and I remember I was upset because I didn't have a beret. I was out of uniform. I mean, all of us were, so we all were just kind of like stranded. . . .

[I got home] and I walked into my house, and there's my entire [family]—my father, my wife, my daughters, all huddled around the TV, staring at what had happened. And I just kind of walk in, without my beret. I just kind of walked in. Well, they were staring at the TV, of the fires that were raging out the windows of my office area, and again my wife had only gotten this very unusual call from a person she didn't know that didn't really make sense. . . . So I walk in like an apparition to this collection of family, and that was a reunion. It took me about five minutes to get everybody calmed down, and then I went up to the TV and I stared at what they were looking at, and it was the first time I, you know, I really realized the enormity of what had happened, because we couldn't see it from where we had evacuated. And that's really when I finally believed that an airliner had hit the Pentagon. Again, I thought it was a, you know, an RPG round or something because—but an RPG didn't hit five meters from my window, but it was an airplane that hit about sixty feet from there.

Well, then the phone calls. The first guy to call me was Ike Skelton, the congressman, who knew that my daughter had been frantic, knew where I sat at the Pentagon. . . . I'll never forget he asked—he said, "What can I do? Bob, what I can do?". . . Of course, having asked first how I was and how my people were and then he said, "What can I do?" And of course the phone call itself meant a lot to me.

Lt. Col. Isabelle Slifer served in the Office of the Deputy Chief of Staff for Personnel (DCSPER). She was interviewed at the Pentagon by Lt. Col. Robert Rossow of the Office of the Deputy Chief of Staff for Personnel on 8 October 2001.

LT. COL. SLIFER: On the 11th of September I actually started my sixth day with the DCSPER section. So going in to work, I went to work with any kind of apprehensions that any new person has; i.e., okay, what is my function, let me read the files that the person that I replaced left me. And I say that because Major Christa Holderman and I did not have a lot of overplay time, but she truly left some great files which at the time I thought this would obviously enhance my ability to do the job, my mission. In fact, the day before I brought in some very, to me, expensive three-ring notebooks because the environment that I was working in was so new, so pretty, for the lack of a better word, that I thought the typical Army three-ring binders wouldn't suffice. So on Monday and in my thought process on Tuesday morning I was putting . . . continuity/smart books together so that with Christa Holderman's files I would be able to do a fairly decent job. . . . It was just a typical Tuesday, very nice, warm, or to be warm, sunny day. I was going to run that day. That's why I brought in my running shoes. I didn't bring in my uniform because taking public transportation I thought, well, running shoes versus uniform. So I brought in my running shoes. Now in hindsight I'm glad I didn't bring my Class A uniforms et cetera because like many people—my colleagues who had their uniforms in their lockers, they don't have them anymore.

At any rate, I got to my desk. And on a personal note, I was—I remember calling my son, one of my two, my twelve-year-old son, before I went into the Metro to let him know that he needed to get up, make sure his brother was up and, of course, make sure that their dad was up. And in hindsight I thought, well, that could have been the last time I ever talked to anybody in my family or my son, one of my sons, let me put it that way. Walked in the building. Again, nothing unusual. Security checks were given, as they are. And again, it was nothing like we're enduring now since the 11th of September. But got to my desk and decided, okay, let me look through some more of my files. In fact, Christa had left some files on the desk, so let me start to file those. Let me complete my continuity/smart books that I was working on. And then I decided, well, let me call my husband because he was taking the cats to the veterinarian. In fact, I called him on his cell phone. He had just returned from getting the cats there. And when he told me, he said, "Hey, maybe you should watch the television because there's been an accident at the World Trade Towers." And as I hung up I heard other people saying, "Hey, let's go into the general's office," and that would be General [Harry] Axson, who was the DMPM and was TDY, "because there's been an accident at the Trade Tower." And I thought someone said a helicopter ran into it. Well . . . by the time the majority of us got into General Axson's office to watch the television, we witnessed in actuality the second plane going into the Trade Center. As everybody would say, a surreal and almost movie-like production.

So it was one of those dazed situations that the majority of us walked out of General Axson's office back into our cubicles, and I know for a fact that a couple of my colleagues were making phone calls home. And I started to, when I heard from a Lieutenant Colonel Jordan that the crisis action team had stood up. Well, being new to the area and the duty position, I thought maybe I should hang around and find out what is needed. Now, at that same time other people, my branch chief, Lieutenant Colonel Deborah Fix, was also coming into this makeshift meeting of sorts and other people were surrounding thinking, okay, what's going on? That was probably around 9:36 when Lieutenant Colonel Jordan made this sort of announcement without alerting everybody, but the people that were in earshot. Just standing around I'd say there was a group of eight of us. . . . Two minutes into this makeshift or just spontaneous conversation about the crisis action team, the building violently, violently—and I can't say it, I can't emphasize it enough—shook. But I also want to say [that] almost as fast as you could snap your fingers, while it was shaking . . . Lieutenant Colonel Deborah Fix shouted, "Get down." And [if] the momentum of the sway of the building didn't throw you down, the force of her body made us all get down. I mean, getting down, I remember this like a mammoth—the only way I can relate it to you is like a flashbulb went out and some people say there was a fireball. Coupled with that and even before the flash was this freight train sound. And when I hear people report on giving explanations of how a tornado sounds, well, I heard the freight train sound with a mammoth whoosh at the same time. That light sensation. And, of course, things were falling. Of course, that was the collapse of the ceiling. Now, we were almost, I don't want to say on top of each other, but we were in close proximity to each other. . . . I believe it was Sergeant Major [Tony] Rose who shouted from a near vicinity, "We have been hit. Move out. Move and move out now. I repeat, we've been hit. Move and move out now." . . .

We all began to low crawl. I'd say we low crawled maybe about forty feet. I sidebar that remark by saying that if anybody told me at my age that I could low crawl as fast as I did, you know, with the combination of I'm sure the almighty God and my adrenalin and, of course, former military training. When we got to the door that led us into the fourth corridor, I remember looking to the right; i.e., looking down to E-Ring and seeing this avalanche of smoke coming towards us. It wasn't black at that time. It was more of a golden brown. When I explained that to someone else later after the incident they said that's because the fire was still inside that smoke. . . . When we got to the fourth corridor there was a yellow haze, so my first thought was we'd been hit by a chemical missile. The same thing when we got to that double door or that door leading into the fourth corridor. We got up off our feet and we made a daisy chain. I remember grabbing onto Sergeant First Class Frazier's belt buckle. [Someone], I believe it was major sergeant, we were holding hands. And someone was holding my backside pants. It reminded me of when my two boys were small. And I don't know who that person was. But it was comforting to have people near you.

However, we got up off our feet and we kept low with this daisy-chain effect. Now, someone recognized the fact that . . . we couldn't get out of that corridor because the firewall or the fire doors had already closed. So someone in the front, and I was only about three or four people—no, actually two or three people from the front—led us into an office that was next door to us, which got us out to the fifth corridor. Getting out to the fifth corridor, it was probably the most beautiful sight in the world because at that time I realized, okay, whatever had happened was now behind me. The emotions that I had going through that experience—and you could have told me it happened in one second, you could have told me it went on for thirty minutes, which I know it didn't. I say that because time stood still. But my emotions were—not scared, not panicking, but I felt calm. I was with my fellow comrades. I mean by that, soldiers. I felt the buddy system was in place. And I knew I was going to get out okay.

Col. Philip A. McNair *was the Executive Officer in the Office of the Deputy Chief of Staff for Personnel (DCSPER). He prepared this account of his experiences in October 2001.*

At the time of the terrorist attack on the Pentagon on September 11th, 2001, I was conducting a meeting in the DCSPER Conference room (2E487). This was a biweekly meeting of the executive officers for the various directorates and operating agencies of the DCSPER. Attendees were Maj. Steve Long (PERSCOM SGS [General Staff Secretariat]), Lt. Col. Robert Grunewald (DCSPER IMO [Information Management Office]), Lt. Col. Dennis

Johnson (DCSPER Mgt Spt Ofc), Ms. Martha Carden (DCSPER front office), Lt. Col. Marilyn Wills (CACO [Congressional Affairs Coordination Office]), Lt. Col. Marian Ward (DCSPER PR [Directorate of Plans, Resources, and Operations]), Maj. Regina Grant (DCSPER HR [Directorate of Human Resources]), and Ms. Lois Stevens (DMPM [Directorate of Military Personnel Management]). Visitors were Col. Thomas and Lt. Col. Nutbrown (DISC4 [Director of Information Systems for Command, Control, Communications, and Computers]). Mr. Max Bielke (Retirement Services) attended the meeting initially but left early to go to another meeting. When the plane struck the building there was a tremendous explosion, and I saw fire erupt through the ceiling behind and above Martha, who was seated at the opposite end of the table from me. Thick black smoke immediately began to fill the room, the lights went out, and we could feel intense heat. Unaware of the attack on the World Trade Center in New York, most of us assumed that a bomb had been detonated. My first reaction was to jump up and say, "What the hell was that!?"

With the conference room in total darkness, getting hotter and filling with very acrid smoke, we moved toward the E-Ring hallway door to exit, but someone yelled, "The door is locked!" I heard Martha screaming, and Lt. Col. Grunewald said something to the effect of "I've got you, Martha!" I recall yelling to the group, "OK, let's get out of here!" or something obvious like that. Despite the confusion, there did not seem to be any outright panic, and we began to move as a group toward the other door, which was next to the stage and led into the DMPM work area. Someone said, "Get down below the smoke!" and we dropped to our hands and knees. There was in fact a space of about two feet between the smoke and the floor, and it was much easier to breathe, so I repeated the comment, telling everyone to get down so that they could breathe. I recall thinking about childhood fire safety training in which you are taught to crawl below the smoke (since smoke rises) and thinking that now I truly understood why they taught you to do that. We crawled along in more or less single-file fashion and exited the conference room. I expected the work area outside the room to be okay because I thought that a bomb had probably been detonated outside the conference room in the E-Ring hallway and therefore when we exited the room in the opposite direction we would have avoided the danger zone. Unfortunately, the DMPM work area was just as bad: dark, smoke filled, hot, and getting worse. The smoke smelled like burning plastic, electrical wiring, and petroleum products, and burned the throat when inhaled.

In the process of crawling, we became separated into several groups, each trying to find a way out. My group included Ms. Stevens and Lt. Col. Wills, and later included Ms. Betty "Doc" Maxfield, who worked in the DMPM area, and perhaps Lt. Col. Ward. Initially I headed toward another E-Ring hallway door near the copier room, around the corner from the conference room, thinking that getting into the hallway would allow us to escape fastest. However, when I rounded the corner it became immediately apparent that I was going in the wrong direction. I could see fire under the door, and it was significantly hotter, so I reversed course and yelled to the group, "We've got to go in the other direction; let's go toward the DMPM's office!" We then crawled through the DMPM workspaces heading generally in the direction of the center courtyard, which seemed instinctively like the right way to go.

Unfortunately, the DMPM work area was comprised of a confusing maze of cubicles, aisles, offices, printer stations, copiers, and the like, which hampered our ability to find our way out in the darkness and smoke. We held onto the person in front of us as we crawled, and occasionally someone would try a turn or move in a direction they thought led to safety. Nothing worked, and breathing was increasingly difficult. We yelled encouragement to each other, and I could hear Martha and Lt. Col. Grunewald yelling in their group apart from ours. Our voices began to crack and get raspy due to the smoke we were inhaling. We entered many dead-end areas and encountered doors that could not be opened and we were increasingly frustrated. I was not sure if we were going to find a way out before being overcome by the smoke, which was intensifying, along with the heat. Things were falling on us from above, such as bits of ceiling, melted plastic, and water from sprinklers. I could hear the crackling of fire, the creaking and crashing of office furniture and building components, and the incessant blaring of fire alarms. We crawled through puddles of water on the carpet, created by the sprinklers, and I scooped up water and splashed it on my face, trying to snort some of it into my nose to combat the effects of the smoke. This helped somewhat, and I showed the others. Lt. Col. Wills had a piece of cloth that she soaked in the water, and we took turns breathing through it to give ourselves a bit of a break from the constant inhalation of smoke. We held onto each other as best we could, though the order of the group changed from time to time as we turned corners or tried different ways to get out. Finally I heard someone yell something about a window, and we moved toward the voice. I saw light coming in through a window that appeared to have been partially blown out, over-looking the service road between the B- and C-Rings. Sitting on the windowsill was Spec. Petrovich. We stuck our heads out the window to suck in the fresh air, which was life-saving, then I got on the sill and together with Petrovich pushed out the window frame with my feet, far enough to be able to get people out. Then Petrovich and I began to lower and drop people through the window (about fifteen feet to the ground) into the arms of people below, who were waving and yelling to us.

We lowered Ms. Stevens, and Ms. Dalisay Olaes (who arrived on the scene at some time unknown to me), and dropped them. Both sustained injuries in the process; Ms. Olaes broke her leg seriously, and Ms. Stevens sprained her ankle. Spec. Petrovich was lowered when he began to have serious difficulty breathing. I learned later that he may have broken out the window himself, or broken it out more after the concussion of the crash caused it to be loosened. We also lowered "Doc" Maxfield and Lt. Col. Marian Ward, who also sprained his ankle in the drop. After the others were out, I attempted to reenter the area while Lt. Col. Wills remained at the window shouting into the room so that others might find their way there, but after crawling in a short distance I found reentry to be impossible due to smoke, fire, and darkness. I returned to the window and told Lt. Col. Wills that we must get out. At this time the smoke and heat from the fire inside the building was being fed by the fresh air coming in through the open window and conditions around us were becoming worse. She did not want to exit because she was worried about coworkers who might still have been inside, but I ordered her to go. We stayed in place for a couple of minutes, yelling back into the room in case there were others who might hear and move toward the window, but finally I lowered Lt. Col. Wills out, then climbed out myself. By the time I got out the people below had moved a trash dumpster under the window, and had propped a ladder on top of it, and I simply had to drop a few feet to the ladder and climb down.

When I landed in the service road area below the window, I found numerous others there, from all services, but none I recognized except for Sgt. Maj. Tony Rose from DMPM. I did not see any of those who exited through the window with me, and learned later that they had been helped to a safer area by people gathered on the road. Turning back toward the area from which I had just escaped, I could see thick black smoke pouring from broken windows all along that section of the building, and two large holes, perhaps ten feet wide, that appeared to have been blown out of the side of the build at ground level. The scene on the street was somewhat chaotic, with thirty to thirty-five people in various disheveled uniforms, all concerned with coworkers left in the building, and all trying to figure out how to help. I climbed through one of the holes in the side of the building, thinking that there may be people trapped there behind or underneath rubble and debris, and several others went with me. Smoke was pouring out and with no light it was almost impossible to see, and the deeper in we went the more difficult it was to breathe. We shouted to alert potential victims of our presence, and heard voices behind a huge metal electrical or air conditioning cabinet, which was too massive to be moved. I grabbed computer parts, ceiling tiles, boards, desk components—anything I could free—and passed it to the person behind me, who in turn passed it to the person behind him and so on until it was thrown out of the building. After digging for a while I could no longer breathe, so I left and told those outside that we would have to work in short shifts so that we could keep going. Others moved into the hole, and I went back in after I got enough fresh air to breathe normally again. It was frustrating work because we had no lights or breathing apparatus, and were unable to move everything necessary to free the survivors. I remember seeing an arm poke out of the rubble, and together with Sgt. Maj. Rose pulled on it and hauled out a Navy petty officer, who appeared to be okay. She had dug her way out from the inside and had met us digging from our side. I don't know how many were rescued in this fashion, but I heard later it was seven or so, between our hole and the other one. The survivors were primarily Navy personnel, who had worked on the first floor below the DCSPER area.

At one point I walked away and attempted to find flashlights or any other tool that might help us. I went down one of the corridors in the undamaged part of the building and looked for janitors' closets, mechanical carts or anything, but found only a painter's mask, which I picked up. When I returned to the street, the rescue efforts were continuing, but it was obvious that the smoke and fire were intensifying in this area at the time, and glass and other building components were falling from above. Flames were visible in the windows above. I saw a group attempting to connect a water hose to a faucet on the wall, but they had no pliers and could not turn the water on because the faucet handle had been removed. Others had gathered hand-held fire extinguishers and were spraying them into the holes in the wall, to little avail. The heat caused the spray to vaporize instantly. I found a fire extinguisher and took it to the second hole, and began to climb inside when someone yelled for me to "watch out!" and I saw electrical wires dangling near the entrance, sparking whenever they touched each other. I went in a short way and found others in there amidst the smoke, still searching for survivors. I sprayed my fire extinguisher at a spot where the smoke appeared to be the most thick, but accomplished little. There was not much room to work inside and I was blocking what little light there was coming in from the hole, so I climbed out, handing the painters mask to someone inside.

Back in the street it appeared that most of the people were beginning to drift away, apparently feeling that further attempts to enter the building were futile. Someone from either the police or fire department told us that we had to leave the area because it was unsafe and another plane was inbound. That was the first time I had heard about a plane, and when I questioned others about it I was told about the World Trade Center attack. I later learned that the holes we had climbed through in our rescue efforts were caused by the nose and landing gear of the plane, though I do not recall seeing any identifiable airplane parts.

I walked down the service road, entered the fourth corridor and exited into the Pentagon center courtyard, where I was mostly alone except for a small group of medical personnel huddled over someone lying on the ground. I heard the name "Yates" and recognized it to be one of the DCSPER folks, so I went over and saw Mr. John Yates being treated by medical personnel. I stayed with him until they evacuated him, then I left the courtyard along with the few people remaining there, at the direction of police and firefighters who again said that another plane was potentially inbound. I walked out into the South Parking area, made my way around to the medical triage area, and was directed by a doctor into an ambulance, which I assume was due to my appearance at the time. I was soaking wet, blackened from the smoke, my uniform was a mess and I could barely talk. I was given oxygen by EMT personnel in the ambulance, which was all I wanted. I told the ambulance attendants that all I needed was some oxygen to help me breathe a little better, and that I did not want to take up ambulance space when there were surely others who needed it more. They told me that because I had inhaled so much smoke and my throat was raspy they could not be sure what might happen to me over the next few hours, so they took me to Arlington hospital over my objections. They cut my pants away from my legs to check for cuts or breaks, but I was okay. My injuries consisted of minor cuts and bruises, mostly on my hands and arms, from digging through rubble and debris, and smoke inhalation. After performing medical tests the doctors decided I should remain in the hospital until my carbon monoxide/blood level returned to normal, which took about seven hours, during which I was administered oxygen through a mask, and put on an IV. I was released about 6:30 p.m., and driven home by my wife. Unable to contact me, she had searched the Internet for hospitals in the area and tracked me down. Fortunately Arlington Hospital begins with the letter "A," so it was one of the first ones she called.

Dalisay Olaes was a military personnel management specialist in the Office of the Deputy Chief of Staff for Personnel. She was interviewed by Frank Shirer and Leo Hirrel on 13 September 2001 at Arlington Hospital.

DR. HIRREL: Well, first of all, did you know about the attack on New York City before it happened or before—

MS. OLAES: Yeah, they were showing it in the conference room and I called my husband, who works over at the Arlington Annex, and I asked him if he had seen it. He said, "Well, the guys were telling me about it and we're trying to retrieve the program in the computer." So I said, "Okay," so I hang up. After I hang up I felt a big, like an earthquake, and then came the fire. . . .

DR. HIRREL: So the first indication something happened was when the explosion came?

MS. OLAES: Yeah, because I thought it was just an earthquake because the first one is a big jerk and then when the explosion came it was like a big blast of fire and it heated up the whole building, so I burned my hair right away. And then all I saw was the filing cabinets flying all over the place, people screaming. They were asking somebody to help them because they were trapped under the filing cabinets. Somebody cannot see. Someone was burning and they were hurt. And everybody was—everybody was trying to find a way out.

DR. HIRREL: How did you manage to get out of the building?

MS. OLAES: Well, the military people, including Lieutenant Colonel [Marilyn] Wills and my specialist, Specialist [Michael] Petrovich, he told me to crawl and not to walk and hold onto his pants. And so I—he said follow his body where he goes and Colonel Wills was right behind me and they were giving instructions to all the, I guess, civilians—because I couldn't see who was there—to lie low, crawl. That way you don't have to inhale all the soot and you won't be unconscious. And somebody found a window and used the printer to crash it so we can get out. And all the other guys came down and they were trying—all the ladies, to catch the ladies. And, well, when they catch me I still fell so I broke my leg. And Colonel Wills was the last one to get out. . . .

DR. HIRREL: What happened after you got out of the [second-floor] window?

MS. OLAES: Well, they—Colonel Wills told me to jump because she's next and I'm scared to jump. I looked back and she said, "Jump!" [*Laughs*] So I jumped and I fell and I broke my leg. It's either jump or get toasted. And then when I was lying down there some civilian and military guys got a piece of wood, long wood, put me on there and carried me to the courtyard.

DR. HIRREL: And what happened in the courtyard?

MS. OLAES: Well, from the courtyard another Army guy took over. He was just coming from the POAC and he said I need a stretcher. . . . They put me on a stretcher but it took like five people because I couldn't move my leg. I was really hurting bad. And then they took me to the North Parking where I was tag number 3 on the ambulance to be taken to the hospital. . . .

DR. HIRREL: How long did it take you to get to the hospital?

MS. OLAES: Maybe thirty, thirty-five minutes because of the traffic. The ambulance couldn't come in. The traffic was really bad. And other people who had vans, they took all their seats out and they were volunteering to take people to the hospital.

DR. HIRREL: Now, do you remember anything about the emergency room when you arrived in the hospital?

MS. OLAES: Yes.

DR. HIRREL: What was it like?

MS. OLAES: It was a madhouse. [*Laughs*] Everybody was holding an IV. Everybody was holding—everybody was yelling, "Take this first, take that first."

Martha Carden was the Assistant Executive Officer in the Office of the Deputy Chief of Staff for Personnel. She was interviewed by Stephen Lofgren of the U.S. Army Center of Military History on 29 October 2001.

MR. LOFGREN: Why don't you begin by your describing your morning on the 11th? Normal morning?

MS. CARDEN: Mm-hmm, normal morning. I get to work normally a little before 6:00. . . . I do paperwork, e-mail, tend to the generals. And that morning we had our biweekly executive officers meeting, which should have been on the Tuesday following Labor Day. But because of the holiday we don't have the meeting the day after a holiday, so it was shifted to the 11th. If that had not happened I would not be here today because my office was basically ground zero.

MR. LOFGREN: What was your office number?

MS. CARDEN: 2E460. We had moved there two months prior. Our meeting was in the DCSPER conference room, which was across the hall and down. . . . The meeting starts at 9:00. It normally lasts thirty minutes or so. But this particular morning it had gone a little bit longer than normal, thank goodness. And we had not yet gotten all the way around the table with people giving their input to the meeting when all of a sudden—I cannot say that I heard it. Everyone else said it's the loudest noise they've ever heard. And I said, "Well, I didn't hear anything." I suppressed it apparently because I cannot call up that noise for anything. I just know that all of a sudden the room became pitch black. The ceiling—I was sitting at the end of the conference table—the ceiling up to my upper left came down.

The lights went out and the room began to fill rapidly with the most acrid blackest smoke you could ever imagine. And the last thing I remember seeing was my glasses being knocked on the table. And strangely enough I remember—I picked up the glasses and folded them up and put them in my left hand. The first thing that anyone heard was Lieutenant Colonel Rob Grunewald who was on the right hand side of the table about midway and he said, "Where's Martha?" And I guess I answered. He said, "I'll get you out." He came across the table to get to me. And in the meantime I'm having trouble getting up out of my chair because of the stuff that has fallen. The ceiling wasn't heavy stuff, it was that real light stuff. But there was just, stuff, and I had difficulty.

But I was finally able to get up out of my chair. And by that time Rob has gotten to me. We try to go out the door that leads onto the E-Ring but it was locked. And we found out later that's a good thing because the E-Ring hallway was an inferno from the fireball. So we then had to get out of the conference room through the other door, which was the other end of the room. From where I was seated at the end of the table to where we finally ended up was the farthest distance to safety, if you will. I was in the very back. And Rob pointed this out to me later, that we had the longest distance to go. And somebody in the conference room said, "Everybody get down." So we all got down on hands and knees. And I had, like I said, my glasses in my left hand and Rob's belt. I was holding onto his belt. The glasses in this hand. And we finally got out of the conference room, which it seemed to take forever to get out of that room. And it was very, very hard to breathe. It was very, very hot. And we got out into this large—people call it a cubicle farm. Again, we couldn't see. I mean, it was just pitch black and that smoke was in there.

MR. LOFGREN: "Cubicle farm," was it?

MS. CARDEN: Cubicle farm, yes. This huge room with cubicle after cubicle after cubicle. We had just moved in, like I said, two months prior. My office was across the hall. I was totally unfamiliar with this area. I knew where some people were. But the whole area itself I had a difficult [time] under normal circumstances finding my way around. But with the lights out, filled with black smoke, furniture and everything is moved around, it was—I could not have done it on my own. I absolutely could not have done it. Rob literally saved my life. There's absolutely no question. And given time I could have done it. But we didn't have time. We were almost out of oxygen. So we're crawling along. And finally the water sprinkler. Well, let me back up. I thought that we would die in that room. I kept waiting for my clothes to catch fire.

MR. LOFGREN: It was that hot?

MS. CARDEN: It was terribly hot. You cannot imagine how hot it was. And you knew that fire was all around us. You didn't see fire. But you—the smoke, oh, it was terrible. Of course, the smell is terrible and it was very hard to breathe, very, very hard to breathe. But you knew fire was around. And then I had the feeling of trying to make myself as small as possible, you know, because I just felt that any moment my clothes were going to catch fire. And I distinctly remember thinking how long does it take to die and how bad is it going to hurt because I was convinced we would die in that room. I do not recall any fear because Rob, Lieutenant Colonel Grunewald, was so calm and so collected that although I thought we were going to die, I was not afraid. And I was totally focused on him. And he was just magnificent. His training—he's an MP [military police]—his training just kicked in I guess. And he just—he was just wonderful. He's definitely my hero. And so the water sprinkler system finally kicked in, and that's the first time that I thought we had a chance to make it.

MR. LOFGREN: This is while you're crawling through—

MS. CARDEN: We're crawling through this huge—maze, if you will, in the pitch, pitch black dark. You cannot imagine how dark it was. And the water felt so good. I cannot tell you how good that water felt. Every time we would try to get up to walk, the heat of the smoke was just so bad, we'd have to go back down. Even after the water came on we still could not get up. We had to keep crawling.

And at one point we hit a blank wall, or we think it was a blank wall. We don't know. And that's when Rob—he told me later that's when he thought we would not make it. But he did not let me know that. And—

MR. LOFGREN: So it was just the two of you?

MS. CARDEN: Just the two of us that we knew of. We heard later that two women heard his voice and followed us. But we didn't know that at the time. We were separated . . . from everyone else. Everyone else went another way. Rob took us a different route. It was—unbelievably quiet. There was no pushing. There was no shoving. There was no panic. It was unbelievably quiet and orderly. Now, we did not know what had happened because we had been in this meeting since 9:00. We did not know about the World Trade Center. We had no clue. My first thought was that it was a bomb. Many people in the room thought that—we were in this newly renovated area. And there were still workmen. We probably should not have moved in. We may have moved in too early. But be that as it may, we were there. Workmen were still there every day doing stuff. And so many of the people in the conference room thought that, "Oh, geez, one of the workers hit a gas line," you know, or something like that. But I thought from the first instance that it was a bomb.

And so Rob and I, and as we learned later two other women, were behind us, kept crawling. And at one point Rob and I became separated probably that much, a teeny little bit. And he and I both remember my saying, "Rob, don't you leave me here." And he was so calm and so good. He said, "I've got you Martha. We're going to make it." And so I had his belt again with my glasses. And we ended up—

MR. LOFGREN: What happened when you hit that wall? Was it a dead end?

MS. CARDEN: We don't have any idea. It was just, you know, you come up on this immovable object. And you know you've got to go one way or the other.

He instinctively knew to go away from the E-Ring and from back here. I don't know how he knew, but he did. I was so totally disoriented. I have since—I've heard a lot of people saying, "I heard so and so's voice and I went to the voice." And I thought, "Geez, I don't know that I would have had the sense to do that." But I have since analyzed this a great deal. And I am certain that once I knew Rob had me, all of my thinking and reasoning powers just shut down. And I was totally focused on him. And anything else that was going on I was just totally oblivious.

The intensity of the fire melted the windows.

I do recall hearing the automated "There is a fire in the building. Please evacuate quickly. There is a fire in the building. Please evacuate quickly." I thought that thing—you just wanted to smack it. It was a very irritating—but it's automated. It's the new—in the new section it's the new fire alarm thing. And there's this noise that goes with it. And it's sort of a siren-type thing. And that just went on and on. And, you know, you wanted to say, "We know there's a fire. We're trying to get out." But we finally end up in the new cafeteria, which is—you have the big cubicle farm and then you have the fourth corridor. . . . And then up in about the B-Ring you have the new cafeteria that has double glass doors that were bolted shut because it had not opened yet. Those doors had been blown off.

And the first thing that we could see were the tables and chairs in the cafeteria. And we did not realize when we had gone from carpet—again, we're still crawling on hands and knees. We did not realize when we had gone from carpet to the tile in the corridor and into the cafeteria. . . . We're in this new cafeteria, realized we had gone too far.

MR. LOFGREN: Can you see anything by that point?

MS. CARDEN: By that time we can see the tables and chairs in the cafeteria. That's how we knew where we were. We could barely make out the tables and chairs. And we go back out into the fourth corridor. And that's where Rob hands me off to a colonel. He tries to go back in. Or he says, "I'm going back in." And I said, "Rob, you can't." We could barely breathe by this time, I think. I said, "Rob, you can't." And he, of course, ignored that and he went back. And so then I came up to the A-Ring and that's where we ran into two other people who had been in the meeting with us. And a major and I literally held each other up as we went out down the stairs and into the center courtyard. We got into the center courtyard and there were lots and lots of people. Well, I would say Rob and I were among the first to get out of the building. When he tried to go back in I don't know if someone stopped him or if he realized he couldn't breathe. But he came out into the center courtyard soon thereafter. So that's why I said he and I were among the first out of the building from this area. And we were among the least injured. We had the longest distance to travel. We got out among the first and the least injured. And that I credit solely to Rob's being so focused on getting us out. . . .

MR. LOFGREN: How long do you think it took you?

MS. CARDEN: We just don't know. At the most ten minutes. Obviously, it seemed like forever. But we just don't know. We just don't know. But then—okay, we get out to the center courtyard and there are many people wanting to help. And, you know, we sat down on the first bench that we came to because, I mean, we can barely breathe. It's just—oh, it was just a terrible, terrible feeling trying to get your breath and it hurt. Now, I'm a thirty-one-year smoker. I quit six years ago. And I think that thirty-one years of smoking allowed me to tolerate it better than nonsmokers. It sounds kind of weird. But I did not have near the respiratory problems that many did. And that theory may be totally all wrong. I don't know. But it seemed that I tolerated it better than a nonsmoker. So anyway, we're out in the center courtyard. Lots of people there. But we're able to walk around. I mean, you know, we're not injured so we didn't need help. Then eventually we were moved from bench to bench. We could look up and see the black, black, black smoke coming out. And here's where we learned that it was a plane that hit the building. Somebody told us in the courtyard. And then we were taken, I want to say, out the eighth corridor.

We ended up near the POAC [Pentagon Officers' Athletic Club] wherever that is, over here, and then on over. And there's a lawn, trees, and grass and then the river. Straight, and then the lawn.

And here we were—of course, we were soaking wet because of the water sprinkler. And although it was a warm day, you know, after awhile you finally start getting chilly in these wet clothes. And there was somebody there to put a blanket around you. And somebody came to me with a cell phone and said, "Can I call somebody?" And I gave her the number to my husband's office. And although he was on jury duty, which I of course had forgotten, I was able to reach his secretary and told her, "I'm out of the building. I'm okay." And then finally they put me in a police car. There was a fellow up front, another injured person. And then they put me with another policeman in the back. And we were driven to Arlington Hospital. The policeman didn't have a clue where it was. That was one of the most exciting rides I've ever taken in my life. He absolutely had no clue. And every little bit he would stop and ask—of course, there were policemen everywhere. And he would stop and ask and they would try to direct him. We finally got to Arlington Hospital. That poor guy. I felt so sorry for him. Of course, I'm sure that wasn't his area. I don't know where he was from. And there were policemen everywhere, just tons of them. I mean, when they were putting a policeman to each person to go to the hospital you had to know there were just tons of policemen around. Yeah, I had my own policeman. . . . There were policemen by the dozens. And so there's no telling what jurisdiction he was from. But anyway, we finally got to Arlington Hospital and I was seen there. And I guess I met up with a buddy, another lieutenant colonel there. And he and I stuck pretty close together. We wouldn't let them split us up. Then one of his buddies came to get him and then they both took me home. And we got home at about a quarter to 3:00 in the afternoon. And my husband was very happy to see me.

MR. LOFGREN: I bet.

MS. CARDEN: Yeah.

* * * *

MR. LOFGREN: You were standing along the river in a blanket and you were wet.

MS. CARDEN: I was in shock. I was in shock. I found a friend who was also in the meeting with us. And she and I hugged. I was glad to see her because I didn't know if she'd gotten out. And this is to show you that the sense of humor is always intact no matter what. I had on an especially good pair of shoes that day and they were ruined. And my friend and I found ourselves propped up against the tree. And I looked over and I said, "Lois, I want reimbursement for my damn shoes." And she looked at me and she said, "Well, I'd like some damn shoes." And I looked down and she had no shoes. She had lost hers in the building. So I said, "Oh, never mind." So, like I said, sense of humor was intact.

Dr. Betty Maxfield was the Chief Demographer for the Army, working in the Office of the Deputy Chief of Staff for Personnel (ODCSPER). She was interviewed in her Pentagon office by Sfc. Dennis Lapic of the 305th Military History Detachment on 16 November 2001.

SFC. LAPIC: Do you recall what you were doing on the 10th of September?

DR. MAXFIELD: On the 10th of September?

SFC. LAPIC: Uh-huh.

DR. MAXFIELD: I was preparing a response to Lieutenant General [Timothy J.] Maude's request that we expand the Army Demographic Brochure to include the Army Reserves and National Guard. So I was working on that data request. . . .

SFC. LAPIC: The day ended typically then?

DR. MAXFIELD: The day ended fine. I knew that I had a lot on the schedule. In fact I had mentioned to my husband as I started the week that this was going to be a "bear of a week" for me because I had so many deliverables that were due. My immediate boss, Brigadier General James Coggin had asked that I generate a list of the issues that the HR should be dealing with. So I was working on a list of hot topics the Army is concerned with from a demographic perspective, and putting the documentation together on that as well as the Reserve/National Guard Brochure. So this was going to be a difficult week. And I had made the comment that I wasn't looking forward to the week. Little did I know that I really wasn't looking forward to the week.

SFC. LAPIC: When do you normally get in your office?

DR. MAXFIELD: Seven-thirty. I normally have stand-up with General Coggin and the senior staff on Tuesdays and Thursdays to brief him on the issues of the week or the day. I come in at seven-thirty and meet with him at eight o'clock.

SFC. LAPIC: So were you preparing?

DR. MAXFIELD: I had finished the meeting with General Coggin and had gone to the renovated wedge of the Pentagon to meet with two other ODCSPER staffers, one for a personnel issue and another for a recruiting issue. Both offices were close to the E-Ring, across the hall from General Maude's office.

SFC. LAPIC: So how did that go?

DR. MAXFIELD: The meetings were over. I was about to leave the desk of Tracy Webb and was standing when the attack occurred, when I heard the collision.

SFC. LAPIC: You had no idea of anything that had been going on in New York up to that point?

DR. MAXFIELD: When I got to the Pentagon, I heard that the World Trade Center had been hit by an airplane and believed that it had been an accident. But I had gone about my business and wasn't watching any of the news coverage and had not heard of an update on the premise that it was a terrorist attack. So I was pretty much going on my business as normal, not focusing too much on it. . . .

SFC. LAPIC: Can you tell me how things went then?

DR. MAXFIELD: I actually was standing up to say good-bye to Tracy Webb, who was the personnel officer that I was talking to. And we, at that point in time, heard an impact noise, several impact noises, probably about four, five, or six. Enough so that we made eye contact with one another and knew that something very, very, very serious had gone wrong in the building.

Frequently when you have construction around here during the renovation time, you'll hear noises that are loud and disturbing. Sometimes people will drop file cabinets and things of that nature. And this was far beyond that, because not only was the volume of the noise very, very loud, but also there was a tremor in the building. And that had never occurred before. And I think in a sense we were all somewhat taken aback by the noise, in disbelief that something was going on that wasn't going to be a good scenario—but we still did not know where it was or what it was.

Within a very short time after the loud impact noise—in my mind, I actually thought there were several bombs that had gone off in the Pentagon—there was a concern that we needed to get out of the Pentagon. But I did not know at that point that the "impact" was in the area that we were located in. And the reason is because the noise occurred maybe two to three seconds before we saw the fireball or everything went black on us. And so I believed it was in close proximity to where we were, but not in our area.

And then within a very short period of time—and probably time-frame-wise I am sure my timing's off because I'm sure things happened quicker, because I think my brain slowed things down a bit. But within a very short period of time, a fireball went passing through the area in which I was standing. And everything went black at that point. The smoke was very, very dense. And the burning ceiling tiles began to drop on us like hot cinder balls. One thing that I remember clearly was that this huge fireball passed through the area, and yet we were all left standing. It kind of came through the ceiling area and I could see it passing through. And I could hear it passing through. But yet the only damage to me personally was that the hair on my arms was burned, but I didn't know that until later when someone mentioned it to me.

I physically did not feel burned. However, I immediately knew that that was very serious and the point of impact was actually not in the distance, but was where we were at that point because the ceiling tiles—which you don't see them here, but in the new wedge they're kind of little squares—they were actually burned and dropping what I would consider kind of like little cinder balls of hot flames coming, dropping down on us. And I was concerned that they might burn us as we crawled because they were falling like a rain. But I didn't see anything in terms of little fireballs around us.

The fireball went straight for the back windows, seeking out, I guess, oxygen, as I'm told perhaps that's what it was doing. But I didn't see anybody in our area that was burned as a result of this. And we all were, at that point in time, in a state of panic.

SFC. LAPIC: Still standing on the ground?

DR. MAXFIELD: Still standing. Furniture and files were falling to the floor and computers were shorting out and catching fire. And there were a lot of people screaming, "Help. We've got to get out of here." Quite a lot of noise. And in my recollection . . . I actually blanked out a lot of that noise and focused on those words that were calm and focused on getting us out of the area.

I was in an area that had been renovated and it was an open bay area. I didn't know the area. So when everything went black and there were no windows close to where I was, I couldn't see but a foot ahead of me. And the first thing that I did was to go to the door that was closest to me, which led to the E-corridor. I wanted to get out of the bay area and into the E-corridor. So I ran to the door and saw the orange glow under the door. And I knew that I couldn't escape via this door—I didn't even put my hands on the door. I just knew from the glow under the door frame that that there was a fire on the other side of the door.

So I immediately turned around and came back. And at that point in time, people who had been in the DCSPER conference room holding the weekly XO meeting were coming into the area where I was. And there were more voices and more panic and more screaming. And somebody—and I believe it was Lieutenant Colonel Rob Grunewald shouted, "Get down on the floor, everyone has got to get on the floor. If we're going to survive we need to get below the smoke."

So at that point, everyone who wasn't already on the floor dropped to the floor and hung on to one another, which was the other survival key, because for me it was essential that I had a hold of somebody because I didn't know the area and didn't know how to get out. And for other people it was a matter of forming up a human chain to be able to get us all together. But for me, personally, I needed to stay with the group to get out because I didn't know the area and if separated from the group, I wouldn't have known where the exits were. I needed the other people in the area to survive.

We crawled in the direction away from the E-corridor. And I heard some commanding voices say, "Stay low. Keep together. Move fast. We've got to get out of here." It wasn't until maybe three or four weeks after the event that one of the guys that I was with, Marian Ward, came by to talk to me and told me that he had been trying to rid his mind of all the screaming and hollering and panicking. And it wasn't until he mentioned it that I remembered that there was a lot of chaos and a lot of screaming and a lot of concern about people dying. I had blocked that all out and in my memory had focused only on Colonel Grunewald's voice saying, "Keep going." So I knew that I didn't want to listen to the sounds of panic because it wasn't helping. The other was helping, so I focused. And I had a kind of a tunnel vision of what all was going on.

SFC. LAPIC: Your analytical way of looking at it when you're in the middle of the situation—don't focus on the emotional but on the technical aspect—

DR. MAXFIELD: And the emotional didn't come out until two or three weeks afterwards, when I actually was concerned with the voice that I had heard. Somebody was yelling, "Help me, help me." And I thought maybe that was one of the people in the area where I was that hadn't made it out of the building, and I didn't go back to help. One of the Red Cross people that was talking to me said, "What would you have done?" And my husband said, "You know, you didn't know the area and going back to help might have meant two deaths instead of one. I mean, if you had left the group to try to help somebody, you probably wouldn't have made it out." But there was still some guilt with not going back to the voice that was calling out for help. And then in talking it over with people that actually were with me, I found out that it was Martha Cardin that was screaming and hollering, "Help me." And that helped in terms of my guilt, because I realized she got out. And it wasn't Odessa Morris, the person I thought it was, that didn't get out. The panicked voice actually belonged to somebody who actually came out with us. So my guilt feeling about helping somebody in need was eased. And my selfishness in staying with people and focusing on my own survival was easier to live with.

SFC. LAPIC: So the chain—

DR. MAXFIELD: Our chain actually was my survival because without them I couldn't have found my way out. At one point I lost my grip on the heel of the person ahead of me, I panicked. I needed that connection to survive. I was calmed when I grabbed another foot and hung on. I remember being very calm and very analytical about what I was doing. But I remember thinking that I may not survive. The smoke was getting closer to the floor and it was getting harder to breathe.

SFC. LAPIC: And you were on the floor?

DR. MAXFIELD: I was on the floor already. And there was a lot of debris on the floor as well as these hot cinders that were falling from the ceiling. But I really did my best to crawl rapidly and grab onto another heel. And I did catch up and grabbed a hold of a foot. And I believe I grabbed hold of Colonel McNair's foot.

SFC. LAPIC: And people were holding onto you—

DR. MAXFIELD: Yes, somebody had a hold of my heel. And I had a hold of someone else's foot—and finally got a hold. And that's how we did it. We moved in concert with one another. And everybody moved. And we all kept moving. And we were moving at a rapid pace to get to the back wall.

And it was surprising with all the chaos and so forth and the furniture being disrupted and file cabinets falling, we did find an aisle that was relatively clear for us to crawl in. We were crawling over areas that had a lot of debris. That's why we sustained burns and cuts on our legs. But we kept together as a unit. And I remember thinking that we were obviously making good progress. We had moved quite a distance and then the sprinkling system came on. And I thought, "Thank God," because, I mean, it seemed to me that somebody knew we were in trouble. And the sprinklers were a great relief because at this point in time, the jet fuel fumes and smoke was very oppressive. And our lungs not only were hot because of the fire, but also because of the fumes and black smoke. And the sprinkler system actually gave a lot of relief to the lungs and made me feel that there was a possibility that we were going to survive this.

SFC. LAPIC: So you worked your way back out of the office towards the—

DR. MAXFIELD: Towards the B-Ring . . . and making good progress. We were really moving fast. We were not wasting much time. And we were all talking as we were moving along. And then I heard somebody holler back, "The door is jammed. We can't get out this way." And I know that at that time I thought we were not going to make it out because my lungs were really very, very irritated and I was coughing. I was getting as close as I could to the floor and yet the smoke was moving down. And the moisture on the carpet felt good. But I knew there was only a small area under the smoke that you could breathe and that area was getting smaller as the density of the smoke moved closer to the floor.

And I felt at that time that this was going to be where we were going to die because we were trapped in the unit. And I don't think I dwelt on that much. I remember thinking about my family. I normally would think that I would panic in a situation like this with my heart racing, but instead there was a calmness. And I've gone to church since the event and talked with people about this, and talked to the chaplain after that. I'm very strong in my religious beliefs, but I never thought I'd be calm about dying. But there was a resolve that, yes, you are going to die here. And you're with people. And there's no way out. And you've done what you can to get out. But there's no escape. And this is how you're going to die. And I thought my family is going to have a tough time with this . . . I think a lot of this flashed through my mind quickly, because within a very short time I heard somebody say, "We've got to try another route to get out."

So again my focus was immediately back to survival and needing to go to an area where there was a possibility of escape. So my survival instincts were good because although most of those that were trapped with me felt we were going to die together, when we discovered that we couldn't open the door to the fourth corridor, we all quickly rebounded when there was an opportunity for another route for survival. And I know Colonel

McNair said this was a horrible way to die. And other folks began to really cry and pray because they didn't think they were going to make it out.

But it was Mike Petrovich who made the suggestion that we try to break a window and go out the second floor windows. And if we could crawl to the windows maybe we could break it, even though the windows are crash resistant—making them virtually impossible to break.

SFC. LAPIC: He was one of the commanding voices you heard?

DR. MAXFIELD: At that point. I didn't hear him before that. But I immediately heard the voice of Mike talking about his plan. And I said, "That sounds like a solution." I liked the idea that we were going to try more ways to get out because I didn't like the idea of giving up and dying right there. I liked the idea that there was another way that we could perhaps pursue to escape. We were going to pursue all the options.

SFC. LAPIC: Well, it sounded like you were tuning out the bad voices and tuning in the correct ones.

DR. MAXFIELD: Exactly. And indeed, I focused on only those things. And I heard Mike and Colonel McNair planning it. And I'm sure there were other voices. But that's what I focused on because that seemed like a plan and something we could do to get out. And I remember at that point going from my knees to my belly, because I wanted to get as close as I could to the ground where I could breathe better. And I wanted to get out if I could. And I didn't know how far I was away from the window because I couldn't see the window. But I also saw the face of another coworker right ahead of me and the desperation on her face, too. And she was very close to the floor, too. And she handed me a wet sweater and said, "We're going to try to go out. Breathe into the sweater." And—

SFC. LAPIC: Do you remember who that was?

DR. MAXFIELD: Lois Stevens. And the sweater belonged to Marilyn Wills, who was a gal who had been holding the sweater over her own face. And Lois Stevens handed it to me and told me what to do. And I breathed in the moisture from the sweater. And then one by one, we were assisted to the window ledge.

I heard a crash, but didn't know until afterwards what they had done. Mike had picked up a printer and thrown it through the window. And my husband was saying how could he have smashed the crash resistant window? The answer is that the window was partially blown from the impact of the fireball, so it was compromised. So it was easier to break. Mike broke the glass out and he and Colonel McNair sat up on the window sill and kicked the remaining glass pieces out. . . .

SFC. LAPIC: Just fell on the ground?

DR. MAXFIELD: Yes, three or four other people gathered on the service road below where we were. The first couple people that went out the window went without assistance. They—Marion Ward jumped out without anybody to catch him. And he sprained his foot. By the time that I was assisted, about fourth or fifth one out, a group had assembled below to catch me. McNair and Petrovich—who was really suffering and should have gone out first—continued to stay there.

They asked me to stand up on a chair and get to the window ledge, sit on the window ledge. They grabbed my wrist and dangled me. The people down below gave the go ahead to drop me. And I just dropped straight down. And Commander Powell caught me by the waist and the legs, and just gently lowered me to the ground. So I had a relatively easy escape even though two people before me suffered injuries, two with sprained feet and one with a badly broken leg. And then Phil McNair and Marilyn Wills came out after I did. And then we were in need of medical assistance. Other uniformed personnel ushered us out of the area and to the center courtyard where we were treated by medical personnel. And that is where we were all grouped, the people that were in our wedge that came out. Some of the people actually had gone out the firewall, had been able to get out the fire door and had gone out the hall and had walked down. There were about seven or eight of us that had to go out the window. But we all accumulated in the center courtyard. And we were given some care there.

And then we were taken to the Pentagon clinic at Corridor 8. And when I was taken into the clinic, they were rushing around and quickly placing us into various treatment rooms where we were given oxygen for our burning lungs and also treated for our burns. There were others in the clinic who were suffering from severe burns and lung damage. So I was there probably about fifteen minutes and received good care. When I walked in I was rushed into a treatment room and taken care of immediately.

Then somebody came through and indicated that we had to vacate immediately—now. And I was in a wheelchair and they wouldn't let me get out of the wheelchair because of the burns to my legs. And they wheeled me out. The nurse who was pushing my wheelchair had trouble pushing the chair up the ramp that comes into Corridor 8. She grabbed a male officer and asked him to take me over to the makeshift triage center. So somebody—and I don't know who this person was, either—wheeled me from the exit to the triage center that was set up across from the river entrance.

And there we were given more oxygen. And a chaplain came by and stayed with me the whole time that I was there, which was probably about twenty minutes before I was sent over to the urgent care center in a private van. Some young man had a van in the parking lot and he went into the parking lot and volunteered his van to transport the injured. He moved his baby seat and four of us were taken to urgent care in his van.

SFC. LAPIC: Out of all of this, is there anything—you covered it very well—is there anything that you really want to point out that I haven't asked you about?

DR. MAXFIELD: From an Army perspective, without a doubt the people that I was with, the Army personnel, did a great deal to form a cohesive group that was going out together. They weren't going to go out and leave people. I was amazed and I was pleased with that. I don't know if that would happen in a civilian organization or if that's just the Army culture or the military culture that you make sure that you've got everybody together and you take care of everybody else. Like Mike Petrovich was very badly burned but was standing on the ledge of this window helping other people out instead of going out himself. And he didn't care. He was burned more than I was. He had smoke inhalation far more severe than I did. But he made sure that I got out.

And I think that's important.

Sgt. Maj. Tony Rose served as Army Senior Retention NCO Career Counselor and ran the Army Retention Program at the Pentagon for the Deputy Chief of Staff for Personnel. He was interviewed at the Pentagon by Sfc. Dennis Lapic of the 305th Military History Detachment and Lt. Col. Robert Rossow of the Office of the Deputy Chief of Staff for Personnel on 23 January 2002.

SFC. LAPIC: So why don't you tell us how September 11th started for you? You came in at the regular time?

SGT. MAJ. ROSE: Yeah, I came in at regular time, got in about 7:00. We usually go down and get a cup of coffee and talk about what we need to do that day and prioritize ourselves before we even look at the e-mail.

SFC. LAPIC: When you say go down, where is that?

SGT. MAJ. ROSE: Down to the cafeteria. In this case, it was the Redskins' cafeteria which is now closed. And that's probably less than a hundred yards from where our office is located. We got back to our office and had just gone over our e-mail and determined what we needed to do for the day when someone told us that we needed to walk down to the general's office and watch the TV because the World Trade Center had just been hit. . . . [M. Sgt.] Fraizer and myself [and] Mrs. [Anna] Taylor, we walked down to the general's office. There were already about fifteen other people in the room when we were watching CNN and they showed the first plane—a replay of the first plane hitting. And then it was—they showed the plane—the second plane hitting. So we stood there and watched that for several minutes and we were just all in shock. And we started filtering out of the office and went back to our cubicle area. Most people were saying, "I can't believe this!" "This can't be real." "Are you sure this is really happening?" None of us could believe it.

SFC. LAPIC: Was anybody suspicious after the second one, the second hit?

SGT. MAJ. ROSE: Well, after the second one hit, it's—you could almost feel it in the room we knew it at that point this was—this was the real McCoy.

SFC. LAPIC: At that time was there any directive or caution given by your higher command?

SGT. MAJ. ROSE: No, this was—this was—I mean, this was only a matter of minutes after just watching this. We had just walked from the general's office to our cubicle, which is less than fifty feet away. I had turned to Fraizer—I had a cup of coffee in my hand—and told Fraizer that we need to be careful and before I got the word careful out of my mouth, the Pentagon was hit. I was knocked to the floor. I couldn't hear for a couple of minutes because—everything sort of happened slow motion. I could see Ms. Taylor, who was walking back from the general's office, falling down. And it looked like slow motion. My ears were hurting from the blast. As I went down off at my 11:00 position because I was facing back towards the general's office, 11:00 position, I just saw this big red flash—black flash. I was on my back for a couple of minutes and the only thing I could think of was, we've been hit. I mean, the building moved. It was—I was just—I was shocked that the building could move. It—it—it just seems like it's so solid. But it did. It moved. And then the—then the noise was just horrendous. And then in just a matter of a little—a little while, my hearing came back and that's when you could hear people crying for help. And that's when the smoke started rolling in. And I got up on my knees and told people, "Let's get out of here," and started to push them toward Master Sergeant Fraizer and told him to take the first group out of the building, get them out to the courtyard.

SFC. LAPIC: Were the lights on?

SGT. MAJ. ROSE: No, most of the lights had been blown out of the ceiling. The Kevlar glass behind us, some it was literally blown out. A lot of it was just bowed out. I remember looking at it later and just thinking how pretty it looked with the spider webbing and with the break. And then the window next to it was totally gone. The people responded—responded very well, military and civilian alike. There was no panic. Nobody was running. Smoke was coming in pretty heavy. At that point black smoke rolled over us when the fuel started burning. And that happened within just a matter of moments after impact. Very quickly we were losing visibility as the smoke was within two feet of the floor within just minutes. And as we were rescued within the next half hour, smoke was within eighteen inches of the floor, white smoke under that. So visibility was pretty low. But by that time all the people that were mobile were pretty well moved out of the room. We were pulling people from this area to get them out of the corridor here toward the escalators because we knew the flash came from this area and the smoke was rolling from that area. Later we found the hole in the floor where the smoke had come up—come through. And then, of course, these windows blown out—This is between the C- and B-Ring. The windows blown out here created a natural chimney for the smoke, so all the smoke just came immediately toward the escape route, which was the windows creating a draft. And it was pulling it down—from the E [Ring] toward the inside . . . C and D at this time . . . is just one open bay and there's no hallway dividing that.

SFC. LAPIC: How long did that process take of evacuating people?

SGT. MAJ. ROSE: The initial evacuation of those people that were totally mobile was easily done in fifteen minutes. People were pretty well organized and moving. Those that—those that had not been harmed and were on their feet were helping those that were not as mobile, or dazed. There was a lot of that. And then when we were pretty well sure that we had this area cleared out here, in this immediate area, Lieutenant Colonel Correa and I started working ourselves back into the office areas to start clearing the hall, clearing the building and moving people out. Once we had worked in General Axson's area and "Colonel's Row," that's when we first saw Colonel Knoblauch coming out with people here. And then we started leapfrogging these aisles and go down and start clearing cubicles and helping people out as we saw them. At this point when we got to here, about midway of the bay, we were on our hands and knees. But at this point the smoke was so thick that we were doing a low crawl to be able to see under the smoke because of the black and white. And it was simply calling out to people, "Can you hear me? Can you hear my voice? Can you see the light? Can you come, can you come—can you come to me? There's a way out here." Anything we could do to let them know that that was a safe haven.

SFC. LAPIC: Were you getting responses?

SGT. MAJ. ROSE: Yes, we were. Some people had been knocked down under the partitions. Some people were under the desk. At that point we had not found anyone that was unconscious or dead in here—in the middle of the bay area. We couldn't work our way back over to this area. . . . That's where all the warrants [warrant officers] for the aviation area were and that's where the admin offices were for the DCSPER area. . . . We got back in here and the smoke was just so thick and rolling we just couldn't get in there and see. And it was a lot of petroleum fuel smell coming out of that area, too. So the first thing we did was make sure anybody we get to, we get them out because of fire.

When we were assured that this area was fairly well clear, we went out into the corridor, Corridor 4. We ran into the fire doors. The first fire door, Colonel Correa held the door back, wedged himself in so I could go down the hallway because we heard voices. We had people calling, "I can't see." "I don't know where I'm at."

SFC. LAPIC: And what hallway was that?

SGT. MAJ. ROSE: Corridor 4, toward the E-Ring. He held the first fire door back; the second fire door had not closed yet. At that point we found Mrs. Tracey, we found Major Grant. They had become disoriented in the smoke and were lost. Major Grant had injuries to her knee and her face. In fact, I was surprised that she was even walking. She looked in pretty rough condition. But I got them back down the hallway to Colonel Correa and then he helped them out—out of the building. And at that point I still heard voices. I went down about another twenty feet and found another person, a lady; I don't know who she was. I just pointed her toward what little bit of light she could see on the floor and just said, go that way, there's somebody waiting for you. And then I tried to get down towards Sergeant Major [Lawrence] Strickland's area. . . . He was clearing his office that day to go on terminal leave, he was down on the E-Ring. . . . At that point I couldn't hear anyone else. There was a lot of noise. You could tell there was a lot of burning. There was a lot of fire. It was hot. Even the smoke was very hot at that point. We didn't have any respirators. The only thing that we had been able to use to help the breathing is we had stopped in one of the latrines and wet down our T-shirts and were using the T-shirts as masks.

SFC. LAPIC: So water was still flowing?

SGT. MAJ. ROSE: Water was still flowing in that latrine, yeah.

SFC. LAPIC: Were sprinklers on anywhere?

SGT. MAJ. ROSE: Sprinklers were not on in the hallways. They were initially on—on over here. But I didn't encounter any. I just know that they were on because people were coming out and some of them were wet with water. . . . Initially I thought there was water on some of the people coming out of what was later determined to be the conference room with Colonel McNair, the XO. I thought his face was peeling off, it just looked so bad. But what it was, petroleum fuel on the face, and it just made it look real blotched and bad and the smoke—it looked pretty bad because he had some burns, too.

But I couldn't tell at first whether that was water or oil. But in the hallway in Corridor 4 there were no sprinklers coming on. In fact, the smoke was so bad that the emergency exit lights could not be seen, the flashing lights could not be seen, and if I could change anything I would have them go in and follow the same things that the airlines do and put landing strips on the floor, because that's where we were at. By the time we got to the second door, we weren't low crawling, we were slithering. Because there were only about four to five inches of breathable air on the floor. And there was no rolling over and looking up for any kind of safety measure. In fact, at one point after—in Corridor 4 I couldn't go any farther, determined that it was too hot—the smoke was too hot and it was time to leave, I turned around and was coming back. And all you could see was about three to four inches of light off the floor that was getting—penetrating the smoke. And that started disappearing. And I realized that the fire door was closing behind me. I scrambled as far as I could and got to the fire door and caught it about twelve inches before it shut.

SFC. LAPIC: Was that hard to do?

SGT. MAJ. ROSE: It was, crawling. And the bad problem of it is, had it closed and someone panicked or just got disoriented going around any debris and lost their angle of exit, they would have turned around and gone right back into the fire. There was nothing on the floor that said, go out this way. There was nothing on the wall that would have lit—lit up and said, this is a fire door, push here to escape. That was just bad mechanics, bad thought process all the way around. Got through the fire door once—I mean, catching it and pushing it aside was not that hard. The angle was simply [tough] because I was lying on my stomach. But in normal conditions it probably wouldn't have [been]. But there's nothing that we could tell there that says, this is a way out. . . . We left out of there, came back down Corridor 4. As I got to the point between the rings here—heading toward the escalator on the C- and B-Ring, we found security guards at that point shuttling people out. I looked out the window and down into the ring and that's when we saw people trying to come out of windows. On the ground there were about four or five people trying to catch them. So I figured it was time to get downstairs. . . . And I went down the escalator or tried to—the security guard tried to stop me is what I should say, but I went down the escalator anyhow. . . .It was not running. And I got down in the center of that area. I saw Sergeant Weaver coming out of the building and they tried to catch him. I saw a lady coming out of the building. . . . And there were about four or five people out there trying to form a hand net to catch them. And then at that point I got distracted because about fifteen feet from that area is where—there was a gaping hole in the wall—just a gaping hole. And later we determined that's where the nose cone of the aircraft had come through. But just to the left of that was a utility room. And the door had been blown open. And the back of the wall, we could hear people crying for help. So several of us just went in the room and started pulling out debris through this hole and started creating a tunnel. That's when I saw Colonel McNair again, working with me and saw that he was not as burned as I thought he was because I thought he was just terribly burned. We started creating a tunnel probably about thirty inches square. It was incredibly hot. What we didn't know at the time was that we were digging directly into the area where the wing fuel was at.

We could hear people calling. We could tell as we dug in the first two feet that it was an office area because we saw a desk. Then we were blocked by obstacles, so we went in about two feet, started digging to the right about three feet to find a space. But it was so hot in there that we would go in and—one person would get inside and pull and we would pass it out. And then that person would have to come out just to get a breather. Again, no respirators. Smoke is pouring out of the hole, again. We're in a utility room on the first floor. There are broke pipes. It's flooding. There are electrical wires hanging all over the place. I mean, we're watching out for each other. I mean, you're pulling stuff out and at the same time you're saying, "Duck your head; there's a wire." As we got into the room about six feet, that's when we saw the first sailor. I don't know any of the names. I know that seven of them passed through us that I could count.

SFC. LAPIC: And they would have been normally on the first floor?

SGT. MAJ. ROSE: I understand that was their office and the ceiling had collapsed right on them. So we were pulling out people one at a time. Someone would go in and work a few minutes. We got to the point where we heard a couple of people but we couldn't get to them because of fire. So we were trying to figure out how to work around this. Now, we're working on our stomachs and our knees to do this. And so we started yelling we needed fire extinguishers. And it totally amazed me, I mean, we had about twenty fire extinguishers in a heartbeat. It was like everybody who could think about grabbing an extinguisher coming out of the building had one. And we tried to hit the flame with the extinguisher but it was so hot in there that the flame—the retardant would get about two to three feet from the flames and just disappear. It was just hot. The guys outside started yelling for us to get out, that the wall was buckling. It looked like it was going to—the wall itself was going to collapse because we're working here in this door, here is the gap for the nose cone and here is the windows. And they were afraid that structurally the side of that was going to break away. We couldn't hear anybody else. We went back in two more times just to see, but at that time we had fire all the way across our front and we just couldn't get in any further. So we came out and started helping the wounded in the corridor area back out into the center courtyard. I got into the center courtyard. By that time there were firemen there. In the meantime, we had been doing all this previous work, there were no fire crews. The only security people that I had seen was the one guy up on the second floor trying to tell us to get out of the building. Everything was being done by military and civilians and first responders at this point.

We got outside in the courtyard, started breaking people up into teams. I saw the fire chief—I knew at that point because of my experience as a volunteer firefighter that he was the captain on the ground at that time until the fire could be contained. I asked him what he needed. He told me that he needed rescue teams, how he wanted them set up and start staging.

The medical personnel had already started staging a triage, a burn area and a morgue. And we just started putting people into work groups—had no problem getting volunteers. By this time security personnel and building personnel were coming out. They had respirators and flashlights. So at least we had that to be able to go back in. The intent was send six litter bearers with each firefighter. A firefighter would have the oxygen in case somebody went down. The six litter bearers would put two—two carrying and two helping move debris. At that point we were getting pretty well organized, breaking up the drink machines, breaking up the soda machines to try to get water to people as quickly as we could. The doctors, the medical teams were very well organized, they triaged very quickly. And that's when one of the police radios said there's another plane in the air and he said, literally, "ETA [estimated time of arrival] fifteen minutes." That initially created some panic but people didn't freak out. We started moving out the victims. We took out litter teams and started assisting the medics to get everyone out. We had to exit out through to the North Parking area of the building because they wouldn't let us out in the South Parking area here. So we exited the building by the—right over here by the river entrance, by the POAC, and by the clinic and moved people to—across the road, the parkway, over by the river where they started setting up triage.

My team was the last one out. When we got here, security was trying to get everybody out of the building, pushing them pretty hard to get here. Doctors were coming back from the triage area, saying, "We need oxygen, we need this"—so about thirty of us turned around and went back into the building, to the clinic, and then we just started carrying whatever the medics gave us. They said, "We need this." We were loading gurneys, litters, boxes, whatever we could to try to get everything out to the triage area. At that point we started reassembling our stretcher teams again and started moving back in. The guards were here. They said, "You can't go back into the building. There's a second plane." And we said, try and stop us. And we took off. At that point there was probably again about thirty of us in teams and we were moving in rank formation, moving very organized. We had a team leader with each one. We knew what we were going to do when we got in the building. We stopped in the latrines just on the other side of the clinic, wet down T-shirts, whatever we had. And then we moved back into the center courtyard again and placed ourselves at the disposal of the firefighters.

At that point I reentered the building with the firefighters to show them where we were located in the building and where we had been pulling out victims and where we had been working. And at that point stayed in—stayed working with them for about another four hours before eventually we pulled back out, pulled all the teams out. Teams in this timeframe had just been waiting in the courtyard to be called, and then moved back around to the South Parking where we went to assist with the morgue. . . . We worked with the morgue and on standby for recovery until about 1800, when General Van Alstyne from OSD [Office of the Secretary of Defense] came up and relieved us. And the Old Guard took over. And they were better equipped. They had helmets and Kevlar. They had boots. They had respirators. They had the things that we didn't have.

Once we turned it over to him, we broke up our teams. Nothing else we could do at that time. I went up the [Interstate] 395 and stuck my thumb out and hitched a ride to Lake Ridge and went home.

* * * *

I was the senior sergeant major in the area, so I knew it would fall to me to try to track down people. And I spent most of the night making sure that we had people accounted for. About 1:00 in the morning I decided to take a bath, and that's when I found out that I had been wounded. I had glass shards in my chest and my back—chest, hands were cut. Arms were cut. Up to that point I thought most of the blood on me was from people we had been helping. But the next morning I went to Woodbridge Clinic, turned myself into sick call and they treated me for smoke inhalation, cuts, bruises, sprained knee, pulled some glass out of my abdomen. I went home and stayed there the rest of the day just trying to track people down.

John D. Yates was in the Office of the Deputy Chief of Staff for Personnel. He was interviewed in his Pentagon office by Frank Shirer of the U.S. Army Center of Military History and Lt. Col. Robert Rossow of the Office of the Deputy Chief of Staff, G–1, on 21 March 2002.

MR. YATES: The week was a typical week. We were—we had just moved like a month and a half earlier into our new space, and, as with any move, you know, taking care of last-minute things to get the space acclimated to us. . . . For the last eight years, I was the DCSPER project officer for this, for the renovation. . . . And

Tuesday was, again, just a typical workday. There was the colonels meeting that Colonel [Philip] McNair, the XO [executive officer], had every Tuesday morning. . . . And that was ongoing in the conference room, started at nine o'clock, as it always does.

About 9:30, 9:25, somebody came over—and I don't recall who it was—came over to me and said, "Hey, do you see what's going on in New York?" So I walked over to Marian Serva's work area. Marian was the CACO [Congressional Affairs Coordination Officer] for DCSPER and had a TV so that she could monitor the House and the Senate on C-Span, C-Span II. And so I walked over and was just watching it with a group of other people. And I watched for, I don't know, five minutes, six minutes, I'm not sure. I walked back to my desk, called my wife, who was at work, you know, to see if she knew what was going on, and she said, yes, she knew, you know, that some of her patients had said something about it. . . . And before we hung up, she said, "Honey, do me a favor," she says, "for the rest of the day work from underneath your desk." And I laughed and she laughed. And I said, "Sure, babe, no problem." I told her I love her and said, "I'll see you tonight." I hung up and walked back over and was again watching what was going on in New York. By this time the second plane had hit the north tower, south tower—I don't know which one—and I had been just, again, standing there for just a—two minutes when there was just this tremendous explosion and just a ball of fire.

I—as I recall vividly, there was just debris flying through the air. I was blown on—blown I don't know how far off my feet and onto the floor. The room was *instantly*, instantly hot . . . I mean, to where it was almost too hot to breathe. The room went dark. There was stuff all over the floor, you know, debris—the drop-ceiling tiles and grids and everything else— and it was all over the floor. Everything that I touched burned my hands because, again, it was just instantly, instantly hot. I took my glasses off because I couldn't see through them because they were covered in what I now know was unburned jet fuel. And I thought I put them in my pocket, but either I missed my pocket or they fell out somewhere because I lost them. I started crawling around trying to find my way out and heard some people calling. I called out. They asked who it was. I identified myself. I said, "It's John Yates," and somebody immediately grabbed the back of my right leg. I didn't find out until much later that it was Major Regina Grant, who is the

XO for the human resources directorate. And I then heard somebody else calling, saying, "Go out through the DMPM [Directorate of Military Personnel Management] door. It's clear down there." . . .

So I/we started crawling in that direction and I just—I crawled until I literally ran head first into a wall. I believe that it was the wall to the copier room that was located down near the DMPM near the C-Ring. I turned right because I knew that I was going in the right direction because it was getting a little lighter and I could feel water on my back from the sprinklers. I turned right and I knew I was going towards the fourth corridor and I came upon a group of people. Couldn't tell you who they were. Somebody just said, "We can't get out that way." And I said, "Yes, we can. Just follow me." And I just—I continued to crawl until, again, I ran into a wall. . . . There were some work stations. By this time, I mean, you could see a little bit but, I mean, I'm crawling on my hands and knees so all I'm seeing is table legs. And I ended up getting out through the doors down on the— where the C-Ring would have been, across from where the new cafeteria was going to be. And I crawled—I mean, when I got there the smoke was . . . it was smoky, but it wasn't that black, choking smoke from the initial explosion.

And I—I just—I kind of looked around and then I just collapsed. And I laid there for I don't know how long. And then I stood up, and I knew where I was, you know? Because I'd been eating, drinking, sleeping, and dreaming about this stuff for the last year. And I started to walk towards the A-Ring.

LT. COL. ROSSOW: You were in the corridor at this point?

MR. YATES: I was in the fourth corridor at this point. I don't know how long it took me to get there. No concept of time at all. I mean, I had a watch on, but I just had no concept of time. . . .

I started to walk out towards the center courtyard when—I thought it was two Navy officers—came up. I know there was one, but I thought it was two. And these—somebody said to me, "Is there anybody left inside there?" And I said, "Yeah, there's a lot of people left inside." And they said "Well, let's get you out of here," and they kind of took me underneath my armpits, and whatnot, and helped me to walk out to the center courtyard.

I received a call on [this past] Tuesday evening from Dr. Georgeen Glands, who is the engineer who works for the renovation project. I had talked to her previous to this and she asked me . . . if I would like to have the name of one of those two men. And I said, "Well, yeah." And so she explained to me that this gentleman—and I'll just use his first name—that Paul—she had interviewed Paul previously and that he had called her recently, I think even that day, and had said that he was on a business trip . . . and was in the airport and picked up the *U.S. News and World Report* and read the article that was in there about myself, and Wayne Sinclair, and some of the other people, and that he—he said—[*pause*] he said that he knew me and that he had wondered what had happened because he didn't know my name, he didn't know what happened to me.

And he relayed to Dr. Glands that when he initially walked up, he thought that . . . I had white surgical gloves on. And then as he got closer to me he could see that my hands were burned and blistered. That's how badly they were burned. And so he and I have spoken. . . .

Paul said that he and this Navy commander walked me out to the doorway going out at the apex of the third and fourth corridors, and that he asked the Navy commander to walk me downstairs out to the courtyard, and that he came back inside. And—and I do remember, you know, walking out to the center courtyard and sitting down in the grass and this Navy commander standing there with me. And then at some point . . . I remember asking how badly I was hurt. And, you know, like any good person would do, they said, "You're fine. You're going to be okay." You know, he obviously wasn't going to tell me . . . how badly I was burned. And after a few minutes—I mean, I was getting cold, because I was outside and I was soaking wet from the sprinklers and I was getting cold. And then a medic from the clinic came up and started cutting my clothes off of me. . . . And then a gentleman who I now know is Don Ellis, who works somewhere for WHS [Washington Headquarters Services], came up in his electric cart, because I remember seeing him drive by. Even though I didn't have my glasses on, I could still discern stuff, even though I'm blind as a bat without my glasses.

Somewhere in here a female doctor, I presume from the health clinic here, came up, because I remember, you know, seeing her. And to the best of my recollection, I recall her saying something about, "He needs to get out of here and needs to get out of here now." I think that was my first indication as to how badly I was burned. I mean, I knew that I was burned because I could look down and I could see the skin hanging off of my fingers and off of my hands. I just didn't realize how badly I was burned. I remember seeing Tracey Webb sitting on the grass next to me and just coughing and coughing and coughing. I remember Colonel McNair coming up and saying that everything would be all right, that they'd take care of me, and to hang in there. . . . At some point during all of this, I remember a DPS officer—I believe he was a DPS officer—walking by saying we had to get everybody out of the courtyard. We have to evacuate the courtyard. That there was an unidentified plane twenty miles out headed this way. And I got scared. I got very, very scared, almost as terrified as what I was when I was trapped inside the building.

Eventually they loaded me onto Mr. Ellis' cart. He put his coat— he took his suit jacket off and put it around me to try to keep me warm. They put me on his electric cart because they were going to take me somewhere. And he was kind enough to gather up my wallet, and my government cell phone, which was still on my hip, [*chuckles*] and my government pager, which was still on my belt, and gather up my trousers and my shirt—even though my trousers were—had been cut to shreds by the medic to get the clothes off of me. And he was kind enough to gather up all of that. Then, at some point they put me on his cart. They couldn't figure out where to take me, so they off-loaded me into the grass, back in the center courtyard.

And then the paramedics and the ambulances showed up . . . mine happened to be out of Alexandria. And the paramedics loaded me onto a stretcher and then took me to an ambulance. And they drove and parked underneath of an overpass because they had been told that there was another plane headed this way. There was a Navy lieutenant who was in the back of the ambulance with me. His name is Lieutenant Greg Goodman, and I have spoken with him and met with him on several occasions. And he sat with me while the paramedic who was driving went to find other—other victims, patients injured who were ambulatory, could walk, and didn't need to be on a stretcher, because I was taking up the stretcher space. I was coherent. I remember asking Greg if he had a cell phone, and if he did, would he please try to call my wife to let her know that I was alive. And he said he did. I gave him all the numbers, but nobody could get through on a cell phone. I mean, they were all jammed.

And then eventually Johnny Marshall, the paramedic who was driving the ambulance, came back and . . . they took me to the triage center that they had set up at—I thought it was at Fort Myers, I didn't know—but I know now that it was at Henderson Hall. And they took me in there and started some IVs. Johnny started an IV also while I was in the center courtyard, I remember that. And he had gotten permission to give me some morphine or something for pain. And then they took me up to, as I said, Henderson Hall, where they started more IVs, and then they put me back onto a stretcher and took me to Arlington Hospital.

I remember going—this is the last thing I really remember until September 13th—I remember them taking me into the emergency room at Arlington Hospital. It was kind of funny. They were just—I mean, they're absolutely wonderful people, and I remember a nurse saying, "Mr. Yates, we're going to have to start a catheter on you and it's going to hurt." And I just— "Okay." And they cut my rings off of me. They cut my watch off. My bracelet I had on. And that's the last thing I remember until the 13th when my wife—well, it's one of the last things that I remember. I remember seeing my daughter and son-in-law. I remember seeing my best friend, who used to work here, you know, at Arlington Hospital. I just remember seeing their faces. I don't remember seeing my wife. I know she was there, but I just don't remember. And then the next thing I remember is my wife waking me up asking me if I'd like to meet President Bush.

As time has gone on, I've remembered more. After being in the ICU [intensive care unit], and being in the burn ward, and talking with my wife, I remember now the helicopter ride. They came in and said that they were going to Medevac me to Washington Hospital Center, and they had to put me on a stretcher, put me in an ambulance, and take me to a baseball field or a park somewhere where the helicopter could land. And I remember going into the Medstar Unit on the 12th. . . .

LT. COL. ROSSOW: It was on the 13th that you met President Bush?

MR. YATES: Yes. . . . I was on a ventilator. I couldn't talk. . . . And I remember he and Mrs. Bush coming into the—to my room, and my wife was up near my head, and then President Bush stood at my arm, and Mrs. Bush stood . . . down near my waist, my hip. And I remember him talking to me. I don't remember what he said. I just remember that as they were getting ready to leave, that he reached down and touched my arm and that—[*pause*] that there were tears in his eyes. And then . . . the next week is a blur, you know?

Maj. John Lewis Thurman was an operations research systems analyst with the Office of the Deputy Chief of Staff for Personnel in the Officer Division of the Directorate of Military Personnel Management. He was interviewed at his residence by Frank Shirer of the U.S. Army Center of Military History on 20 September 2001.

MR. SHIRER: What was your office number within the Pentagon, where you were assigned?

MAJ. THURMAN: We were in the new area . . . second floor D-Ring 491, which was off of the big large bay numbered 2D451.

MR. SHIRER: And where were you when the attack occurred?

MAJ. THURMAN: I was seated at my desk in the smaller office off of the large kind of bullpen area. The bullpen being 2D451. My small one being 491.

MR. SHIRER: Had you heard news of the attack upon the World Trade Center in New York?

MAJ. THURMAN: Yes. The first indication was that we had heard that a small commuter jet had clipped the World Trade Center and that escalated to a large plane going into the World Trade Center. Then we heard that the second plane had hit the World Trade Center. . . .

MR. SHIRER: Please describe what happened upon the impact of the aircraft.

MAJ. THURMAN: I had just gotten off the telephone with a friend who had called to say, "What's going on in New York?" And we kind of talked, "You know, terrorists, blah, blah, blah. I can't believe they hit it again in so many years. It's crazy. Good-bye. Click." I'd gotten an e-mail from my father saying that my sister had just broke her water. They were off to the hospital. Keep me posted. And what's up with that and stuff in New York? Wrote back and said, "Great. I'll be around my desk all day and at home this evening." And he said it looked like terrorists since it was hit twice. So I said, "Keep me posted and give me a call." Hit send. I called up the *Washington Post* Web site again just to see if there was a further development. At that time they had the streaming video, where you could actually watch the second plane hit the towers. And then that's when the explosion happened. So I was seated right at my desk staring at the computer. The E-Ring would have been to my left. So I was facing towards the fifth corridor, E-Ring to my left, facing the fifth corridor. And when the explosion happened, it, to me, seemed in two parts. A kind of percussion whoosh and a crunching sound. I definitely remember it just seemed like suddenly there was a huge wind and whooshing and the crunch sound at which time my chair— which was one of these ergonomically correct padded, got you in all these positions—went flying against the backside of my cubicle. And then I dove under my desk. Luckily the chair went back. . . . So if I'm facing my desk here, the chair just kind of went back this way. . . . So the chair pushed me to the point where I was then facing the E-Ring, and I dove in under the desk to my right. And then that's when it seemed like—and I can't tell you whether I was diving or had dove at that point— when it seemed to me that the second part of the explosion happened. And that's when a definite explosion sound and the false dropped ceiling then dropped onto the ground. All the fluorescent lights seem to come down. The lights obviously went out. The wall that separated our smaller office was just drywall. It was just a false wall. And I think they only build those things up to the acoustical ceiling tiles so that you can continue to run pipes and computer lines and the like. So I was looking up to my left. If my head was oriented toward the E-Ring and I look up to my left I then could see fingers of flames shooting over that wall in the area of the false ceiling under the tiles kind of just arching over like fingertips were coming through. And then immediately the room began to fill up with smoke. And the sprinkler system came on, but it didn't seem to be doing much. It seemed like a squirt gun. It was just like I could feel spatterings of water. And I thought that was kind of strange. In hindsight I guess it was the lack of pressure. Then the room immediately

Snapshots of simultaneous activities: fighting the fire, providing assistance, and evacuating the wounded

began to fill up with smoke. . . . At that point then I low-crawled out from my desk. . . . I'm in this room that's rectangle and the long access is pointing toward the E-Ring and the short access of it is perpendicular to that. There was a spine in the center of the room where cubicles could be on either side. And then cubicles on the side closest to the bullpen and across the wall that would have been closest to the E-Ring. In the corner that was the farthest away from the E-Ring there was a small conference table and a lot of file cabinets. I then crawled out.

And the other thing is that when I was under the desk it felt—I'm from California—and it felt like an earthquake had hit. Having gone through those and I could feel that everything had shifted. And my first thoughts at that time were, "How very clever. They planted bombs in the new construction and someone either command-detonated or they had them on a timer because they thought this was going to be the day that they wanted more mayhem in America." And to me it seemed like this had been a bomb. But as the room began to fill up more and more and more with smoke, I thought, "What has caught on fire?" We have these new-fangled fire-resistant carpets and office furniture. You know, someone sold the Army a hill of beans or there's something much worse about it. But still it wasn't until twenty-four hours later that I knew that . . . it was an airplane.

MR. SHIRER: So you didn't even think about an airplane even though you had heard about airplanes—

MAJ. THURMAN: Right, no. I, for some reason—just Army training and observing fire out on mortar ranges and field utility ranges and that kind of thing—for some reason it had just stuck in my mind, "A bomb in the building." Because I, you know, just had this feeling of the Pentagon's a stalwart fortress and no one is going to do that. . . .

I'm now beginning to low-crawl out of my desk. I quickly realized the only place there's oxygen is on the floor. And I had to keep my nose on the ground. I called out immediately, "Who else is here? Who else is here?" because there was just a dead silence after that initial explosion and then you could hear the water. And then you could begin to hear some other noises like things moving it sounded like. So then I called out, "Who's here? Who's there?" And two office co-mates who would have been—if I was here, if this is the spine and I'm on this side, their stations, their carrels were here. And wall lockers and file cabinets had fallen across. And so it was a matter of me pushing and opening those and getting some leverage and pulling one of my colleagues through and then another colleague.

MR. SHIRER: Who were the colleagues that you pulled out of there?

MAJ. THURMAN: I know who they were. And this is official record. It was CW4 Bill Ruth, William Ruth. He was the first one of the DCSPER to be released on the deceased list, to move from the missing to the deceased list. The other was Lieutenant Colonel Karen Wagner. And there was a third person that was back there that I believe must have been knocked unconscious immediately because I was unaware of it until days later that there was a third person in this office. So I was able to pull them through. Mr. Ruth, to me, seemed obviously injured. And I—because it was pitch black in that room—I could not even begin to estimate what his injuries were or the extent of them. But he was not in a good way. But he did have the strength to be able to call out and make his way to the one side of the wall.

MR. SHIRER: Now, you had to carry him out then?

MAJ. THURMAN: So once I was able to pull him through, I said, "Okay, we've got to stay down. We've got to stay down. We have to get out of here now." And I said, "Let's"—now, there were two doors to the room. One was here. And this door led to the main bullpen area. And it's what everyone used. And this bullpen went from halfway on the D-Ring all the way back to the edge of the C-Ring. So it's quite lengthy. And the D-Ring doors to that new area perfectly lined up—because I'd always tell people to come in the D-Ring door at 2D451 and then just keep walking in a straight line and you'll come to the door where my office was. . . . So I told the other two, I said, "We've got to get out of here. Let's try to get to the door," thinking that possibily there would be some way to either run out to this D-Ring door off of the fourth corridor. Or you could turn up—we call it colonels' row. There was a lot of colonels' offices right here. And we could run up this way and then go out the C-Ring door to the fourth corridor. Well, when we crawled to this door here. It was off its hinge. And I could feel, not see, that the smoke and heat was more intense coming from that room. And so I said, "We've got to turn back," because as you approached it you really couldn't breathe even though your nose was touching the ground and you're just down.

And the smoke was really coming in. And I knew, though, that we had to quickly get out because the smoke just kept getting more and more intense. And I didn't know if it was coming from the door or over this wall, but that it was important to get out. And so we retreated back a little bit, and there seemed to be more air in the area of my desk. But the problem was, again, all this furniture had moved. Unfortunately Mr. Ruth at that time, I lost contact with him. He stopped speaking. And I believe he succumbed to smoke inhalation at that point.

And Colonel Wagner was beginning to really breathe very fast and she began to pray. And I had shouted to both of them, I said, "We've got to get to the back door. And everybody's got to be looking. We've got to look all for the back door." And so I pulled her. And I kind of sensed at that point that she was not doing well. And, in fact—so then we began to turn this way and it was blocked. Wall lockers and now the landscape was totally unfamiliar and you're feeling with your hands and you can't feel too far up because you're immediately, again, getting the smoke. And so it was at that point that I had a real sense of desperation and thought that this was game over. You're trapped and you can't get through. And I tried to stand up a couple of times, but the heat—you could just feel the heat. But I couldn't feel any way to begin to crawl over.

MR. SHIRER: How high up could you get your head before you had to drop back down to literally nose on the floor?

MAJ. THURMAN: I want to say that it seemed to me that I had about six to eight inches of oxygen on the floor, of breathable air I should say. And I don't know. It seems like that's—you could kind of get up on your knees and get up. But the heat then was just too much. And, you know, I don't know whether this is—you know, I guess I'll just say it right now, I think it's Army training. The individual kind of drills that the Army teaches you—that allows me to be speaking to you today—to know to drop immediately on this kind of noise—stop, drop, and roll. To instinctively low-crawl out, to wait until everything stops moving, and then to start low-crawling and then physical ability. Just, you know, the Army is PT, PT, PT, PT [physical training]. And those things I think instinctively—and I look at my actions there and, you know, it's typical rally—now we search out. We rally back to the last safe point. We then, you know, okay now patrols, and we're going to rally, you know, back and then make a decision and go. And so I—somehow I was able to move some furniture. Don't ask me what it was because I have no idea. And I was able to find a path that came back this way. And I was calling, "Karen. Come on, Karen, follow me." . . . I tried to, you know, get her to listen to my voice and follow. And at that point in time I didn't hear her any more. And I was able then to crawl over a couple small pieces of furniture. I think there was a small file cabinet or something like that. There were the big two-by-twos. We call them two-by-twos where you put in files and then there's a lever on the floor you push and it causes the whole thing to turn around. . . . Those had been over surrounding this conference table. And they had all fallen over and all the contents of them because they were generally in an open position.

MR. SHIRER: Are those also what you refer to as wall lockers?

MAJ. THURMAN: No, no. In the new design everybody at their cubicle had a wall locker that had a little narrow thing the length of it that you could hang uniforms and put your backpack in. And then it had some file cabinets and then it had an upper door where you could put in—they had shelves where you could put in whatever you needed. And then also most people had a little wheely—file cabinets this size with two hanging file doors. And those had kind of rolled around. . . .

So let's see, I'm low-crawling and I've now made it over—the other door was here—towards the E-Ring opposite side of the room. . . . And I knew the approximate distance, don't ask me how, that I should begin to be looking for this door. Again, pitch black, full of smoke, nose on the ground. And I gazed up and thank God for OSHA and their little glowing red signs because I was able to see up in the smoke just a faint glow of the red exit sign. And I knew the red glow had to be where the door was. And this is one of these doors—they hadn't fixed it completely yet—with a bar on the inside, no handle on the outside. And it was going to be alarmed, one of these doors you can't go through without setting off all the emergency alarms for the whole building. And it was one of these vertical stairways that are in the Pentagon. They're sometimes in the middle of the corridors that you can traverse floors. It was kind of a small square room and on the other side of that was another door leading to the old side of the Pentagon. We were right on the seam there. So now you're in the D-Ring. And you could head out to the fifth corridor. So I knew that if I let go of the one door that I wasn't—I was hoping that Karen was behind me and that she was following. And suddenly opening the door— because what was so strange was that when I opened it the lights were working in the stairwell. And at that point I knew that I was okay.

Did I mention the whole thing about when I was trapped and we couldn't find a way? Army training again. I got sidetracked. Something came over me. And all of a sudden I said, "I'm not going to let these guys do this to me. I'm not going to lose. You know, you're going to have victory from this. You're going to not let these guys do this to you, your family, the ones that love you. And you're going to see this thing." Thoughts of my new-born niece came to mind, my parents, my sister. And that somehow reinvigorated me to really start searching knowing that time is running away.

Back to the stairwell—but I knew that I needed to get assistance because I knew I probably couldn't go back in the room again without dying. So I took off one of my shoes and put it in the one door. And opening the other door I noticed that it was already off kilter. So for some reason the frame on that door was a little kooky. So I ran one-footed down and as I did shouting as best as I could. And then down that hallway my division chief, Colonel Karl Knoblauch. . . . He's the Chief, Officer Division, DMPM. . . . He was very involved in the whole rescue and pulling people out. So then he and some other people with him they carried me back toward the door. And I said that they were in there. And we were shouting into the room. But the thickest, blackest smoke that you could imagine was pouring out of the door from the top of the door down to the bottom of the door. And some people tried just to go ahead in and just it was impossible. And unfortunately, I think at some point Karen had succumbed to the smoke also. And, again, the third person there I didn't know. [*long pause*] There were two other people that were in the room. They were very close—they were closer to that door, a Mr. Barr, Andy Barr, and a Mr. Eggleston, both warrant officers CW5s. . . .

So then two people assisted me. They didn't have to carry me, but I had my arms around them. We went out through the fifth corridor, down the fifth corridor, past the Redskins' Lounge and then down into the Center Court, at which time they left me there with some medical folks. And so then they went back to try to help pull out some more people. And I don't know what the medical folks had determined, but they said, "Get him to the clinic now." So they took me. Two people, again, putting my arms over their shoulders. And at this point I'm just coughing and coughing all this black tar and stuff out of my lungs. And they took me to the eighth corridor health clinic, where I was treated. And then the doctor there had decided that I needed to get out to North Parking because they knew that's where they were doing the ambulance triage. And she wanted—I think it was a he, I can't remember. They put me on a gurney at that point and then wheeled me out to North Parking. Or they carried me. I think I was on a gurney because it was on wheels. I thought we were going to tumble. And then no ambulances were readily available. So this Air Force doctor got someone to get their minivan and pulled out the backbenches. We put the litter in that. And she went with me to Arlington Hospital. . . .

MR. SHIRER: How long were you in the Pentagon clinic and what was your treatment there?

MAJ THURMAN: Just oxygen at that point. Because my main complaint was that I was bringing air into my lungs, but I wasn't breathing. I had no obstruction of my windpipes or anything. "This is useless. It's not doing me any good." And I can feel I'm totally light headed and I kept coughing all this stuff up. I want to say they had me there for maybe ten minutes, maybe fifteen minutes. And then going out to the North Parking area, where they did the triaging for the ambulances, I knew I was going into shock at that point. And someone else has said, "You were in shock when I saw you in the Center Court." Because I all of a sudden just got freezing cold and they couldn't put enough blankets on me. And then all of a sudden I was sweating to death.

MR. SHIRER: That's shock. And that was in the Center Court?

MAJ THURMAN: No. Where I noticed that I was doing that was as they were taking me out on the gurney to North Parking. And I said—I was telling this story to a colleague. And she said, "Oh no. I saw you in Center Court. And you were in shock there. You looked like a wild, crazed man." I kept repeating, "Karen and Bill are in the room. Karen and Bill are in the room. We've got to go in and get them." Because somehow in my mind I thought that someone could maybe get firefighter masks and they could go in. . . .

MR. SHIRER: You were saying it took forever to get to the hospital?

MAJ. THURMAN: It seemed forever because I was lying in the back of the minivan. So [my] only perspective was kind of lying in the back and looking up and seeing trees and bridges go by. Whoever the driver was he was honking the horn. And the doctor had to hold up her stethoscope all the time. And there was another fellow who was just holding my oxygen mask. And of course, I know how this happened and I don't mean to—it's just that, the way things happened. The oxygen tank, and I'm sure some poor medical specialist grabbed as many oxygen tanks as he could out of that clinic and hauled them over to where they were triaging, but halfway there it ran out. And so the whole thing of pulling air and not breathing started in again. And by the time we got to the hospital my legs had totally gone numb. My arms had gone numb. I could feel like my neck, the whole neck, was going numb. And I know I was panicked in that regard because just nothing was working right. It wasn't working. And so they got me in the hospital. They gave me a paralytic and then immediately injected my body with all these IV lines and whatnot. And then they intubated me. And then at that time they anesthetized me, and I was out. . . .

Let's see, so I guess that takes us to Tuesday about two hours—I don't know—two hours after. And they knocked me out with morphine. Had me on the respirator until the next day when I woke up. And then they came and extubated me and kept me in the ICU there until that evening when Walter Reed sent an ambulance and came to pick me up. And then I was in Walter Reed until Friday evening.

Col. Edwin Morehead worked in the Office of the Deputy Chief of Staff for Logistics. He was interviewed at the Pentagon by Stephen Lofgren of the U.S. Army Center of Military History on 30 October 2001.

COL. MOREHEAD: At the moment of attack I was in my office. . . . My office is physically located in the fourth corridor right at D-Ring. . . . Third floor. . . . Was at my desk—working on my e-mail when the plane hit the Pentagon. It was obviously a very loud thud and then a muffled type sound. And when it hit and that muffled type sound, the only structural damage in our area at the time was some tiles fell from the ceiling and stuff. And everybody started exiting out the door. Where my desk is located it's right—there were some double doors just to my back area, and people were rushing out that door. So I got up.

MR. LOFGREN: Those doors open into the corridor?

COL. MOREHEAD: Yeah, they open into Corridor 4. . . . I went out. As soon as I went out there were people rushing out, going out. And the smoke was already about down to your waist instantly. It was amazing. By the time I got out in the corridor smoke was already down to your waist. I looked down to the E-Ring . . . and you could see some kind of destruction-like and the smoke boiling. Really I couldn't tell where it was coming from. But I went down to this direction [*pointing to diagram*] and I was more or less squatting right here and signaling people to go down the corridor this way [toward the A-Ring], because you could look down the E-Ring here—and the floor hadn't collapsed at that point. I don't even know. I've heard it collapsed in thirty minutes, I've heard fifteen minutes. So I don't know when it collapsed, but I know it wasn't collapsed then. There was all kinds of damaged stuff lying on the floor here.

So I was telling people to go down this way. . . . And at one point, and I don't remember when I did it, but I know another colonel was with me. He told me later that we went into another room. We went into this room and looked at it, and flames were all right here. The flames were lapping up here. And, at one point, I went down and there are rooms, offices, down here. And I went in and started going into these offices and helping people. . . . And, at one point I tried to crawl in this. . . . We tried to go in this room here. And I say "we." There was a contractor, a young contractor kid that I don't know who he is, but I know he had a contractor hat on, and he had a shirt wrapped around—or a cloth wrapped around—his face and at that point I didn't have anything. So we tried to crawl into this room here and it was just—the flames and smoke were just so bad that I don't believe I got within maybe five, maybe ten feet. I don't know if I even made it that far, it was just so bad. But so we backed out of there and that was—and I don't remember the sequence, I truly do not remember if I went in there first or I went down here—but I went down and started helping people in these rooms. We'd go into them. I know in one of these rooms here, the whole wall or window was missing and the flames were just—there was nothing but a wall of flame from the, I guess, the ground to the ceiling. I don't know. We were on the third floor and it was just a solid flame. I mean, the whole wall was missing. I don't know if it was wall or a window had been blown out, but it wasn't there. Whatever it was wasn't there.

There were other people in here helping people up and helping them to the doors and get out. And so what I did, I just went down from one room to another. And at one point I got . . . about to the end right where the new construction began or stopped. People coming in were trying to go this way. Well, the damage was even worse this way. And I know for a fact that General Webster, Brigadier General [William G.] Webster [Jr., Director of Training, Office of the Deputy Chief of Staff for Operations and Plans], came out of his office when I was down here. He was helping some people. And I tried to get him to go back this way, and he shot right past me. Now, I talked to him later. I ran into him in the building here, and I asked him if he remembered seeing me. He said, "Yeah." And I asked him how did he get out, and he said well, he saw me when he went and ran by me. He ran this way, but then he ran into some other people that said the flames were even worse here, so they turned around. And, anyway, we helped and got people to go back this way . . . because there were no flames here. . . .

It was the E-Ring here—and there was stuff lying, you know, all these offices, stuff was collapsing, falling on the ground. There were lights and everything. . . . I did not see the floor cracking, because you were stepping over stuff. You're stepping over stuff that had fallen from the roof and stuff. But at some point we know that it cracked and collapsed. But what General Webster said—he had seen it where the floor had actually collapsed, was cracking. I didn't see that. There was so much stuff lying on the floor and fire and smoke. You know, the smoke was just so bad. And you were down, low, because the smoke—the black smoke was just so bad at certain points. . . .

And so at one point I ran into CW5 [Chief Warrant Officer 5 Paul D.] Heggood, who was in here helping me. . . . When we started pulling out and thought everybody was out—and here's where I have one regret. If I ever have a regret, I have a regret. A good while, maybe two weeks, after the attack, I found out there was a major and a secretary killed in this office that I could not get in, and I, [*pause*] I regret that, because maybe I could have gone in there further. But at that time I couldn't. At that time I felt like I couldn't. . . . So at one point, at some time, we started pulling out, coming back down Corridor 4 on the third floor.

Myself and Chief Heggood met some Navy guys. I don't know who they were, but there were about three or four of them that came up the hallway and they asked us if we would help them go up on the fourth and fifth floor to clear the fourth and fifth floor. . . . So Chief Heggood, he held the door open. There's a door to the stairwells. He stayed at the door because there are no lights. There were absolutely no lights anywhere. We couldn't see s——t. At this time I had a fire extinguisher. I do not know where I got that fire extinguisher. During the whole time that I was up here, I had a fire extinguisher with me. I don't know where I got it. I have no idea when I picked it up, but I had it the whole time. I know I had it when I went in these rooms because when I went in this room and that fire was so bad, I really felt like, "What the hell, you know, there's nothing I can do with this little fire extinguisher." Anyways, so we went up to the fourth floor just out the stairwells and the smoke was so bad we just were yelling for people. . . . And I don't recall anybody coming. Maybe they did. I don't know. There were like four or five Navy guys and myself. And then we went up to the fifth floor and did the same thing, just went up the stairwell and yelled for people to come to the stairwell. . . . I went down to the second floor, and went down and just screamed. But I don't think I went to the first floor. . . . I know I went down to the second floor and just kind of stepped out and screamed for people. But it was so—it was like you couldn't see in front of your hand. First off, it was dark and then the smoke was so bad you couldn't see anything.

MR. LOFGREN: Were you having difficulty breathing?

COL. MOREHEAD: I don't remember. You know, coughing and stuff, but I wasn't choking per se. . . . We weren't doing this but a matter of minutes. You know, we were running up and down the stairs screaming and hollering for people and then running up to the next floor, screaming and hollering. . . . We came back up to the third floor where Chief Heggood was holding the door open and somebody had a flashlight because that helped us get back up the stairs. I don't know who that was, but somebody had it. You know, you couldn't see faces. And we went out at that point here, ran into this Major [Michael J.] Kerzie who was holding this door open, this fire door. It was one of these spring doors in the new area. They built these doors that would close by themselves. And so he was holding it open so we could get out. So we went out, went down to the second floor on the escalator, and then went out into the courtyard, down the stairs, the outside stairs. And when we went down the stairs, this Major Kerzie who was with me said, "Sir, I can hear the people screaming. We need to go back in. We need to go back in." . . . So we walked down and were standing right at the doorway. There's a doorway right there at Corridor 3 and 4. And there was a bunch of Navy guys that were kind of trying to like take charge, and they were taking everybody's fire extinguishers. . . . And so we were standing right at the doorway, the three of us: Chief Heggood, Mike—Major Kerzie, and myself. Major Kerzie kept saying, "Sir, we've got to go back in. I can hear them screaming. I can hear them screaming." You know, I said, "Mike, just hold off. Hold off." So they took my fire extinguisher and just a second later they said, "We need some people to go back in." So the three of us volunteered to go back and went back in.

And what we did, we went back into Corridor 4 on the first floor . . . to that breezeway area [on A-E Drive]. . . . When you went in through Corridor 4 on the first floor, you go past the escalator and then there are the doors. You go outside the door and there's that passageway where handicapped people could park and where people smoke and everything. And it was total disaster out there. That was where the hole was punched through and there was a doorway. And there was an area that I think it's—I don't know if it was the Navy Ops or what area it was . . . and that's where this Major Kerzie says he believed that he could hear these people screaming back in there. So somebody handed me a shirt, and I don't know who it was. It was a white shirt and I dipped it down in the water. There was water about four to six inches deep. The whole area was flooded at that point. So I dipped it, that T-shirt or shirt—it wasn't a T-shirt, it was a shirt—in the water and wrapped it around my face. I had picked up two fire extinguishers, where they had collected these. So each one of us picked up two fire extinguishers as we went in. And there were other people, too. I don't remember who all they were. Again, I don't remember faces. It was just everything happened so fast. I know Mike Kerzie and Chief Heggood were with me. I know that much just because I know them. They work for me.

Two views of A-E Drive

So we went into that area and we went in—I don't remember if it was the doorway or the hole, but we crawled in an area. I went in this area, and I can remember I saw a guy take a flat screen monitor, one of these very expensive flat screens, and he just took it and kind of pitched it. I can remember thinking, "Holy s———t." You know, I just bought my son one about two years ago and it was about eight hundred and some odd dollars. Well, we proceeded into the hole—I think it may have been the doorway—and you almost had to walk up on stuff because it was garbage. And I can remember there was a big—one of these lights was in the way and I picked it up and I threw it outside into the corridor area, in that breezeway area. . . . You had to not crawl, but duck-walk kind of, up to the fire, and you had your towel on or whatever you had on your face, and you would spray the fire because there were people back in there. So I—it was my turn. I had my fire extinguishers. So I crawled up as close as you could get to the fire, and you just held the fire extinguishers, held them down until they expended. And by then you probably couldn't breathe anyway. For me that's what happened. By the time I ran out of fire extinguisher it was so hot and you needed fresh air. So you'd crawl back out the hole. And I grabbed two more fire extinguishers, wet my towel, and went back in and did the same thing.

And there were other people doing it, too. Major Kerzie and Chief Heggood were two of them, I know. And we did it—I know I did it two times. I may have done it more. I don't know. But I know for a fact I did it two times. Then we ran out of fire extinguishers. You know, we'd go back outside and there was—I've seen pictures. There are fire extinguishers all over the place and those were the ones that we would carry in there and squat and spray and spray. And I remember, fuzzily, if that's a word, I was standing there, standing outside the hole and I think it was a young Navy kid—he was dressed in white, that's all I remember—ran out of that hole, laid down in the water, rolled around in the water to get wet, I guess. I don't know. Rolled around in the water and jumped back up and I'm almost certain he went back in that hole. To this day I believe that's what he did because he came out of the hole, he wasn't on fire, flames. I think he was wetting himself so he could go back in there. . . .

And so we were out of fire extinguishers and so I decided, well, I was going to go look for a fire hose. Well, I started walking down that [road]—if you're looking at the hole to the left, I just started walking by myself, walked around to the first turn. Well, there was a steam cleaner, pressure washer, you know, a great big Honda engine, I think, pressure washer. So I thought, "I got me a damn firefighter here." So I turned the switch on and pulled the cord and the damn thing cranked right up. And I started pressuring and it started shooting some water. Well, I thought, you know, if I could pull that nozzle off I could get some water. So I shut it back down, and I went and I was able just to grab the hose by my hand and I took the hose off the faucet where it was hooked at the wall. So I dragged this thing, pulled it. It was on wheels. I pulled it down to the area where we had been going in that hole. Then some other people saw me and they helped me, you know, pull it up. Around that corner you couldn't see me, so I dragged it around the corner, and then other people saw what I was doing and came and grabbed it. You know, "What do I do? What do I do?" Well, I saw that there was a faucet and I told them to hook it to the faucet. So somebody grabbed the end of the hose and went and hooked it to the faucet. As they were doing that, I cranked the engine back up. Well, we didn't have a wrench to turn the water on. The water was turned on at that other place, because when I unhooked the hose, water shot all over the place. It took a square wrench, one of those little square wrenches. . . . We didn't have anything to turn the damn water on. So we're about helpless at that point because we'd used all our fire extinguishers and couldn't get that damn steam cleaner to work, or we could get it to work, we couldn't get the water turned on. If we could have got it turned on, we could have at least, if nothing else, kept the hose and used the pressure washer to spray, to get up in there. It may have been a mist, but I was thinking if I took that nozzle off the end that it would shoot, just shoot water versus a mist. At least give us some fire fighting capability, because there were no fire hoses anywhere. . . .

About that time somebody, a policeman I think it was, started telling us to get out of there, that a second plane was coming or something. Anyways, they were telling us to get out of there. So we all, everybody in that area—I say everybody—most of us started pulling back through Corridor 4, the doorway to the breezeway. We went into the courtyard. . . .

When we pulled out of there, Major Kerzie, I don't know where he went, but Chief Heggood, CW5 Heggood stayed with me. And they started bringing casualties out, or there were some there so we—there was a guy they brought up and he had a bad cut in his—well, let me tell you this, another strange story. As I was walking out of this area here, at the men's latrine was a janitor's cart. And I don't know why I did this, but there was a roll of paper towels in that cart, and I just grabbed that roll of paper towels as we walked by, which came in handy here. These are the strange things you do. So we walked out there and there was a guy lying on the ground. As we got there, they brought this guy out from someplace. Anyway, he had a bad cut in his head and he had a cut in his chin. So Chief Heggood and I started helping with first aid. And initially I picked his head up and I stuck that paper towel [roll] under it, and at that point, that's when I noticed he had a big cut in the back of his head. And I guess everybody thought he just had this in his face—on his chin here, because he had a piece of rag or something that he was covering it, but there was nothing here, and this was a big gash here. So I said, "Holy s——t." So I took [the roll] back out and had the chief unwrap some of that paper towel and he gave it to me and so I applied it on his head. And so we just held it and at that time some medics came up and were trying to give him oxygen. And so then somebody started yelling about this second plane coming. You know, we had put this guy on a stretcher and then

A view of the hole that Flight 77 created through the inner C-Ring wall, opening onto A-E Drive *(Note the FBI markings and the designation "Punch-out [hole]."*)

they decided—before this happened, we put him on a stretcher, and they said no, they needed a stretcher to bring some more people. So we took him off of the stretcher and we started to put him on a blanket. And then somebody started yelling about a second plane was headed to the Pentagon, and that's where they—people kept talking about this damn second plane. That was another problem. So at that time somebody yelled, "Well, here's an ambulance." So we grabbed this guy up, three or four of us. . . . So we took him over and put him in that ambulance.

And then Chief Heggood and I went back, and they were telling everybody to leave because this second plane was coming. Well, as we walked back to where this triage station was, we started picking up some medical supplies. There were these like footlocker things, green footlocker things where you open them up. Well, we grabbed the two halves and just kind of stacked them on top of each other. We didn't close them. We just stacked them. He had one side, I had one side. Then I grabbed another little blue thing. I don't know what it was. We started to head out—we went up this way and then people telling us, for some reason, don't go that way, so we went down to—I think it was Corridor 9 and 10. Wherever it was, we went and started going down the tunnel to get out. We were following other people.

We got about halfway down that tunnel and there was a little electric cart, one of these little orange carts. And so I went over to it and tested it to see if it worked. Well, it worked. So s——t, we put the medical supplies on the little orange cart, stole this cart, and started driving down into the tunnel. Well, there was some kind of gate or something—the people that were in front of us, they were already turning around because you couldn't get through that gate. So we turned the little orange cart back around. . . . So we came back out. As we started heading down this way there was a medic, a lady with a blue vest on, a medic was running down here. And as we were driving down this way we asked, "Do you need medical supplies?" and she said, "Yes." . . . "Where?" And she said, "Down here." So we drove . . . back in, actually drove into the building, as far as I could. The doorway between B- and C-[Rings], out in the little breezeway area, you . . . can't drive through there. So I stopped the cart and I tried to turn it around there. Well, I backed it into the wall, and when I backed it into the wall, it killed it. It wouldn't run. So I didn't want to leave it blocking—because it was actually diagonal in the hallway—so Chief Heggood and I pushed it around, so it was just against the side so people could get by it. When I hit that wall, I had the whole damn hallway blocked.

So we grabbed those medical supplies and went back out to the same place where we had been. By then, there were some firemen that were out there. What they were doing, I don't know. They weren't doing a damn thing because they were just standing there. They didn't have fire hoses. They didn't have anything. They were standing down by where the hole was, just looking in. When we came through—as we came through underneath—they told us to wait right there. There were other people there with stretchers, military people standing there with stretchers and stuff, and we had the medical supplies for the medics and there were medics, but they were waiting to see what those firemen were going to do. Nobody was going in the hole or anything at that time because the firemen wouldn't let them go. But they weren't doing anything but looking. But then they started yelling at us to leave, again. And so we went back in, grabbed our little medical cart, and I drove it back down, drove it back out here and all those medical supplies were still there, and there were some other medical people who were picking up the supplies. So I stopped the medical cart there, and we loaded up everything and anything that we could, we put on that cart. And then one of those medics sat in the seat and drove my medical cart, drove my little cart off. . . .

About at this point, they started yelling, "Run. Run. The plane is inbound. The plane is inbound." So as we went down Corridor 8, as we got down right by the DiLorenzo Clinic, there's a medical person—again, I don't know if they were a nurse or what— standing there with a blue vest on, because that's how you could tell. And that's a good thing. You knew who the medical people were because they had these little blue vests on. And she was just standing there and so I asked, "Do you need help?" She said, "Yeah." There were a couple people behind me and Chief Heggood was one of them. She said, "In here." So we just did a right turn into the clinic. "What do you need?" And she said, "Grab anything you can. Just grab anything. It doesn't matter. Just grab anything."

So we ran back in the back following some people, and I can remember somebody coming out with a cart that had a bunch of towels stacked on it. Some of the towels fell over right when we got to them, so I just picked those towels up and we ran back into the back of the clinic. I had no idea where I was because I'm not familiar with the clinic. And there was a medical cabinet that they were trying to pull out, a big six-, seven-foot medical cabinet, plexiglass sides and everything. Well, they didn't have the keys for the medical cabinet. . . . So there was a three-seater couch, one of these three-seater couches that have legs, like just open legs. So I told Chief, "Grab the other side." So we grabbed this three-seater couch, turned it sideways, and we took the legs and busted the cabinet. And then I gave the towels to the people, and they laid the towels out and just started putting supplies into the towels.

And then that's when this policeman came down there and kept telling us to get out, get out. And about that point they figured out how to get the wheels to move. . . . So they got that first cabinet to start rolling. Well, there was another one, so I went back to try to get it, but its brakes, I couldn't get the brakes off. And then this policeman just ordered me to get out of there. I had to leave. So I was about probably one of the last ones out of there. As I was walking out with that policeman, another thing I grabbed—I don't know why I grabbed it—but as I went out, right at the counter, if you go in the clinic, there was a big set of bolt cutters. . . . So we went out to the triage site. You go out 8 Corridor out on the river. They had a big triage site set up there. And then there was another medical cabinet that had got out there, and they couldn't get into it. They didn't have the keys. So I had those bolt cutters, so Chief Heggood and I started busting the plexiglass. I was busting it, and he was pulling the small pieces, so we were able to bust that open again, and they got the medical supplies to treat the patients there.

There were some other people at that point, after we busted that out, stopping some cars, trying to get help. . . . So I started talking to some of these doctors or something, and then I walked up to a young airman, airwoman—she was female—and asked, "Is this your car?"—she was driving this van. She said, "Yes." I said, "We need to use it to carry casualties." Or whatever I said, "injured people." So like [*snaps finger*], like that, that thing filled up with about five people that could walk.

MR. LOFGREN: Were there a lot of injured people?

COL. MOREHEAD: Oh, yeah. Yeah. And then somebody yelled, "We have a life or death." So I went back to that van where that airman was driving that van. I said, "We need you people to get back out. We've got a life or death." And these people had, you know, they were walking. Well, we couldn't get the damn seats out of the van, so we couldn't put a stretcher in there. . . . So there was a police van pulled up and I went up to this guy and said, "We've got a life or death. Will you transport them?" And he said, "Yeah." So I went around to the back of the van and I tried to get the back of the van opened. I couldn't. And then somebody else opened the side door up, and so I walked around the side and there's a damn German shepherd in there in a cage. And I said, "You've got a damn"—you know, I'm talking to this policeman—I said, "You've got a damn dog in here." He says, "Yeah, just let it out." I said, "There's no way I'm letting that dog out." And about that time another van, and this is where a Lieutenant Colonel Russell was driving . . . pulled right beside that police van, and a couple people, including myself, asked him if he would transport a lady to the hospital and he said yeah. So I ran back and grabbed one of the stretcher points and we ran out and carried her in. And I got up inside the van, you know, so I dragged her in the van like this. Well, once I got into the van with her there was a doctor. I think he was either a doctor or a PA [physician's assistant]. I don't know. And this other doctor started talking about, well, who's going to go. And then they started asking me and Colonel Russell, "Do you know where the hospital is?" "Yeah, I know where the hospital is." I had no idea where the hospital was. So they talked for a few seconds. It seemed like forever. Then they decided that the guy that was already in the van, the one PA—he's a major—he would go with us. So it was Colonel Russell, myself, and this PA. They shut the van and he took off.

Well, we took off down on [Interstate] 395 South and as we were going down 395, people were slowing down to look at the Pentagon. So I was holding the IV bottle at that time, and I gave it to the PA and said, "Here, you hold this." Because he was giving her oxygen at the time. So I crawled up in the front seat and got up on the door—I lowered the window—and started telling people to get out of the way. Well, so people would get out of the way. Colonel Russell would blow the horn and people would move. Well, once we got down to Glebe Road, right at Glebe Road, traffic was bumper to bumper. So I got out and I started getting people to move their cars away, and we'd drive a little ways and I'd get out and I'd beat on the cars.

MR. LOFGREN: Walking?

COL. MOREHEAD: Walking, yeah. Running in front of it, beating on them. And it was just bumper to bumper traffic both directions. And so we got down so far, and there was a police car. A state police car was coming the opposite direction, and he was more or less stopped in traffic. So I jumped out at that time, ran over, and I said, "We need an escort. We've got a life or death." And he said, "I'm going to a lot of life or deaths." And I said, "That's exactly where we came from. We just came from the Pentagon." And I think he said, "God damn it." But he did a U-turn, drove over the curb, and got in front of us. And he was kind of slow—to lead us, to try to get us through, he was kind of slow about it. It was obvious as we went, you know, 100 yards, he was just kind of taking his time, beeping his horn once in a while. And then you could tell he got mad. He got on the . . . PA system, and he was just screaming at people. He was cussing at them. Now, he wasn't cussing at them, but he was screaming, yelling at them, [blaring] the siren. And what people would do is they would pull aside and let him through, but then they'd pull back in front of us. And so I would get out and beat on the side of—I mean, there's a lot of Mercedes and cars that have got big dents in their side because I'd beat on the side. And then sometimes I'd run in front of the police car and get people to move over. People just did not want to open up to let us through. And anyway, eventually we got her to the hospital. . . . I don't remember the lady's name, but I know they were talking about doing a tracheotomy on her, and that physician's assistant or the doctor, whatever he was that was with us, he didn't think she would live. And I haven't—I don't recognize her name. I'm hoping she didn't pass away. But anyways, we got her to the hospital as quick as we could.

And then Colonel Russell drove us back to the Pentagon because we thought we'd be transporting more people. By the time we got there, though, there were a lot of ambulances and they had triage. And then I went back over to the riverfront with that major, and they wouldn't let me back into the Pentagon. The triage station right where we had transported that lady from, there was nothing going on there at that point. They would let him back in the Pentagon. They wouldn't let me.

So I walked back down—the policeman told me where to go—so I walked back down there on Army-Navy Drive. And I got down to an intersection right at Army-Navy Drive. . . . This side of the Doubletree [Hotel], there's an intersection, Eads or something like that. That thing was one big spider web. It was all tied up. And there was a policeman there, and he wasn't doing anything. And so I got out there and started directing traffic. And the next thing I hear, I hear, "Hey, Colonel Morehead," and here comes my chief, my CW5 Heggood. He comes walking up. He stayed at the triage station and had gone back in the Pentagon to help out. They formed some teams that went back in, and then they pulled them out, let the firemen and stuff do it. But he came down. So for about three hours, until 3:30, or whenever it was, we didn't leave until about 3:30, 2:30 or 3:30. . . . We stayed there and directed traffic, because ambulances and fire trucks would come down through there. So what we did—and that policeman just let us do it, he turned it over to me, Chief Heggood, and this Lieutenant Colonel Taylor who is in DCSLOG [Deputy Chief of Staff for Logistics], he came up minutes after I got there— and we all three started directing traffic and just took over that intersection. And the policeman let us do it. He just stood back. And then, you know, we'd let the fire trucks through and let buses [through]—they were forming up buses down by Macy's, I think, to start transporting people. Because we couldn't go anywhere. You couldn't get south on 395. And about that time, when they opened up 395, once the traffic lessened—it was a big mess there because people couldn't get on 395, so they were just going in circles—but once 395 opened up, the traffic started opening up, and people could get up on it, it wasn't such a big traffic jam. And we left then.

Lt. Col. Adrian Erckenbrack was a defense congressional fellow in the Office of the Chief of Legislative Liaison. He was interviewed at his office in the Dirksen Senate Office Building by Sfc. Dennis Lapic of the 305th Military History Detachment on 16 January 2002.

SFC. LAPIC: Why don't we go into the 11th. Do you recall how that day went?

LT. COL. ERCKENBRACK: Yes. I got there at my normal time, 6:30 or 6:45, and do the normal stuff. Kind of try to track down that first cup of coffee and get charged up and just reading through some e-mail and getting some paper organized for the day.

I guess it was about 9:00-ish. I really don't know what time it was but I heard a scream down the hallway, which got my attention. I got up and walked down to our travel section, which is about a half a hallway down, where they had a TV on. I walked in and all three gals were standing there watching TV of the Trade Towers, one of which was burning. Of course, I asked them what happened and they said a plane had hit the building.

I stood there talking to them a little bit. While I was standing there the second plane hit the second Trade Tower and any doubt in your mind that it was anything other than a deliberate attack on the building dissipated because you're looking at the TV and it was blue skies, broad daylight, so you knew it was a deliberate attack at that point. The room started filling up with people because it was one of the TVs in the area, so I went back to my office . . . because I have a TV just above my desk, and I turned it on to the same channel so I could watch it. I stood there just watching it. As was happening in the other rooms, more people started filling around. We just watched it. It was at the point where there was nothing I could do from here where I was at. I sat down and started to continue going through my e-mail. People eventually went back to their desks where they had TVs over their space. I don't know what time it was, but I'm sure it's recorded somewhere, but the plane hit the Pentagon. In our office the effect was the whole office shook. Some of the ceiling tiles fell out. Lights went off and on, and [there was] the over-pressure associated with a large demolition.

I could feel the concussion so I knew from my experiences as a Special Forces guy that an explosion had occurred. What had caused it I didn't know but, of course, everybody started to panic. Not everyone. Certain people started to panic. Others were just in a daze and wondered what was going on.

SFC. LAPIC: Power was still on?

LT. COL. ERCKENBRACK: Power was back on.

SFC. LAPIC: It had gone off for a bit?

LT. COL. ERCKENBRACK: Yeah. It flickered and went off for a bit and came back on. Some people were screaming. Others immediately evacuated their office space. I kind of took a sense of what was going on around me and made a decision to move to the hallway and stay in the corridor because I didn't know— at the time I didn't know if the Pentagon was under attack by a ground force. I listened in the hallway for the repeat of any weapons. I didn't hear any. Of course, people were running up and down the hallway trying to get out. I eventually moved into the hallway and out of the building where I noticed off to my right immediately that the chairman and, I think, the Secretary or Chief [of] Staff of the Army were being evacuated in their parked cars. I watched that for a while. I used my cell phone to call my wife to let her know I was okay. Then I still didn't fully know what was going on because while I was watching all this I still had not seen the fire and the smoke from the aircraft hitting the building.

SFC. LAPIC: So you don't recall, or do you recall what corridor you came out of?

LT. COL. ERCKENBRACK: I really don't. I kept my back to—this is all in retrospect. I kept my back to the fire and the smoke because I didn't know it was there. The way I found out is I heard someone scream and I looked to my left and I saw two people running back toward the other side of the building. At the same time I noticed—that's where I saw just a huge fire and smoke from the impact of the airplane. I took off running with them. I think one guy was a Marine and another a civilian. As I ran out of the corridor of the Pentagon that was my first view of the physical destruction that the plane had caused when it hit the building. Just everything at point of impact was on fire. Everything was smoking. I mean, just huge billows of black and gray smoke, rubble, debris at various places out to twenty to fifty yards from the building. As I was running with these guys, I didn't know where they were going but I knew somebody might need help.

I started running back towards the building and I spotted an arm come up over—come out of some of the rubble. I started running towards this guy and crawled up through the rubble. It turns out it was a guy. I crawled up into the rubble and dug this guy out. These other two guys crawled up in there with me. Once I got him out, between the three of us we carried him down out of the rubble. We got him to a location where a medic—I don't even know if it was a doctor—showed up and started working on him.

SFC. LAPIC: Any idea who he was?

LT. COL. ERCKENBRACK: No idea. He was covered in concrete soot and black burnt material. He was still alive. It didn't appear he was bleeding from anywhere. He was just lucky enough to be in an area where the impact had destroyed part of the building but had not burnt it so he was still alive. We got him out of there. About that time somebody screamed another plane was inbound so we ended up pulling this guy out and moving him away from the building. Everybody was being pushed back so we got him away from the building. Eventually the medics took over or the medical people took over.

They started pushing us back even further and I ended up under the 395 overpass with just a small group of 10 or 15—I mean, maybe 25 people of all kinds and sorts. I didn't know anybody. At that point I started using my phone a lot in terms of just calling. There's a lot of people around me that hadn't told their family members that they were still alive or that they were unhurt or just where they were at, so I started calling my wife and letting these others give her their name and number to call to let their relatives know they were okay. The phone system was just—I don't want to say collapsed but it was overwhelmed. For some reason my cell phone was getting through so every so often while we were standing there I would make a call. These people would tell her their name and number.

I eventually ended up standing next to a doctor, and where he came from I have no idea. I think that he had been in Crystal

City or was driving along and saw what happened, parked his car, and was walking over to try to help, so we started talking. I had ended up with a pair of gloves on and a respirator from somewhere so I don't know if he thought I was another health care provider or whatever, but we started talking. While we were talking I heard somebody over near the building scream for medical help. He took off and I took off with him. We started running back towards the building. When we got there, there was nobody who had screamed for help so we went inside the building to see if we could help. We climbed up through and got into a corridor area that was still intact.

SFC. LAPIC: Was that the first level or second level?

LT. COL. ERCKENBRACK: I think it was the second level. We were able to get into the corridor that was leading back towards the crash site. As we were moving our way down the corridor it was just full of smoke. I mean, smoke all the way down to probably about hip high. So we were moving down the corridor and almost simultaneously I heard a scream or screams. One was off to the right and one was off to the left.

The doc, because he was on the right side, he responded to that one. As he peeled off, I peeled off to the one on the left. He disappeared inside one of the rooms. I was at the room where I thought I heard screams. I tried to enter the door and couldn't get through because of the heat or maybe the building had shifted. I don't know what happened but I couldn't get through the door. I finally managed to get the door open and just as I opened the door, of course—this office had an outer office and an inner office and the outer office was just full of smoke—so as I opened the door the smoke, which there was less [of] out in the hallway, it poured out. Just as I crawled through I saw a person who was completely on fire. . . . He came out. He fell through the door and collapsed in the outer office. While he was in the outer office I crawled over to him and found a coat that had been hanging there for some reason. I grabbed the coat and put it on him and tried to put the fire out. The guy was on fire. He was just on fire from head to toe completely. It had to be jet fuel because I couldn't put it out. Eventually I got it out and the guy, believe it or not, was still conscious. He was conscious enough to say—I got close to him to see if he was still alive and he was barely breathing. One of the things that he was saying was that you had to get help to the other people. He just kept on saying that.

SFC. LAPIC: Who were these other people?

LT. COL. ERCKENBRACK: I had no idea. I couldn't get to them.

SFC. LAPIC: They were further in?

LT. COL. ERCKENBRACK: My assumption was they were in a room that was on fire. . . . So I grabbed the guy and put his arms over his head and grabbed his forearms and tried to pull him out of the room. As I tried to do that, he was burnt so bad that where I grabbed his skin, his skin pulled away from his forearms. His shirt was still intact so I grabbed the back of his shirt and we started low-crawling out of his office and into the hallway. . . . We just kept moving up the hallway until I was about halfway up, I guess. The firemen showed up with a paramedic. Between us we got him out of the building, got him outside, got an IV into him. I was holding the IV bag.

While we were standing there somebody said they needed people with stretchers in the Pentagon. There was a guy who just happened to be standing next to me with an orange stretcher so I handed the IV bag off to one of the firemen that was standing there. The four of us went running down the hallway. We got up into the corridor. So we started running down the corridor toward the courtyard area. We get to the courtyard area and there was nobody there. I only mention it because I've been there a number of times and there are always people there. It was like a ghost town. I turned around and looked at the fire, just thinking, "Somebody is going to need these stretchers but there's nobody here."

We said we were going to do whatever we think is right. When we did turn around we said, "Okay. How can we get at the fire or get to the crash site?" We found a maintenance corridor that was running somewhat parallel back to the crash site. The four of us started moving through the corridor in just pitch black because there were no lights. As we were moving through we crossed through the A-Ring. . . . We cleared the B-Ring and got to the breezeway between there and the C-Ring. I looked left and I saw this huge hole and [what] looked like a piece of the landing gear. The wheel and a piece of landing gear, about ten feet of landing gear had just sheered off and punched a huge hole in the C-Ring wall and had come to a stop against the backside of the B-Ring wall. Along with it there was probably a four- or five-foot-high, 10-foot-wide pile of debris. As it turns out later it was like somebody had taken the plane and turned it into a syringe and everything that had been in the plane moving at 300 miles an hour had come to an immediate stop and shot forward. . . .

The debris . . . was burning. It was aircraft parts, plastic, brick, people, everything. We went over there and found—I mean, went into the hole. I was the only guy with a respirator on so everybody else when they got to the hole had to stop. I went in just a little bit further and was looking for anybody that might need help. But I couldn't really see too much just because there was so much smoke and there were electrical lines that were arcing and pieces of building still falling. I got as low to the ground as I could and just kept looking around and listening. I started listening more and looking. I didn't have anything to cover my eyes and the smoke was just so acrid that you involuntarily had to close your eyes.

SFC. LAPIC: You were in the D-Ring?

LT. COL. ERCKENBRACK: I was in the backside of the C-Ring.

SFC. LAPIC: Okay.

LT. COL. ERCKENBRACK: I couldn't hear anything except for the electrical lines arcing.

SFC. LAPIC: You're saying the plane penetrated the C-Ring?

LT. COL. ERCKENBRACK: Yes.

SFC. LAPIC: But the landing gear was between C and D.

LT. COL. ERCKENBRACK: It was in the breezeway between the C-Ring and the B-Ring.

SFC. LAPIC: But it partially punched a hole?

LT. COL. ERCKENBRACK: Yes. It means—E, D, C. It had punched a hole through the C-Ring wall and stopped against the B-Ring wall. I listened and couldn't find anybody alive. I shimmied back out of there and we basically just looked around to see if there was anybody that was alive or needed help. We couldn't find anybody.

Soon after that the firemen showed up. We started helping the firemen feed hoses in and turn water on for them. More people started showing up with stretchers. I started organizing stretcher teams to make sure they had water, make sure they had commo. Flashlights showed up from somewhere. People with radios showed up. We had funnel lines that we made sure everybody had commo, water, respirators, and a stretcher.

It turned out there wasn't anybody alive. The FBI showed up, so all of us just started helping pick up forensic evidence. We picked up body parts and just material we thought the FBI might think is useful for the investigation. Eventually I started feeling kind of useless, so me and my team and a number of the other teams, after we had picked up as much as we could, thought we would get in the way more than anything else. So we moved back into the courtyard area where we found there were a lot of people now and they had set up an evacuation point for people they were pulling out. I sat there for a while just taking my socks and shoes off—because we had been standing in water up to our knees for a couple of hours—and trying to wring some of the water out.

We were there for a while and eventually somebody came in—and, again, here is that generic word, "somebody" or "they"—came in and said they needed two hundred people with stretchers to help evacuate people on the outside of the building from an entry point that they apparently created to get people out. Everybody that wasn't involved in providing care or some other critical need there, they had a stretcher and were on the stretcher team, lined up and got out of there and moved back towards the outer part of the Pentagon and back towards the edge of the crash site. And that's where we stood for a long time . . . where they thought they needed all the people. They didn't because there just wasn't anybody alive at that point.

After that I just started—I can't remember the general, but some two- or three-star general showed up and just kind of assumed de facto charge of the site. I was helping him in basically whatever he needed. If he needed some commo or needed more people here to do that or whatever. There was a lot of emergency aid that was starting to flow in. At that point the honor guard showed up and started securing the site and getting some tents set up. I told the general, "I don't know if I can do anymore for you here," and just went home. I ate dinner and came back for about an hour. Basically the same stuff. I helped the general out for a while and just went home about 9:00 p.m.

Robert L. Jaworski was the Director of Resource Services–Washington. He was interviewed in his Pentagon office by Capt. George Dover of the 46th Military History Detachment on 11 December 2001.

CAPT. DOVER: When did you become aware of the attacks on the World Trade Center.

MR. JAWORSKI: Well, we had heard about it on the radio. One of our individuals had been listening to the radio and heard that a plane had crashed into the World Trade Center and then we obviously had turned on the other radios to try to get a sense of what was going on. But it was strictly by accidentally having the radio on as opposed to any formal notification process or anything like that. . . .

CAPT. DOVER: Did you take any actions at that time after learning of the attacks on the World Trade Center?

MR. JAWORSKI: Well, at the time, we didn't know they were attacks. The first indication was that a plane had crashed but nobody had highlighted whether it was deliberate or not. It was a plane had crashed. And when the second one crashed, somewhat later, then at that point I think people started to sense there was more going on than they might have originally thought. I know in my case, I was sitting here talking with one of our analysts who, as it turns out, would have been in an office that was where all the individuals were killed. And on 11 September, he happened to be here talking to me and a news bulletin had come on the radio saying they believed it was a terrorist attack.

And I remember remarking to the individual, you know, if anybody wanted to attack at ground zero, this is the likely place for them to attack, and within fifteen or twenty seconds, we felt the shake in the building and heard glass shattering. And at that point, unfortunately, reality started hitting home that there was more going on than just what happened in New York.

CAPT. DOVER: What's your office?

MR. JAWORSKI: Okay. I'm up here in 3D735. We were slated, as a group, to move down to 1E, the 1E400 area where most of our folks lost their lives. But because all the rooms had not been made ready, the furniture positioned and so on—our budget and accounting folks had moved—my particular office, the folks you see here, was slated to have moved in that first phase but because the room had not been laid out correctly, we were then incorporated into the next phase, which would have occurred in October. . . . As it turned out, the office that we would have been in was being used by one of our employees who was critically injured in the attack. Fortunately he's now out of the hospital but literally he was burned over the vast majority of his body. So it's safe to say had we been in that room, we'd have probably suffered similar if not worse consequences.

* * * *

CAPT. DOVER: Mr. Jaworski, could you describe in detail what happened when the attack occurred and how your office responded?

MR. JAWORSKI: Well, when you talk about our office, we were in several different—are still in several different parts of the Pentagon. I was physically located in this office here when it occurred. Our manpower folks were across the hall. We had two other groups in the building at other areas. Our financial management folks were on C-Ring up here on the third floor. Our financial accounting services group was in the 1D600 area on the first floor. And finally, the group that was decimated by the attack was in the 1E400 range. So each of those groups was impacted to a different extent and I'll go through it just to kind of give you an idea.

We, here on the third floor, felt the building shake, heard falling glass coming down from outside, heard the alarms go off and, recognizing that the building had moved, the glass was falling, we didn't wait to see if it was a false alarm or not. Everybody basically started exiting. As we exited down seven corridor, when we got to A-Ring, then you could actually see over Center Court. All you saw was night, just smoke, it was dark and at that point, I think people realized that something severe had happened. And when I say people realized, those were the folks on the third floor here.

Our folks on the first floor actually had a wall fall down, part of a wall come down on them and they were they could tell firsthand that something serious had happened. Whereas here, it was just a shudder but not anything as dramatic as a wall buckling or anything like that.

The folks who were in the 1E400 area, basically they didn't have a chance. And as we found out later, the only two people who were physically in that area and who survived happened to be in restrooms on the corridor right outside E-Ring and were they not in restrooms at the time, the odds are they would not have survived. The reason I say that is because all the people who were on E-Ring, on the inner corridor, nobody in that room managed to escape. The people who were on outer E-Ring, we had three survivors and a fourth person who initially survived but who died in the hospital.

So the impact on the organization really was a function of which part of the building you were in at the time. Obviously the folks up here didn't realize the severity of what was going on until they exited the building. The folks who happened to be closer, the ones who had a wall come down, in another case the folks who were in the restroom, realized that something had happened because the smoke and air was just so—they literally couldn't breathe and had to run to escape for their lives.

CAPT. DOVER: What were your immediate actions or reactions?

MR. JAWORSKI: Well, as I mentioned, we didn't know what had happened. Basically until we saw, and I'm speaking for myself and the folks here on the third floor, until we saw the smoke over in the Center Court and just how dark it was outside, that was the first indication we had of the severity of what had occurred. Even when we evacuated the building and I and a number of our folks walked across South Parking to the side of the building with the heliport where they could see the smoke coming up— we literally were in lane one and then moved up onto the grassy knoll near the highway there—and we still could not tell, and this was probably within five or seven minutes of when the plane had actually hit, we could not tell what had happened. It was just smoke and fire. You couldn't even see the hole in the building. And the only way that folks were even imagining what had happened was somebody indicated that a couple of the light poles had been knocked over alongside the highway and that was the only indication that a plane had caused this as opposed to, somebody had driven a truck with a bomb or something like that. But the smoke and fire was so intense that you honestly could not tell what had happened. . . .

I don't think anybody knew that it was an attack. Everybody was— the people that we saw were obviously concerned. There was a lot of uncertainty about what had happened. Many of them had seen smoke or had some indication that something serious had occurred but I don't think anybody realized the severity of what had happened. And people were just—they were reasonably calm but they were concerned about getting out of the building because of the uncertainty about what had actually occurred. I think people realized this was not any false alarm but they didn't actually know what happened and they realized that exiting was the right thing to do. . . .

In terms of exiting the building, basically, the folks here on the third floor, we had pretty much exited together. The folks who were on other floors had used different exits . . . and were located in different areas outside. As a matter of fact, when I evacuated the building, I actually ran into one of the folks who had been in the restroom in the 1E400 area. When we talked to him and said, "Where are the rest of our folks who were down there?" his first thought was they were on the other side of the building. But he couldn't verify what had happened because he had to exit the restroom quickly when the blast occurred and he had to go to Center Court to evacuate, so he couldn't tell, with any certainty, who was where. . . . The other thing that I think was also a cause for concern was, when you exited the building, the police basically were pushing everybody as far away from the building as they could because they understood that there was a real possibility of another plane, an additional threat and so on. So essentially you didn't really have the capability to regroup. . . .

CAPT. DOVER: Of those people that were out that you accounted for, did you send these people home or did they remain somewhere here on the Pentagon grounds?

MR. JAWORSKI: Most of them wound up going home. A few of them stayed. . . . My understanding was that most of our folks had been pushed so far away from the building by security, that there really was no alternative but for them to try to get home.

The other problem we ran into [was] there was virtually no way to communicate with anybody because no matter what cell phone you used, who you tried to borrow one from or what have you, the cell phone service was just not working. It was just so overburdened or what have you, and the only way that we were able to call our families was to go over to the area around the Macy's store. We wound up actually asking somebody to see if we could go up to their apartment and use their regular phones because there were—the stores had started to close down and things like that, and there was no way to get in contact with anybody. . . .

CAPT. DOVER: How many people did you lose?

MR. JAWORSKI: We lost thirty-four people in terms of fatalities. I believe we were the organization that lost the single largest group in the Pentagon. We also had four folks injured, seriously injured in this and one of those is included in the thirty-four fatalities because she died in the hospital several days after the attack.

* * * *

CAPT. DOVER: How did you get home and when?

MR. JAWORSKI: Getting home was an interesting proposition that day because we tried to, well, I was with, as I say, one of our folks who had been in the restroom and we were also with another colleague who was visiting from another command who I happened to know for probably twenty-five years. And we were trying to, well, we all thought we had to do several things. Before we even thought about going home, we tried to contact our various relatives or offices to kind of let them know that we were okay. And that was a challenge because, as I mentioned, we had to kind of depend on the good graces of one of the tenants of the condos near Macy's who let us in. And the irony of it is here we are across the highway from the Pentagon watching what's going on on a TV screen while we're trying to contact relatives to let them know we were okay.

So our primary focus was to at least let people know we were alive. I know in my own case, it took a while to get through because my wife had been evacuated from her job on the Hill, couldn't get through on her cell phone, so we wound up having to leave, for example, a message on the voicemail at home. You know,

I finally reached my daughter at school, just knowing that her Mom would wind up going there to pick them up.

Is it okay to relate an anecdote here? It's one of those kinds of things you're going to remember as long as you live but it's really not part of this history. I finally got through to the school after about five or six tries because all of the parents were calling. I asked for my daughter and got put on hold for five or six minutes. And I had told the lady I needed to talk to her to let her know that things were okay, not being sure what the school knew about what had gone on or what they had told the kids.

And the lady came back and said, "I can't get your daughter, she's in the last two minutes of art class." And I just about lost it because here I am trying to call and tell her I'm alive because my wife knew that we worked in the side of the building that had been hit and I kind of let the lady have it. In the end, I said, "Hey, I'm calling to tell my daughter that I'm alive. I don't care about the last two minutes of art class." I think it was a little more graphic in what I've said than that. So finally she gets my daughter on the phone and I said, "Libby, I don't know what they've told you but if your Mom comes, just tell her that Dad's okay, he's trying to figure out what to do. We'll try to hook up with you whenever we can but just let Mom know we're okay." And, you know, as long as I live, I'm going to remember that last two minutes of art class explanation. I'm going to tell you, after you've seen what's gone on on the TV, you've been evacuated, you see the damage and all that, to hear something that trite, just sets you off. I mean, you just want to shake the person and say, "I can't believe that answer!" I found out afterwards some of the parents were calling but they couldn't get all the kids and all that. But the way it came across was the last two minutes of art class. I hope I never see the last two minutes of art class. . . .

We finally managed to talk a taxicab driver who didn't want to give us a ride into taking us on as fares by promising to fill his gas tank, and also we had learned that he had spent so much time tied up in traffic in the area that he wanted to go home. Well, when we found out home was in Annandale, "Hey, we'll go home with you because where we need to go is near Annandale." So we talked him into taking us to a gas station, we filled his car up, and then we went on backstreets to drop the person off who was visiting from Hawaii at the place where she was staying, and then we dropped myself and my coworker who had been in the restroom off at the school where my daughter was.

And, in the meantime, we finally, using a cell phone, we had reached my wife because the traffic had eased a little bit and wound up meeting at the school. But it probably took us, I want to say, about two and a half hours once we tried to figure out a way to get home, to get to our destinations. And in a number of points, the traffic was just so horrendous that we seriously considered trying to walk. It would have been a long walk to get to where any of us were trying to get to. But the good news is that the cabby got a free tank of gas and a fare, and because we were lucky enough that his home was in Annandale, we convinced him that he really wasn't going that far out of the way. So the three of us were able to get home.

Of course, all along, we're not sure what has happened to anybody else. All we knew is that the police had scattered everybody and basically said get away from the building and the impression was, at that point, you were on your own. You just had to figure out how to get home, get away from there. They were not going to let you anywhere near the Pentagon anymore.

* * * *

CAPT. DOVER: How long was that before you realized how many people you had lost?

MR. JAWORSKI: Well, we started—we had myself and a number of folks calling around just trying to understand. Clearly we didn't realize that [on] Tuesday, the day of the incident. And one of the reasons . . . is because we kept hearing that there were a lot of unidentified in hospitals. So between that and what later turned out to be a somewhat erroneous impression on my part—frankly, I thought most of our organization was located closer to the tower than they actually were. In other words, when you looked at that side of the building, there was the control tower there and then there were a range of a number of rooms between the tower and where the plane had hit. My feeling was we were more towards the tower and less towards the—where the plane actually had entered the building. As it turned out, most of our folks were to the right of the tower as you were looking at the building. And given the intensity of what had happened—and we didn't know this at the time—whether you were at the tower, slightly to the left of the tower, slightly to the right of the tower, given what had actually happened, it really didn't matter. You basically did not survive or the odds were against you.

So we were optimistic when Wednesday came around and we're still talking to various families and they're telling us they've been canvassing hospitals and there's nobody by that name. Obviously we're getting more concerned but we were aware that there were folks who were unidentified who were in the hospitals. But I think we started to realize there can't be thirty-four. And clearly by, I guess, Wednesday evening, at that point there's still hope, but it's not the optimism that you had Tuesday or even Wednesday morning—that the more you start hearing that their folks had talked to various hospitals, the relatives are not there, they're calling and saying, "Well, have you heard or has anybody heard?" then you start to realize there's more, there's more to this than you first thought. When we reported the information into the central clearinghouse the Army was running and it was, "Okay, have you heard from any of these people?" and they indicated that relatively few had called in—we might have crossed off half a dozen names who were out of the building or on leave or what have you—it became even clearer that a lot of our folks could not survive or could not have survived.

I think what was troubling is normally you're able to talk to a first-level supervisor or a second-level supervisor to find out who was at work, who wasn't, where folks might have been. We lost the whole group. So you could never be sure who was there, who wasn't, who was on leave, who wasn't, who was in a meeting in a different part of the building, until you were either able to get hold of them or they had called in. And the good news was we found out a number of folks had survived, but it turned out that most of them were either in the restrooms, on leave, or were in the hospital critically injured. As it turned out, other than the three who were in the hospital and are now being released, as I mentioned earlier, none of the folks on the interior part of that ring or of that area had survived. And once we knew they hadn't called in, you know, and we started to hear more about the severity of the fire and things like that. I think it became a grim reality that they were not going to be found and if anybody were found it would be by luck, not by numbers.

Arthur Santana was a reporter for the Washington Post *covering the D.C. Superior Court beat. He was interviewed by Stephen Lofgren and Capt. Timothy Frambes of the U.S. Army Center of Military History on 5 March 2002.*

MR. SANTANA: So here I am at about 9:15, 9:30, coming to work from Alexandria on this beautiful clear day on the Washington Parkway. So I'm coming down from Alexandria to D.C., and I normally take the 14th Street Bridge from the parkway and then cross over and head to the courthouse, which is normally not more than a 30-minute drive, especially at that hour. You know, rush hour is starting to slow down.

So I am coming in and I see this huge black plume of smoke sort of starting to rise out of the trees in the distance. I was heading north, so it was to my north. I knew, from my experience as a police reporter, that it's a general and generic rule that black smoke is not good and white smoke typically is okay. Black smoke means something is on fire, fuel of some kind. It means something is wrong. Typically—not always. And so I knew something was wrong and I saw, as I was driving in, this smoke just rising and rising and rising, really starting to rise. And I thought, I don't know, something was on fire. Then I got a call from my wife on my cell phone that the Trade Centers had been hit in New York, and I knew immediately something was wrong. And I turned on the radio and, I guess, it didn't—actually, it didn't occur to me immediately that there was some kind of coordinated attack. I thought, "Oh, no, here is another Oklahoma City, it's Oklahoma, New York, we're going to hear about this for months and months and months and how terrible," you know, and I was, of course, curious. And so I ended up turning on the radio and, of all things, there was this, like a disc jockey, a radio disc jockey. They had stopped all their music and they had started, you know, receiving calls from people. And that's how I actually heard that a plane—the early reports, these frantic calls into these radio disc jockeys—that a plane had hit the Pentagon. And suddenly everything clicked for me, that this was a coordinated thing, and this was huge, and this was unbelievable, and just shocking. Just shocking.

Waiting to help

So immediately I knew I was close to the Pentagon and I knew I just had to get there to find out what was happening. And I knew I had a particular vantage point, being close. So instead of taking the 14th Street Bridge to cross over, I kept going straight past the bridge a little ways, and it started getting really congested, because there's fire trucks and cars starting to move real fast and everybody else was starting to get just locked in, in what was becoming a really bad traffic jam. So I did—of course, this is probably illegal—but I did a U-turn across this grassy embankment to head back south to catch the [Interstate] 395 exit to the Pentagon. So I jumped the curb and I turned around and headed back south, just a little ways, and took the 395 exit and suddenly I was right there at the Pentagon. And, of course, everything was crystal clear in my view, this huge plume of black smoke rising, this mass exodus of people leaving the Pentagon, just crowds and crowds of people just pouring out. And I put my car on the side of the freeway and just left it there, and grabbed my note pad and my cell phone, and that's sort of how I got there. How it all started.

MR. LOFGREN: What time do you think it was when you got there?

MR. SANTANA: It could not have been—I think the Pentagon, I seem to recall, was hit at 9:40 or something, I don't remember—but it could not have been ten or fifteen minutes after it happened. It probably was five or ten till 10:00 that morning. I must have seen the accident happen. I mean, seeing the smoke, in the minutes after it happened. That must have been the smoke I was seeing. Yeah, I'm guessing.

MR. LOFGREN: You parked your car and got out.

MR. SANTANA: Yeah. So I started being a reporter. I started interviewing people and I ran into a lieutenant colonel, I forget his name, his name is in my note pad somewhere. His arm was bloodied up and he was gracious enough to take a few minutes to talk to me about how he was near the explosion site, and he and his staff were in a meeting, and they just got out of there as soon as they heard this massive explosion. After him, I interviewed a few more, a few others who were coming out, military and nonmilitary.

At one point—it was kind of strange—because at one point . . . I was going around, I was trying to make my way to the other side of the Pentagon, the crash site, ground zero, so they say. And I was alone with—I think there was one other person walking with me, maybe intending to walk to the other side, and these agents, some federal agents, I don't know if they were marshals or FBI or who they were, secret service, but they started yelling at us from up above the street that another plane was on its way, to get out of there. . . . Three or four of them just yelling at us, screaming at us to get out, get away, get away quickly. So the people who were straggling behind were beginning to run away from the Pentagon, and myself included as part of that group. It's also an interesting scene that's never made prints, but there was an interesting scene, where I was coming back to where people were, I guess, taking cover. Because all these people were lying down on their stomachs. . . . They were lying down with their arms out. It was a weird scene, to see all these military guys who were taking cover and they were, like I said, just sort of in the grass, sort of on the downslope of a hill, and I think had been ordered to get down. So everybody was down and it was surreal to see this.

MR. LOFGREN: Where was this?

MR. SANTANA: This was—I don't have the map, but there's a body of water just northeast of the Pentagon. . . . So right on that bank, there is a grassy median, sort of a hill, and people were taking cover there. There must have been hundreds of people. . . .

And then something strange happened, something weird happened. I ended up putting my note pad *away*. Because eventually after that I started walking around and came across this sort of medical triage area, where there were victims who were being pulled out, and they were being—it was just sort of the immediate makeshift triage area, and they were being placed in this area . . . on the street between the grass and the Pentagon, and there must have been a dozen people, bandages, and really badly injured. And they were being transported in private cars. In other words, people weren't waiting for ambulances. There were too many people, and they were starting to take them in cars. I don't know if they were federal or law enforcement or civilians, but they were taking these plain unmarked cars and taking people out.

In the meantime, they had set this triage area up where there were medical carts and oxygen tanks and bandages, and all these things had suddenly sort of materialized in this sort of triage area, which is pretty impressive, so soon after everything happened. And this was the place where people were being treated and they were pushing back photographers who were first on the scene. There must have been just a few of them. And I put my note pad away and went in there and I actually found a guy, I think it was [Maj. T.] Ryan Yantis. . . . I think he was the guy that was out there, and I asked him, and he eventually said that it was okay for me to be there. But when I was out there, I just started helping out and I started helping move these tanks, and they had all these surgeon's masks and these latex gloves. And for a while there, I wasn't a reporter anymore. I was trying to help out. It just was a strange and crazy time during that whole—and there's really some, what appear to be some badly hurt people.

And eventually, a few minutes later, they started—I'm not sure who, I don't know if it was Ryan or somebody—but they started organizing. They told everybody they needed to get people to line up in columns, and they were going to hand out these masks, and we were going to go into the courtyard of the Pentagon, and we were going to help set up the triage area there. We were going to essentially transfer it from where it was outside, we were going to transfer it inside, because they were expecting a group of people to be rescued from inside and that the more effective triage area would be in the courtyard. So they started lining us up in columns and they were handing out gloves and masks. And I found myself behind a medical cart with the gloves and masks and was sort of corralled into all this. So the next thing I knew, I guess it must have been 10:30, maybe 10:45, when I found myself in the middle of this smoky courtyard of the Pentagon.

So that's essentially . . . how I got in there, and that's sort of really how it all really started. It was probably a little bit before I identified myself to Major Yantis, I think. . . . We started talking. He said, "I see you're helping, so long as you don't bother anybody, it's okay." And I told him, "Look, I'm with the *Post*. I intend to record my observations, although I don't intend to interview anybody. I'm going to look around and eventually I'll probably report my observations to the paper for publication, but I'm not going to bother anybody with a note pad in their face." That was the last thing on my mind.

So I continued there in that courtyard probably for an hour or so just helping out. These firefighters were going in and coming out, just with soot and sweat all over them, and these guys were unbelievable. I mean, they were just going in there, I guess, looking for people. In this courtyard area, we had a makeshift CPR training by one woman. I think she was a reporter herself for like *Stars and Stripes* or something. She . . . gathered a group of a dozen or so people and she started reminding everybody how to do CPR, and I was part of that group watching. And we started putting together—you know, I'm handing out towels to firefighters and bottles of water and sorting medical equipment and moving it around. Everybody was doing something, getting ready for what we thought were going to be victims who would be coming out.

At some point, they organized us into groups of—like five or six groups—and every group of about maybe a dozen or so people had a role, and like one group was supposed to be helping with the medical treatment, another group was supposed to give that team medical equipment. Another team was specific medically trained people who were going to treat the wounded. So very organized, it was really impressive. I got into a group which was a group that was supposed to provide equipment to the medical personnel. So we started putting together gurneys and ripping up sheets to make these swathes to tie down people or [bind] their wounds, if need be.

Nobody ever came out. No wounded ever came out. We were there for a while, and I would say, I guess, maybe an hour, maybe two hours. Maybe two hours.

And during the slow times, I went back and I called in feeds. It was incredibly difficult to get through with a cell phone. But I would call in feeds to my city desk. My editor, Gabe Escobar, is our city editor. It was funny, because I told him—because we were breaking up, it was a touch-and-go feed—and I told him, "I'm in the courtyard." And I was supposed to have worked at the courthouse, so he heard, "Oh, you're at the courthouse, okay, fine." So I had to repeat, "No, I'm in the courtyard," which, of course, he was surprised about. And he patched me through to a guy by the name of Tucker, who was taking feeds and transcripts. So we come to find out I was the only *Post* reporter that had that kind of access. And throughout that whole thing, this was sort of the beginning of what would be a sort of—a kind of a struggle, sort of a coming to terms with trying to find my role and understand my place in this whole thing. That was sort of the beginning of it. I wasn't sure to what extent I was supposed to be a reporter and to what extent I was supposed to be a human being, and there was some grappling with that and it continued to the next day, all night to the next day. Anyway, he sort of hinted, work things out that way, you know, to myself and for myself, all the while identifying myself to people as much as I could. And at the direction of my city desk, he said, "You need to tell them who you are. We're not tricking anybody, we're not going to surprise anybody with something. Just be up front." Which is our policy and it's a good policy.

So eventually we—I can't remember what time, maybe 12:00, one o'clock—we were given the instruction, this group in the courtyard—probably about a hundred people, maybe more—we were given the instruction that we were going to move the triage center to ground zero. We were going to move around through one of the corridors on the southwest side, maybe just the west side. We were going to travel around two panels of the Pentagon and we were going to end up in that northwest yard, that helicopter landing pad. . . . I was walking with a military person, a woman who was beside me on a cart, pushing a cart, and we came around this, and we both sort of commented to each other, because as soon as we came around, we were getting our first up-close look at this crash site. It was still burning, smoky and burning, fire, and there were fire trucks and crowds and crowds of people who had gathered at that lawn, this lawn, just bunches and bunches, must have been three hundred people, military and emergency. I made some comment, or she made the comment—we made the comment to each other—like, "If I lived to be a hundred, I never thought I'd see such a thing." It was just shocking to all of us who were walking around because here we were seeing this for the first time. This huge gaping hole in the side of the Pentagon.

CAPT. FRAMBES: Had it already collapsed?

MR. SANTANA: Yes.

CAPT. FRAMBES: You were looking at the hole, the right side.

MR. SANTANA: It had already collapsed. The reason I know that is because people had said that they heard this huge, loud bang, almost a second explosion, when it fell. I don't remember hearing that, but I heard people talking about it. So, yeah, there was this—it was like—the pile was such that you couldn't actually even see the plane, because it had fallen and sort of covered the plane. This huge wall had collapsed over it and you couldn't actually see any part of the plane. So, yeah, I imagine that it had collapsed and I imagine that if it did thereafter, I would have noticed, and I didn't.

So this began what would be thirty-plus hours on that lawn. I busied myself the same way I busied myself in the courtyard, which was helping people with medical equipment. We had created a triage area, a huge—a bigger tent this time, moving water, bottles of water and medical equipment, masks, gloves.

It dawned on me after a while, we must have been there for thirty to forty-five minutes and it dawned on me. . . . Everybody was doing something, but really doing nothing. I mean, everybody was hurrying and they were rushing . . . but at the end of the day, they were really doing nothing. It's like they were moving bottles of water from this stack to this stack. Or they were moving ice from here to here. And you really did nothing, you know, except busy people, you know, like they were doing something. There were constructive things going on. This medical triage center was created and people were being organized, but it didn't seem like—it was like everybody was hurrying up to do a lot of nothing, it just seemed to me. . . . There was this frantic need, I think, on the part of everybody there to *do something*, to react, in some constructive way. But with what we had before us, how could you really do anything? Unless you were a firefighter who was sent in there to go put this thing out or get on the roof and start what would be a day-long spraying of these hot spots? I mean, how could you possibly be really doing anything except maybe feel like you were doing something? So I was part of that. I was moving around. People were telling me to do something and I did it. . . .

At some point thereafter, they started forming one of these groups of columns again. . . . It must have been a group of what was now becoming all men. At some point, people were starting to leave and it was almost all military and/or emergency, and there were a few civilians like myself who were hanging around, who, you know, were helping or trying to help. At some point, these guys had—they ordered us to sort of get in line, like a single-file line, these columns, and to have a buddy. So we quickly looked around and found somebody and we were standing two by two in these lines of probably a dozen guys each, in what were probably a dozen columns. And our instructions were we were going to go in and retrieve bodies. This was strange, of course, but it was sort of, how could you say no? You were there to help.

So they gave us masks and they gave us latex gloves and they gave us some bottles of water to stick in our pockets and they said we're going in and this is what you should expect. And they started to tell us how there's deceased and a lot of them are not what you expect. You know, there might be people that look just as alive as you, except they died of smoke inhalation or something. Anyway, we're in there to get them out of there. So we were fully prepared and there was this sort of eerie several minutes when we were ready to go in. We were just sort of—minutes turned into thirty minutes, and then to an hour, and then at some point, the guy who organized it called it off, saying it was still—it was too smoky to go in there.

So after that was over, we disbanded our group and we began to busy ourselves again with—you know, at this point, the Red Cross started coming in with food and water. And so more stuff for us to move around, to organize, to sort, and situate.

* * * *

One of the things we started doing, at least I did, we started picking up pieces of the airplane, and they were everywhere, scattered, and in chunks two or three feet big, and then as little as little nuts and bolts, and they were just everywhere. The FBI—some guy, I'm not sure, somebody in the FBI— started handing out another order to start putting them in piles. So that was one of [the] things I busied myself doing, and I spent a couple hours collecting parts of the airplane, which was a strange experience for me. I'm not crazy about flying to start off with, and it just wasn't doing any good, I can tell you that. And there were huge chunks, and there was actually one chunk that was so big you actually could see the C, the red C in the word American. And there were big and then there were small, and we put them in piles. . . . We put them in piles just at different places, and these guys would then come over and stick them in bags. Some were tiny little bags, some were huge bags.

I was involved in that, and, again, what I was told to do, I did. If somebody told me to do something, I did it. If I was carrying something and somebody said go get me a bag of ice, I'd go and put what I was doing down and get a bag of ice. That's how it went all through that day.

Maj. Craig Collier worked in the Office of the Chief of Legislative Liaison. He prepared the following account for his family in September 2001. He submitted it to the U.S. Army Center of Military History in November 2001 with a cover note that read, in part: "One thought not on here is that I wish we had ignored the security guards' instructions to clear out of the area for the second incoming aircraft that was supposedly on its way. I talked with several individuals who did just that, and they managed to get inside the building and save lives."

Yesterday the Pentagon, where I work, was hit and partially destroyed by a hijacked airliner. . . . This short entry is an attempt to capture my experience before time dulls the details as well as to comply with the instructions of my father, who regrets not keeping a diary to record his participation in WWII (The Big One).

I am currently assigned to the Office, Chief of Legislative Liaison (OCLL), in the Pentagon, Room 2C638 (second floor, "C" Ring, room 638). . . . The day promised to be rather slow, as the one scheduled meeting for the day had been canceled. Just after 0900 I returned to the office from picking up some equipment from a conference room in the "E" ring (the outermost ring; the "A" ring is the innermost). Shortly after I arrived and with most of us in the office, Mr. Winchester, who specializes in Army liaison with the Senate and House Intelligence Committees and always has his office TV tuned into CNN, walked in to let us know that one of the World Trade Center towers had been hit by an aircraft and was on fire. We immediately turned on a nearby TV to NBC just in time to see the second aircraft plow into the other tower. I called [my wife] Linh on her cell phone to tell her that she probably wanted to get to a TV to see this. . . .

One of the members of the office whose background is force protection and counterterrorism casually speculated about what else they could do if they could coordinate two major attacks at once. Ironically, at about that time Katie Couric mentioned the same thing. Moments later the building jolted and we heard a muffled boom, then a rumble. Some loose plaster and dust fell from the ceiling, but otherwise there was no other indication of what had just taken place about two hundred feet away. All of my peers in the area are experienced combat arms officers, and we quickly agreed that it sounded and felt like a bomb. Most of us stayed in place watching the news and waiting for more information as one or two officers walked out into the hallway to see what was going on. Remarkably, my boss walked in and asked us what was happening. He had been in the latrine next door and hadn't felt or heard a thing. Within about two minutes the TV banner below the video of the burning towers changed from "World Trade Center" to "Pentagon," but before I could hear any of the details the word came to evacuate the building. Two of our female civilian secretaries bolted out of the office but the rest of us took the time to calmly turn off our computers, call our wives, grab our bags, and exit. Unfortunately I did not take the opportunity to call Linh, thinking that I would wait for more information on what happened and borrow someone's cell phone outside. That was a bad decision.

On the way out I didn't see any fire and only caught a whiff of smoke just before I exited the building. After we walked out of the Mall Entrance we made our way to the heliport side, where a large crowd was gathering near the freeway [Route 27]. When we rounded the corner of the Pentagon we saw that the center of that side was engulfed in flames, along with several trees, a few vehicles, and what appeared to be a truck. Large amounts of debris littered the area in front of that side, some of it still on fire. At least one wounded person was being attended to by what looked like an Emergency Response Team member. Pentagon security guards kept the rest of us back. Emergency vehicles were already arriving on the scene, and highway traffic was backed up and barely moving, as motorists made way for the fire trucks and gawked at the spectacle. Most of us still believed that a bomb had exploded, and it wasn't until we looked around us and saw what looked like pieces of aircraft that we realized that the same thing that happened in New York had just taken place here, and we were standing in the debris field three hundred meters away from the impact. We also noticed that, ironically, the area hit was the newly renovated section, specifically the area where our canceled meeting was supposed to have taken place.

Every other person standing around had his cell phone out. We overheard one sooty and scraped Air Force lieutenant colonel talking to his wife. He was in the B-Ring near the crash site. The explosion knocked him and his colleagues down and dropped ceiling tiles, but everyone in his area had gotten out alive. From that info and from what we were witnessing we figured that C- and D-Rings had been hit hard, probably destroyed. Clearly, the middle area of E-Ring was destroyed and on fire. One man from across the road screamed to passing police that he thought there was a pipe bomb in the road. Everyone ignored him, correctly believing that what he saw was a piece of the airplane.

About ten minutes after leaving the building a marine officer ran up to the crowd from the crash site and asked for any military men to volunteer to act as stretcher bearers for casualties. A few hundred of us, from all ranks and services, dropped our stuff and ran over to help. A female Army major appeared to be the senior medic on the scene. She asked if anyone had medical experience, then attempted to get us organized into groups of one medic with two or three stretcher-bearer teams each. Unfortunately she asked the nearest most senior officer in view to do this for her, and the marine colonel tagged hesitated and did not appear ready to assume control. Soon, however, one of the ERT [Emergency Response Team] members called the group over and we rushed to near the fire, which by now several firemen were trying to get under control. At this point my four-man stretcher team happened to include a civilian, one of my coworkers in Legislative Liaison, and SMA [Sergeant Major of the Army Jack] Tilley. I found it difficult to take my eyes off of the blackened façade to our front and the burning, gaping hole to our immediate right. The ERT guys gave us gloves and we were poised to enter the building, when a fireman came out and told us there were no survivors in that section. Our sobered teams began moving to the South Parking lot on the other side of the fire to try to approach the damaged area from inside one of the rings. As we were moving, the local security, increasingly augmented with arriving police from everywhere, began screaming for us to move to the other side of I-395, as there was another aircraft inbound just minutes away. While moving we heard a sonic boom and moments later an F–16 buzzed the Pentagon. We wondered if we were about to witness an American fighter shoot down a civilian passenger aircraft before our eyes, and where would be the safest place to witness that? Black smoke filled the air over the Pentagon as the fire spread.

After waiting in Pentagon City for about twenty minutes I crossed back over the police line and made my way back to the Pentagon, where a group of about two hundred service members waited to assist in any way they could. By this time we had heard all sorts of rumors: an explosion at the base of one of the towers had collapsed it; both towers had collapsed; Camp David had been attacked; the State Department had been attacked; the Mall had been attacked; the Old Executive Office Building near the

White House had been attacked; another aircraft went down in Pennsylvania, possibly shot down; a fifth went down somewhere in or off the coast of North Carolina; other aircraft from Europe were unaccounted for. More and more emergency personnel arrived, and we all tried to find out what was happening outside of the Pentagon. I tried to call Linh several times on borrowed cell phones, but most of the time all of the lines were tied up. Typically, once someone in a group managed to contact his wife, he passed around the phone so she could contact everyone else's.

Soon after returning we again split up into teams and my group moved to inside the Pentagon courtyard to again attempt to pull out casualties. By now there were plenty of doctors, paramedics, nurses, corpsmen, and medics available. Once we arrived at the courtyard we made several false starts, as firefighters would not let anyone else in due to the fire, which despite their efforts was continuing to spread. The FBI began tagging pieces of aircraft metal that had blown over the building into the courtyard from the initial explosion. Within our holding area lay a partially melted tie and bloody underwear from one of the earlier treated victims, thankfully the only gore I would see. Several of us milling around expressed our frustration at not being allowed into the building to look for survivors, but it was becoming increasingly obvious that the fire and smoke were successfully resisting the firefighters' efforts to contain them. It was also becoming obvious that the chances of anyone surviving the fire and smoke were slim.

After a few hours in the courtyard the marine colonel doctor in our team told us that the mission would most likely change from casevac [casualty evacuation] to recovery. Anyone who did not want to participate in that potentially gruesome mission, he said, did not have to volunteer. The number of firefighters continued to grow, and the medical personnel and assets kept getting pushed further away from the building. Sometime around 1400 all of us moved back to outside the Pentagon, where we joined the rest of the volunteers still waiting to assist. Since it looked like we would not be used anytime soon due to the fiercely burning fire, I went looking for my jacket and bag that I dropped, only to be told by security personnel that it was probably picked up by the FBI when they combed that area for evidence. Around 1600 came the word that there was nothing we could do, and Army [Lt. Gen. John A.] Van Alstyne released the volunteers. I left the FBI evidence team my card in case they came across my bag and jacket, walked a mile to the Metro at Pentagon City, caught the train and made it home by 2000. Linh met me at the door and gave me a long hug.

Maj. Jeanette K. Stone worked for the Environmental Law Division, U.S. Army Legal Services Agency, and was attending a Base Realignment and Closures (BRAC) meeting at the Pentagon on 11 September. She submitted the following account of her experiences to the U.S. Army Center of Military History on 10 October 2001.

[*After feeling the impact, Major Stone joined her colleagues in evacuating the building.*] I moved very quickly toward the nearest exit that I knew, the Mall Entrance. Many of the people around me were clearly panicked, but for the most part the evacuation was orderly.

I left the building through the Mall Entrance and headed in a ten o'clock direction. When I got to the side of the building, I saw that the façade of the building was on fire and that there were small machine parts scattered everywhere on the grass. I later learned that these were pieces of the plane that struck the Pentagon. . . .

Staring at the Pentagon while it burned, I felt like I should be doing something, and noted that that feeling seemed to be collectively felt among the military personnel as they began to slowly gravitate together into little groups and edge back toward the building. At that point, a fire truck with a bullhorn informed us that a second plane, headed toward D.C., was twenty minutes out, and that everybody needed to get as far away from the building as possible. We did so, looking anxiously to the sky. A few minutes later, a second bullhorn announcement came informing us that that plane was no longer en route; presumably, this was the one that crashed in rural Pennsylvania. An F–16 flew overhead then, and someone said, "It's about time!"

At that point, I began feeling ineffectual again, and so I looked around to see if someone was taking charge of the military personnel. I noticed that an Army O-6, a Colonel Powell, seemed to be forming a group, and so I went to him and joined up with a few Army field grade officers. Within minutes, this group quadrupled in size. At that time, Colonel Powell was forming four-man litter teams. Because the forty or so personnel that had formed up at that point were male, and because they were all physically bigger than me, I feared not being included and so I produced a BLS [basic life support] certification card from my wallet. Having that card gave me the credibility that I lacked physically, at 62 inches and 120 pounds, and, later, allowed me to move up onto the first litter team.

Of the four-man litter teams that formed initially, none remained intact. Instead, we would form and re-form into new groups many times before the day was over because of tasks that arose that separated us and because the number of military people that were on-site and volunteering to help continued to grow as the day progressed. For brief periods of time, though, we came together, exchanged first names, talked about where we were in the building and what we had experienced at the time of impact—and bonded, I think, from a combination of stress, adrenalin, and a growing awareness of the enormity of what had occurred.

Our litter teams, led by Colonel Powell, approached the civilian police that were attempting to cordon off the area. The police appeared initially resistant to the idea of assistance from us, even though they were insufficiently manned, but we managed to persuade them that we could be of help. We were at that point permitted onto the roadway directly adjacent to the point of impact. The fire was raging, and the smoke pouring out of the windows and emanating from the roof was dark and thick. The firefighters were aggressively attempting to control the flames, but they continued to spread. The fire appeared to be traveling to the left, from the fifth to the sixth corridor, and would seem to jump from office window to office window. It also began shooting up off the roof. The responding fire departments were not, at that point, even sending in their own personnel because the combination of fire and smoke was too great. Then, at what I estimate was about 1030 hours, the façade of the building collapsed. It was a horrific site, and there was a collective gasp. To the best of my knowledge, there is no videotape of the collapse but it is burned into my memory as vividly as is the impact.

The military personnel, stunned by what we were seeing, were more than willing to assume risk in order to effect a rescue effort and voiced as much, but we were not permitted to do so; the civilian agencies were very much in charge. Rationally, I took their point—the building was structurally unsound, the fire was unmanageable, the smoke itself could be lethal, and we had no equipment—but emotionally . . . it was difficult to stand there and do nothing while people inside were dying. The experience was both surreal and numbing.

Because we were not going to be utilized in the near term as litter teams, we individually began to volunteer to assist the various agencies with their manual labor needs. I and others around me (the number of military present at the scene grew large as the day progressed) off-loaded pallets of equipment, set up tents and triage areas, assisted with the set-up of medical equipment, and formed numerous makeshift assembly lines for the purpose of quickly moving donated items of food and water to central locations.

As for the tents, they were heavy and required four people to unload them from the various trucks that they were delivered on. At one point while unloading a tent with three others, I noticed that the man to my left was Lieutenant Colonel Robert Grunewald, my primary instructor in MP OBC [military police officer basic course], whom I had not seen in over twelve years. We recognized each other at the same time, and he hugged me. At some point later that day, he told me the horrific story of his own escape—in the dark and through the smoke—from the building. He said that he worked in the DCSPER, and pointed to the collapsed façade to show me where his office used to be. He also expressed his distress as to the whereabouts of his coworkers, many of who were in a meeting being held by Lieutenant General Maude. I subsequently learned that many that he worked with, including Lieutenant General Maude, died in the attack. . . .

Despite being on the first litter team, neither I nor any of the evacuated military personnel were ever permitted to reenter the building. At the end of the day, [Lt. Gen. John A. Van Alstyne], who had come to update us twice before, told us that the Old Guard had arrived for duty and that we were released. He thanked us for our help, indicating that, realistically, it was all the thanks that we would probably ever get. He also added that it was not what we had done (which was, essentially, wait for a call to help that never came) but what we were prepared to do. I was impressed with the way that he phrased that, and with his clear sincerity.

Assistant Fire Chief James H. Schwartz was Assistant Chief of Operations for the Arlington County Fire Department.

CHIEF SCHWARTZ: The order for no more military personnel to go in the building came from me. . . . And the reason for that was that on the west lawn on that day here we have this incident command system that we have established. . . . I have assigned people responsibility, giving them tactical assignments and giving them the resources to carry out those assignments. On a normal incident, we have clear way to do that. In fact, by law we have a clear way to do that, okay? But on the morning of 9/11 we had a sea of well-intentioned people who were, for lack of a better description, getting in the way *and* posing a risk to both themselves and our responders in terms of the actions that they were taking. And I'll give you a great example. This is the one time that I left the command post after I had all this established. I am getting reports from my EMS branch that he cannot get the orders that I have given to him carried out. And the people under him cannot carry out their taskings because there are military people, mostly military people, that were getting in the way, trying to get in the building and posing a risk to themselves, causing us to have to draw them out. When I heard this, it was the one time I left the command post. And when I went out on the lawn I found in one instance a line of about ten people, Army people, with dust masks on. And they are lined up ready to go into this building where six thousand gallons of jet fuel are burning. And they somehow think that this dust mask is going to protect them. At the time, the highest-ranking guy was a one-star general who was at the back of the line. And I stopped him and I said, "What are you doing? Where are you going?" And he said, "We're going in there." And I said, "No, you are not." And that's when I gave the order that nobody else without proper protective clothing and under the incident command system is to enter the building.

Now, there are a couple of extremely compelling stories . . . about some of the circumstances surrounding that order and its implementation. . . . Including one that . . . has been recounted back to me from several sources, [who] recognizes now that the somewhat of a—if not a skirmish then a scuffle—that he got into with some of my people, when they prohibited him from going in the building, he in retrospect recognizes that, in fact, his life was saved as a result, because it was shortly after that order was given that the building collapsed. And had he been in there at that time, he surely would have perished in not only that collapse, . . . but also in what amounted to a flare-up of that fire that came out as a result of that collapse.

So we were trying to manage all of those issues. So if you're talking about in those early stages, that order came from me. And the reason that it came was that as we were—you have to remember that the incident command system is designed for nothing else other than safety reasons. Like on a military battlefield, you have to have one person calling the shots. And that can be through span of control filtered down through various subsystems. But freelancing is inexcusable, and freelancing leads to death and injury. And that's what we were trying to stave off.

And I have nothing but the highest regard and respect for what those people were trying to accomplish on that day. Every time I have done a presentation about the Pentagon, I don't get ten minutes into the presentation before I let the audience know that there's been a lot of attention focused on what the fire service and what the emergency response community gave on that particular morning. But truly heroic acts were exhibited on the parts of both military and civilian personnel who were residents of the Pentagon, who saved *far* more lives in those first few minutes, okay, than we saved at any time in that incident. . . . What those people in uniform and out of uniform did on that morning were truly heroic acts that should not go unrecognized and should not be somehow subordinate to the acts of the fire and EMS community on that particular morning. But I as the incident commander, who am charged lawfully with the authority to manage that incident, could not in good conscience let that level of chaos continue, knowing that it could have resulted in far more casualties than we had to go through.

1st Lt. Steven Cunningham was a platoon leader in Company B, 1st Battalion, 3d U.S. Infantry (The Old Guard). He was interviewed at Fort Myer, Virginia, by Stephen Lofgren of the U.S. Army Center of Military History on 2 October 2001.

MR. LOFGREN: Steve, can you tell me what you were doing Tuesday morning? Was it a normal day?

1ST LT. CUNNINGHAM: It was a normal day, sir, in the respects of what we do here in the Old Guard, preparing for missions in the cemetery [Arlington National Cemetery]. Actually, our company was getting ready for the Spirit of America, which is a public affairs–type forum where we put on a ceremony for the American public, just to display what the Army has done in a historical perspective. We were getting ready for that rehearsal that day. In addition, one of our platoons, Second Platoon, was also getting ready for civil disturbance operations in conjunction with the World Bank protest that was supposed to occur this past weekend, I guess, the twenty-ninth and thirtieth. . . .

My platoon, I would say around 1500 to 1600, we were actually tasked to go down to the cemetery, itself, and to help the National Park Service Police get everybody out of the cemetery. Because at this point, of course, the media is going down there to the cemetery, trying to find out what's going on. But then you had just, you know, people that were in the cemetery, tourists that were in the cemetery, or people actually driving, were trying to get down to Section 70, which is right across from the Pentagon. It's no more than fifty to seventy meters across from the Pentagon. And from that vantage point, you can clearly see all the damage. And from what they had cordoned off, that was actually the best view point. So my platoon was tasked to go down and sweep out the cemetery, link up with the Park Police and make sure that there was no media in the cemetery, itself, and that there were no civilians in the cemetery trying to get down there. When I linked up with the Park Police, they had just recovered a piece of the plane. And up until that point, they hadn't found any parts of the plane or whatnot, but I don't know, five or ten minutes before I got down there, they found a piece. And he showed it to me so I would know what to look for and tell my guys what to look for. And it was actually—it looked like the—I don't know what you call it—gasket head, or whatever they put on top of a propane tank. It was the top of that, and it was in the grass. And he rolled it over with his foot and it said, "American Airlines," and it had all kinds of serial numbers on there. And so I got together with my squad leaders and told them, hey, you guys, in conjunction with making sure you clear out the cemetery, if you identify any parts of the plane, not to touch it and then we would get the Park Police in. Consequently, they had contacted the FBI and they sent an FBI team to come in and pick up the plane parts that had actually gone into the cemetery. And we found quite a few parts, smaller parts, but quite a few parts of the plane. . . .

There was one breach in the fence line that we knew about, over where they conduct a lot of maintenance behind the columbarium. And I immediately sent one squad over there to basically make sure people weren't coming in where the fence was breached. There was a hole in the fence. It's been there for awhile and it's heavily wooded, so you're not going to see anybody that's trying to sneak in. So I sent a squadron over there. And then the other two squads, one was over by the maintenance building, itself, because there was a gate. And that's, in fact, where all the media and people were congregating there. So I had a squad down there and then the other squad was basically helping sweep the several sections to find plane parts and whatnot.

My initial impression when I got down there [near the Pentagon] was, there was a pretty big hole. I didn't know what the extent of the damage was, just from that viewpoint. I could only see the hole in the side of the Pentagon. There weren't a lot of people down—from my opinion, it didn't seem like there were a lot of people down there at the Pentagon, itself, helping out. At that point, they hadn't—obviously, they had stopped traffic but it didn't seem like any kind of—there was no security, no kind of security perimeter put up except . . . the police that were blocking the various roads coming in. They were keeping the media back in the distance and then us in the cemetery, and that was it. About 1730, I had linked up with Mr. Metzler, who is the Arlington National Cemetery superintendent. And he is the one that asked for the help clearing people out. I linked up with him, and he said that the Park Police had the situation stabilized and security was now getting set in, so we could go back to the barracks. Once we got back to the barracks, we were pretty much on standby for any mission that the Old Guard was going to get tasked for. And at that point, I think my platoon was the ready-reaction force. Basically, we were going to deploy to augment any of the MP companies and we were pretty much held in reserve overnight. The company spent the night here in the barracks waiting for, you know, any kind of word or anything that we would get tasked for.

Assistant Fire Chief James H. Schwartz *was Assistant Chief of Operations for the Arlington County Fire Department.*

CHIEF SCHWARTZ: It was somewhere around that time frame, 12:00/1:00/two o'clock in the afternoon, something along those lines . . . I was out checking on the welfare of the guys, how they were doing. And I came across our technical rescue team, who is very similar to a USAR [urban search and rescue] team except that they're local only and they don't travel a lot out of the area. And I asked them, "Do you need anything? How is it going?" You know, that sort of thing. And one of the things they told me was, one of the very first things they said was, "Chief, our boots, you know, we're breaking our boots climbing over all of the rubble, and we need more boots." So I called logistics. I told them we have a special boot that we wear. I don't wear it, but the guys in the field wear them. They're called Pro Boots. That's the name of the manufacturer, Warrington Pro. And I called logistics and I said, "Get me a truck load of boots, okay?" Logistics called our vendor, Maryland Fire. Maryland Fire called the factory in Wisconsin. They loaded a tractor trailer and it was here the next morning from Wisconsin. They drove all night, put a tractor-trailer load of boots in South Parking as a part of logistics section, and we started, you know, issuing boots as they were needed. To me it's always just a great anecdote about how our needs were met. We had virtually no logistical gaps. You know, what we needed we got.

Col. J. Edgar Wakayama *was in the Office of the Director, Operational Test and Evaluation, Office of the Secretary of Defense. He was interviewed in his Pentagon office by Stephen Lofgren of the U.S. Army Center of Military History on 27 September 2001.*

[Colonel Wakayama evacuated the Pentagon after the impact and then assisted the Red Cross on site throughout the day.]

COL. WAKAYAMA: Oh, another thing I did was, since I was in the area on Tuesday—and I know that everybody left the office without securing classified information—so about six o'clock or so I went in the office, turned off most of the classified personal computers. . . . Then I sealed our vault, which you need a combination pin number to do that, and I signed out, and I counted something like forty-some classified files that I have to check, because I don't want any of this to leak outside or we are in big trouble. So I check every one of those file cabinets, classified file cabinets, to make sure it's secure, and then I date it, initial. I go through this whole procedure, and then I turn off all the lights, and then I finally secured the outside door. And I feel very secure now that none of this information leaked out.

MR. LOFGREN: When did you do this?

COL. WAKAYAMA: I did it on Tuesday night, about 6:00 p.m. I went in there—it's very dense smoke, I could smell the smoke, and as a matter of fact, we were not able to get in Wednesday morning because of the smoke in the area. So we went to plan B and went different places, and I believe we came back to our office, you know, everybody came back to our office on Wednesday afternoon. So anyway, so that's another thing I did, because I was worried that the classified information may leak out, so make sure that everything is secure, because everybody just left, and I was worried that someone has to go in and do something, so that's what I did.

* * * *

Arthur Santana was with the Washington Post.

MR. SANTANA: One of the things I saw that night, it must have been, again, 2:00 or 3:00 or 4:00 in the morning, very surreal, because all these Army guys were—they had camped out in groups. . . . And they were asleep on the grass or like lying down in the grass, and . . . I felt like this is—I mean, it's almost—is this a war zone or what is this? Where are we? And these guys are in their full camouflage gear, they're lying down on their helmets, just kind of leaning their heads back. They're lying down on their backs, with their helmets, and they were sleeping—whole platoons of these guys scattered all over the place. A couple of guys were awake and I went up and asked one guy, "What's

The Pentagon continued burning during the night, creating an image that Capt. Lincoln Leibner described as "Atlanta burning."

going on? What are you doing here?" And he said something like, "I don't know" or something, which I thought was funny or interesting. Anyway, firefighters were doing the same. They were scattered everywhere.

Again, the whole place was lit with these humming generators and the whole place was lit with these big overhead lights. And, by this point, the fire is out and they've got these construction crews in starting to put in support beams early in the morning. And at about 2:00 in the morning, like out of the blue, these guys on the roof draped that huge American flag, just threw it over the side, and the only people that could see it were the people that were up and awake and this sort of din of cheers went up, for those that were awake, construction workers that were at the site, at the ground zero area.

Lt. Col. Tracy Bryant was Deputy Commander of the 3d U.S. Infantry (Old Guard). He was interviewed at Fort Myer, Virginia, by Capt. George Dover, 46th Military History Detachment, on 29 November 2001.

CAPT. DOVER: Describe how others were acting and how the attack affected them. You said some of them had a particular mode they were in. Overall, how did the people around the post . . . handle it? . . .

LT. COL. BRYANT: The general mentality was, "I'm here, I'm a soldier, I want to help. I want to do what it is that I've been trained to do. I don't want to be, you know, not doing anything." And people were coming up with, "Let me go do this. Let me go do that." Or, "I think we need to." You know, things like our medical platoon pretty much rolled itself out of here. "Yes, you can go." But they didn't wait for us to say, "Medical, get your ambulances, get your medical bags, get ready to go." They were ready to go. There were—our support platoon, our headquarters company commander, people were like, "Hey, there's a crisis here. We've got to roll. We've got to do something." People were taking action and doing things, without having to be told. If anything, we were having to say, "Okay, wait a minute. Let's think about this before you go off and do this. Is this the right thing to do?"

On a broader perspective, what interaction I had with other people around post here, there was a fair amount of shock. Most of the employees here at Fort Myer are civilian. There was a fair amount of, "Oh, my God, what's happened?" But I didn't see many of them get in their cars and heading home. They were here to work. The dining facility opened and stayed open to feed soldiers who needed to eat, who were now on the clock twenty-four hours.

So I was amazed at the level of support, the desire to work. You know, you would think that there would be a lot of people who would say, "Hey, a plane just crashed into the Pentagon. I could be next. I'm going to my house and I'm going to crawl in the basement and hide." I didn't see a lot of that. I saw people coming forward saying, "I want to help. I want to do my part. I want to be involved."

CAPT. DOVER: Did you get to make a trip to the scene at the Pentagon, and if so, describe it for me, please, what you saw upon arrival at the Pentagon.

LT. COL. BRYANT: Let me tell you a little bit about how we got to the Pentagon. Initially after this thing happened we were starting to get, you know, an hour or so into it we were starting to get some reports from the Military District of Washington. They were starting to ask for things and tell us to do things. And we pushed our medical platoon forward, the ambulances and all of the medics that we had. We sent them over to help start treating casualties. Soon after that happened, Colonel [James] Laufenberg, the regimental commander, got in his Humvee, he drove over to the Pentagon to make an assessment for himself of what was happening. And I can't comment upon all of the things that happened over there for him, but I know that within an hour and a half or so of the crash, we began to move our soldiers and supplies forward to the Pentagon to help. I stayed here in this building here in our headquarters to honcho the staff and to make sure that we were providing staff products, operations orders, frag orders, warning orders, and logistical support to those people who were deployed over to the Pentagon.

And I stayed here the remainder of September the 11th and through the night into the 12th. On the morning of the 12th then the commander and I talked and I decided to go forward over to the Pentagon. And when I arrived there midmorning on the 12th, I was absolutely amazed at what I saw. The first thing that took me was the physical damage to the Pentagon itself. It was still burning. There was still smoking coming out. The fire departments were putting water on it. And I was just, the physical damage to the building itself. The smell, the smoke, you know, [all] the burned materials and stuff was there and present. But then the next thing that took me was the sea of people and equipment that had assembled around the helipad and the west side of the Pentagon there. Fire trucks everywhere. Rescue squads everywhere. Policemen, police departments, military. Just this sea of people who had magically appeared in the last twelve, twenty-four hours to help handle this incident. And, in fact, that west side of the Pentagon, what used to be the helipad, was literally covered with rescue equipment and people. Tents had been erected for people to work out of. Big tractor-trailer rigs had been brought in with equipment for rescue squads. There's armed guards around. The second thing that hit me was the number of people, civilian relief agencies, that had come forward to support the effort. The American Red Cross, the Salvation Army, church groups, religious organizations, Burger King, McDonalds, who had pushed forward support. They were not asked. It was just there. We went through this big deal as to whether we were going to have to mobilize a mess team to feed our soldiers who were working over at the Pentagon. If we had done that, they wouldn't have eaten a bit of food that we prepared because all these relief organizations were just pushing food. Volunteers riding around on golf carts handing out soda and water and cold towels and all sorts of stuff. Just unbelievable.

Assistant Fire Chief James H. Schwartz was Assistant Chief of Operations for the Arlington County Fire Department.

CHIEF SCHWARTZ: There was, in fact, a tremendous [fire] suppression effort going on from the Center Court, okay. We had established a division in the Center Court. And I had a battalion chief back there that was directing all of the units and resources assigned to that division for an interior firefight that came from the Center Court. You've got to remember. . . . We are the Pentagon's fire department. . . . We respond to the Pentagon virtually every day. Not always for a fire, but we go there normally for EMS [Emergency Medical Services] incidents. That's the most predominant type of response that we make there. So we are very familiar with the Pentagon. And we've had a number of fires there over the years. . . . So almost all of our incidents that we go to the Pentagon for that are fire-related, we operate from the Center Court, okay. Because that is our best vantage point to get to the corridors and get to wherever we want to go. It makes a great place to get the resources that are coming out of the Pentagon that we need to interface with. . . .

We did our own water supply. We did not use the internal system. We used the hydrants from outside the building. In other words, we did not use the stand pipes from the building because we did not have a lot of confidence in them. And certainly in the area of the crash itself they were unusable. We drove into the Center Court through A and E Drive, which is our typical method of entry there. Virtually all of our apparatus fits underneath that overhang. And the interesting story here is that over the years the Pentagon has repaved that road. And as they have repaved that road the height of that tunnel, if you will, has been reduced. The clearance has been reduced. So for a number of years now our ladder trucks have not been able to get down there. Now, our engines can get in there. Our command vehicles, our ambulances can all get down there. Our ladder trucks, however, cannot. And, in the past, for smaller fire incidents that has not proved to be a major obstacle because we've just hoofed equipment in there. And quite honestly, nobody was paying attention enough to us to want to remedy that situation until after September 11th. . . . One of the ladder trucks that we needed to get into that Center Court, because it did not fit, there was a communication given by, at that time, the operations section, back to command saying that they could not get access and they were recommending that they alter the vehicle—I'll put it nicely. We cut the roof off the tiller cab of one of the ladder trucks. We took a Saws-all and we cut the top off the tiller cab and through that we were able to make access. We did what we had to do at the time.

* * * *

In the early stages the crash trucks are in the front, on the west lawn, and all these resources are in the Center Court and doing manual suppression, stretching hose lines as long as eight hundred feet. Now, just to give you a point of reference here, the longest hose line that we carry pre-connected is three hundred feet. And there's only one of those. Every rig has one. But they're only [three] hundred feet long. So to go eight hundred feet, you know, is a pretty significant distance on a hose line. Also, because of the building configuration and size, the guys going in were not necessarily following the kind of safety practices that we encourage on the average fire. Meaning, they were not putting on their respiratory protection until they got as far in as they could stand it, and then putting it on, knowing that if they did so when they first crossed the threshold, they'd be out of air before they got to a place at which they were able to do any kind of significant tactical operations. Their descriptions of those events were that they encountered some of the highest heat conditions they had ever experienced in any fire anywhere—interestingly enough, in many cases without smoke or visible flame. It was essentially the radiant and convected heat off that fire that was coming from the center area of the crash site.

We did an excellent job of containing the fire. And, in fact, by late afternoon on the 11th the interior portion of the fire was largely contained. We worked to control hot spots for several days after that. But we largely had the bulk of the fire knocked down by late afternoon on the 11th. But the fire got into the roof structure. Now, if you're not familiar with the roof structure, the roof of the Pentagon is a concrete deck. It is a flat concrete deck and the structure that people see on the outer ring and over top of the corridors is actually an add-on, okay. I sometimes refer to it as a rain roof because, you know, it's primarily designed to get the water off. It is a heavy timber structure that is covered by slate. That kind of construction, back in those days, you know, sixty years ago, was rather common. I'm not sure the next element of the construction was, because on the interior of that structure was insulation—the best I can determine, horse hair insulation. As the fire got up into the roof structure, okay, it was running underneath that slate deck and being fueled with that horse hair insulation.

Well, as night fell on the night of the 11th, as darkness fell on the night of the 11th, I had a great concern about that roof as a working platform. It is a huge roof without a whole lot of room for error given the spaces that are in between the rings of the Pentagon. Given the structural damage, given the darkness and what I deemed to be the structural instability, I made a decision to change our strategic approach from an offensive attack to a defensive posture. Now for us, what that means is that we go from those positions at which we have hose lines advancing on a fire, okay. We pull back to a certain position. And we typically use things like master stream devices, those large elevated streams off ladder pipes or large monitor nozzles to try to hold the fire. I had some hope, some expectation, that we had enough control on the fire, including the roof fire, that we could contain it overnight, that it wouldn't spread very far. Unfortunately, it was a bad judgment. Because at the time, I did not know about that insulation, I didn't know about that until the next afternoon— maybe next morning, maybe midmorning—but I didn't know about that insulation and its contributing effects to the fire-spread until the next day. So when we went back to work the next day, the roof fire had pretty significant headway on us. Again, we had dealt with most of what was going on in the building. And the fire that was on the roof was not critical in terms of structural stability. It was not going to cause additional collapse or even in my mind pose a large risk, which again contributed to my decision on the night of the 11th to withdraw. I didn't see that much more of a risk of a life hazard being associated with that other than to the responders, you know, and what jeopardy they might have been in being up on that roof.

Unfortunately, it was, again, quite a graphic event for those watching, including the Secretary [of Defense] who constantly wanted to know when the fire was going to be out and he could have his building back. And again, this is where [Maj.] General [James T.] Jackson, [Commanding General, Military District of Washington] played such an important part, because he became the intermediary for us to say, "Look, you know, they're working at it. They're doing the best job that they can. You just have to let them use their professional judgment and work through this." And the secretary was great in that regard. But, obviously, the news is watching the Pentagon burn. The world is watching the Pentagon burn. At least that's what they think they're watching.

And so when we went back on the morning of the 12th what we had to do was go back to an offensive operation that was largely—you know, you could probably associate the manual labor effort of the day before and crawling down those hallways on eight-hunred-foot lines in the highest heat conditions they'd ever experienced, that was one kind of manual labor. You know, very closely associated with that was the manual labor necessary to work that roof fire. Because in any installation where we find that kind of roof, there's only one way to get to it, and that is sledge hammers and a lot of hard swinging down on that slate and heavy timber, breaking open holes, busting it all back, getting hose streams under there. That enabled us to wet down all of that insulation and stop the development of the fire. . . .

You know, I've been to a lot of big fires in my life. And I've never been on a roof that big with that kind of fire. It was a huge effort. It was massive. Most of the guys working that fire had a great deal of fear about—when you're up there that long, you know, do you fatigue enough that you pay attention to what you're doing? Can you continue to concentrate on the safety aspects of working on that kind of platform? We were greatly concerned about all of that throughout that portion of the fire. And that took us to about the evening of the 12th, fighting the roof fire. Until late in the afternoon or early in the evening, we finally said, "That's contained. We have that fire out." We were still going to do mopping up of hot spots, but largely we felt like we had that under control.

Brenda Hirschi was Chief of Military Personnel, Army Division, in the Army Budget Office, under the purview of the Office of the Assistant Secretary of the Army for Financial Management.

MR. LOFGREN: So what happened the next day?

MS. HIRSCHI: The next day?

MR. LOFGREN: Did you sleep at all that night?

MS. HIRSCHI: No, that was terrible. And I had all this stuff down in my lungs and stuff in my eyes. It's like that stuff that was floating down. It just would burn. It felt like sand in your eyes. It was really hard to get the stuff out.

The next morning I got up and went to get my ID cards and driver's license and start putting it back together. [My colleague] Joan thought that [the crash] wasn't that close [to our office], but because I had seen the fire, I knew that there was going to be nothing. So I just said, you know, you get up the next day and you start putting it back together. When I was a young girl our house burned, and so I had kind of like, you know, I just—I was eleven years old again and I started just putting things back together. That's what you have to do.

Then Thursday I came back to work.

MR. LOFGREN: Where did you go?

MS. HIRSCHI: We came back in here [Crystal City]. We came over here, and we just started putting things back together—because we'd lost everything. We'll be reconstructing and putting stuff back together for months to come, because we had a lot of information on hard drives, and it's just lost.

MR. LOFGREN: How did you know to come over here? Did you talk to somebody?

MS. HIRSCHI: Yes. We had like a roster and talked to each other. So what I told my staff to do is come back when they could, when they felt like they could get back in. . . . But everybody was back at work on Monday. They all came back in on Monday and—

MR. LOFGREN: How goes the work reconstructing your data?

MS. HIRSCHI: You know, we're doing pretty good. We brought one of the retirees back in on an emergency appointment. That really helped us out. He came back and he's helping us, you know, to reconstruct the files and the worksheets.

Maj. Gen. John R. Wood was the Director of Directorate of Strategy, Plans and Policy (DAMO-SS), Office of the Deputy Chief of Staff for Operations and Plans (DCSOPS).

MAJ. GEN. WOOD: I went into work the next morning at just generally the same time. I was in about 6:15. . . . But there wasn't anywhere to go to. I didn't have an office. I didn't have a space. I didn't have a clipboard. I didn't have anything. But you have to—you have to get on with it. I found some spaces down in the Army Operations Center that they put aside for us, because clearly we were going to have to do some immediate planning, immediate strategic planning on a host of things—how we were going to respond, how we were going to take care of our people, what was—what kind of attack we were under, what was the nature of this terrorist threat. And it was about—not that day but the next day is when the chief asked me to put together the Army's plan and response to this, including a strategy for response. So that occupied the next three months.

Charlene Ryan served as a customer liaison/computer specialist with the Information Management Support Center Requirements, Analysis and Design Branch. She was interviewed at the Pentagon by Leo Hirrel of the U.S. Army Center of Military History on 18 January 2002.

MS. RYAN: I came back the next morning, not knowing the situation about our office. But it was all cordoned off, they weren't letting anybody in. The smoke; you could smell diesel fuel, you could smell smoke, it was awful. . . . People were going around in masks. . . . Everywhere you went it was like a fog in the building. I learned from somebody, from one of our neighboring—one of our other branches, that we were all regrouping in an office down across the building. Talk about the logistics of all this. We were—our office was scheduled to move into the new Wedge One space on October 11th. It was thirty days after the event, and we were going to be right in harm's way if we were going to be there. And our move was rescheduled from August. If it went on as usual, we would have been part of the casualties. So we are already realizing this; where [the building] was hit, what—we weren't there, we were—planned to be there—you know, all these logistics started crunching in our mind, and it was affecting our emotional stamina really bad. We would see fellow office workers or people that we know from other parts of the building in the hallway, it was common everywhere to see hugging, crying, "So glad you're okay," you know, it—the day— the morning after was incredible. People coming back into the building, beginning to deal with this, and it was—we went down to the space where we regrouped to the new BMDO [Ballistic Missile Defense Organization] area, which was—is located under the concourse.

DR. HIRREL: In Crystal City?

MS. RYAN: It's down here in the building, and it's the other side of the building, under the concourse, which is where the stores are. The bank and the drug store. It's newly renovated, and our SASS area [System/Application Support and Services]—division was moved down there literally five days before the crash, they just got moved in. That weekend before—they didn't have time to put the room numbers on the rooms, they didn't unpack their boxes yet, it was literally that soon. Here we are invading on their space, we've become three and four deep in every cubicle, we commandeered the conference table they had in the area, we were sharing—they set up five or six computers with fifteen or twenty people trying to get on those computers to check our mail.

DR. HIRREL: Was the server working?

MS. RYAN: The server was working—yes, not that day—it was working by Friday. What they did was when I came and reported to work, they told to me to go around and go home and wait for a phone call. So they—our server, our mail server came up the following day and we were able to log in from home to see our mail, which was so amazing. I think it was the next day. I didn't report back to work until Friday morning, and it was after a couple of days of "you're scheduled to come in [at] seven p.m." We were—we turned into a 24-hour-a-day schedule.

On 17 September, the Information Management Support Center (IMCEN) reestablishes operations at the Taylor Building in Crystal City, Virgina. *Top:* New offices are wired; *bottom and top, facing page:* a new cable plant is installed; *center, facing page:* new Dell laptops are stacked and ready for issue; and *bottom, facing page:* Neal Shelley, *center in red,* briefs Director of the Army Staff Lt. Gen. John M. Pickler, *left.*

DR. HIRREL: Why was that?

MS. RYAN: Because all these people who lost their office space and their desktops, we had to get them new computers, and set them up in new space, temporary space someplace else. And so we managed to get Dell, I think it was, and a couple of other vendors to deliver thousands of laptops that we set up overnight, working around the clock. Not me personally, but our division. . . . And we were given a building, the Taylor Building in Crystal City, so we went in and picked a floor where we could set some people up in temporary space, had them come in the building and we set laptops up and had them go through some kind of—a line where they signed for them, giving them a logon ID, and giving them a laptop. And I understand the fourth table was a McDonald's meal that McDonald's provided, because they set up operations in South Parking. They brought a whole bunch of food over to the Taylor Building to pass out to people who were relocating. So that's how we got a lot of the people working, we didn't get them connectivity to their network, but we gave them a laptop first off, and then we worked on the network after that.

Maj. Craig Collier was with the Office of the Chief of Legislative Liaison.

MAJ. COLLIER: When we returned on Thursday the 13th security was exceptionally tight. We passed through several cordons, most manned with either MPs with M14s or cops with submachine guns. The area near the Red Cross office was filled up with tables and a long line of blood donors. Legislative Liaison met in the basement of the Pentagon, since our offices near the impact were closed. Several of us tried to get to our office to gather up some of our more important items, but guards posted at all of the corridors prevented us from getting in. Our end of the building clearly suffered significant smoke and water damage.

Sgt. Maj. Tony Rose served as Army Senior Retention NCO Career Counselor and ran the Army Retention Program in the Office of the Deputy Chief of Staff for Personnel.

LT. COL. ROSSOW: Sergeant Major, would you please tell us about the continuity operations that followed once you moved to the Hoffman Building? How did DCSPER work with the remote location?

SGT. MAJ. ROSE: We moved into the Hoffman One and the Hoffman Two [Army buildings in Alexandria, Virginia]. We were split up. They found room for us wherever they could find room. But within a matter of hours of our arriving at the Hoffman Building they had desks for us. They had computers set up for us. We were on the Internet, we were on the LAN [local area network]. I was really impressed at how fast they just got everything together and took care of us. We were working out of very small cubicles, out of corners, out of closets, wherever they could put us. But at least we had a room. And we were actually worldwide operational in that time frame. So we stayed there till just about a week before last, about the middle of January when we moved back over here to the Pentagon.

LT. COL. ROSSOW: Do you recall the specific date that you carried your box up here?

SGT. MAJ. ROSE: I didn't have a box. I have nothing. Everything that we generated in the Hoffman was done electronically. In fact, I went to Fort Myer the other day to collect supposedly five boxes of personal belongings they found. It was not really five boxes. I walked away with the ribbons that were on my shirt and my name tag. That was the only thing that they found. . . .

SFC. LAPIC: Any final words?

SGT. MAJ. ROSE: Yeah, I don't want to do it again.

Col. Henry A. Haynes was the Pentagon Chaplain. He was interviewed by Frank Shirer of the U.S. Army Center of Military History on 26 February 2002.

CHAPLAIN HAYNES: Thursday [13 September] I spent time in the hospital and returned back to my office inside the building right here I guess about 7:00 in the evening. I immediately got a call from one of the [Department of Defense] under secretaries. . . . She was asking me, "Chaplain, are you aware of the fact that the President has declared tomorrow (which would have been the 14th) a national day of prayer? What are you doing for that?" At that point I just told her, "Ma'am, there's a message here lying on my desk saying that tomorrow is a national day of prayer. I've been gone and I really haven't thought about it, but I'm sure we will be doing something. I just don't know exactly what." She said, "Do you need some help?"

You need to understand at this point I had no help. I was the only Chaplain here. I had an assistant, but my assistant was on leave. I had not been able to contact him. My computer was out and the phone wasn't working.

I said, "Ma'am, what kind of help can you offer?" She said, "What do you need?" She said she would volunteer to give the word out to the media. She volunteered to reserve the auditorium for me and to clear it all day for my use. She did those things. I said, "I really need someone who can type that has a computer that works." She said, "There's a colonel here in my office who would be more than happy to help you with whatever you need to type." I said, "I need flyers typed so I can get the word out to people." She said, "He'll be happy to do that for you. I'll put him on the phone." He got on the phone and he said, "Tell me what you need." He worked with me and printed up several thousand flyers. Then we began to call various individuals and ask them if they would be willing to participate in the program tomorrow. Everyone was more than accommodating and willing to help out. To give you an example of what kind of help I'm talking about, the colonel [Col. John Adams] and I who were working on putting the program together for that night didn't leave here until after 12:00 [midnight], and that was after going down to graphics and getting poster boards made and put up. As people entered the building they would be able to see that there was going to be services tomorrow and the times and locations and all that information that they needed.

We had all that stuff in place by 4:30 in the morning and we were back here by 5:00 passing out flyers and stuff at the entrances as people came in. We started doing services at 10:00 that morning.

We did three services of prayer and we had a mass at 12:00. Each service was packed. There was standing room only. It was just something the people really needed. I suspect if we had the resources we could have done a service from 8:00 to 8:00 and every one probably would have been packed. That's how intense it was and seemed to be needed by those in attendance. . . .

It was amazing because it was a full-fledged program. I mean, I even had a Navy commander who took a flyer and came streaming down to my office and said, "Hey, Chaplain, I see you're doing the services of prayer. Do you have music?" I said, "Not unless you're going to offer it." She said, "I'll do it." I said, "For every service?" She said, "Every service. Whatever you need." That was the attitude of the people. The generosity of the people, the love, the support. Whatever I needed, it was there. I mean, I didn't have to ask. Most of the time they were telling me, "I can do this for you. I can do that," and they did it. It was great.

Spec. Lauren Panfili was a flutist in the Fife and Drum Corps, 1st Battalion, 3d U.S. Infantry (The Old Guard). She was interviewed by Stephen Lofgren of the U.S. Army Center of Military History on 17 October 2001.

SPEC. PANFILI: I joined the Army under the impression that my sole duty station would be Fort Myer, Virginia, playing with the Old Guard Fife and Drum Corps, a purely musical MOS [military occupational specialty] without any other typical military duties thrown in. I went to basic training over the summer and, after a brief period of leave, I arrived on Fort Myer on September 8th and reported for my first day of duty on the 10th and then of course the 11th of September we all know what happened. . . .

The first few days of—whenever you report to a new unit, the first few days are filling out a lot of paperwork, going around post to all the offices you have to go to and filling out the forms for this, that, whatever. So that was pretty much the first day, well, actually, that was all of the first day, and then the second day I was actually on my way up to Walter Reed to be fitted for earplugs for performing—Walter Reed Medical Center. We were about to leave, I was going to be driving up with one of the staff sergeants, Staff Sergeant Hubbard. As we were on our way out of the building we saw everyone crowded in the day room around the big-screen TV and they said the World Trade Center was on fire and we were of course stunned. So we sat down and we watched the second plane hit the other tower and it was just rather shocking.

It seemed very surreal, like a movie more than real life. Then we got up and left and went to go to Walter Reed and we stopped to get gas and some of the fire trucks from Fort Myer were going by as we were leaving the gas station. Drove down the road and got to [Interstate] 395 and we were forced to go south instead of north because they had closed the north ramp. We actually saw—we didn't see the plane hit the Pentagon but we saw the fire and everything and actually got into a car accident because we were both looking at the Pentagon and not at the road. But it was just a very disturbing experience in general. . . .

We tried to get back on post and right before we got there they had gone to ThreatCon Delta so we weren't considered mission essential because, of course, we're just fife players, what can we do, and we were turned away at the gate. . . . So we just finally made it to Sergeant Hubbard's apartment and we just stayed there and waited to hear news from the corps. We figured they would try to reach us eventually and they did. Our group leader called us, Sergeant White, called us and told us to just stay put, that the corps was guarding the headquarters of the regiment and they were being issued gas masks and Kevlar helmets, which kind of shocked both of us, made us realize just the gravity of the situation—that the day that they issue gas masks to the Fife and Drum Corps is not a good sign.

Since I had come recently from basic training I was actually very comfortable with a lot of the things so in that regard I was more comfortable than a lot of people in the corps. I knew how to put the gas mask together and clear it and seal it and I was actually still qualified with an M16. There were maybe three or four of us who had gone to basic training in the last year that would still be considered qualified. But of course we don't have an arms room here. None of us were issued weapons of any sort except for . . . eighteenth-century weapons. . . .

Wednesday night I think I actually was able to go back to the barracks to sleep in my room. Then Thursday went out to the Pentagon to help out there. It seems like a very long period of time but it was actually only two days later. We got there and there were of course so many people wanting to help and to do things and only so many things that needed to be done. They had just put the fire out and they were trying to get things organized in the building so that more people could come in and help with the recovery effort.

Shoring up the E-Ring

MR. LOFGREN: Had you been told you were going to do anything particular before you got down there?

SPEC. PANFILI: No. There was the potential that some of us might be part of a body-recovery team, so they asked for volunteers to do that. I didn't volunteer just because I wasn't comfortable with something like that, not that anyone is really trained for that. Some people are, but some people in the corps were more willing to go face that. But I still wanted to help, so we were there and it turned out that a lot of people were needed for the recovery and I was sitting back going, "Please don't need me."

It turned out that they needed some other people to go help with the light labor crew that was helping the engineers to shore up the building so that it wouldn't collapse. So I went over and helped with that. There were three of us from the corps that went. It was just basically carrying 4 x 4s back and forth. They were cutting them to different sizes and we were taking them to wherever they needed to go. So that was what I ended up doing for part of the day.

But most of the day was just sitting and waiting for an opportunity to do some more, because there were so many people helping with each task that it would get done right away, and then we wouldn't be able to do more until this person over here got caught up with what they were doing. . . .

We were within one hundred yards of the building. Then I actually carried the wood to the building and I actually went in once, but I wasn't supposed to but I didn't realize that. I was just following someone who didn't know where he was going. So I did actually get to go inside but just briefly.

MR. LOFGREN: What did you think when you saw it the first time?

SPEC. PANFILI: It was a lot worse from the inside than it is from the outside. The extent of the damage was much more obvious. What used to be a building was just a giant hole. There were no more levels, floors. It was just very black and the air was very thick and dark and creepy, very creepy. And wet from all the water. . . .

MR. LOFGREN: When you weren't actually doing specific work—

SPEC. PANFILI: Then we would go back. They had a lot of tents set up that were out of the sun and so we would just hang back there. . . . By the time we got there things were fairly well set up in terms of if you needed food you had to go over here to get it. Over here is where they're doing the construction or whatever. This part over here, where they're doing the body recovery. It was a large work in progress. It wasn't chaotic; all things considered, people were very calm and very helpful. Attitudes were very minimal. It was just a very common goal to focus and everyone working together and doing whatever they could to help. In a way, it was really kind of heart warming just to see the amount of people that were there wanting to be of use.

MR. LOFGREN: I'm just curious what . . . your strongest impressions were that—when you think back—that are stuck in your memory.

SPEC. PANFILI: The support of everyone, especially the civilian support that we got just being military. It was really amazing, it was very amazing. The people knew—they didn't really know what we were doing but they figured that we must be doing something important and they appreciated that. It was a good feeling. Even though of course we weren't doing much, but we were doing more than a lot of people could do. So, from that perspective, we were doing what they couldn't do. So they were trying to support us because they couldn't actually be doing any of the real work.

[*Later, the Fife and Drum Corps, on twelve-hour shifts, assisted the Fort Myer Military Police at the post gates.*]

. . . Friday was a full day of standing out at Hatfield Gate searching cars for bombs.

MR. LOFGREN: Did you get any sort of training or briefing on what to do or what to look for?

SPEC. PANFILI: No, it was sort of a learn-as-you-go thing and all of the MPs were telling us different things. Each one had a different way of doing things so whoever we were working with we tried to just go with what they were telling us to do. But then if someone else would come to relieve them, we'd kind of have to figure out what their modus operandi was and go with that. But it was—I didn't feel I had any—I was not qualified to be doing that. And I think a lot of us had that feeling that what if we were to miss something that we should have seen, because we don't really know what we're looking for. It would just—it was very hard to understand why we were the ones that were out there. Of course, they needed people to help but at the same time we were not armed, we had no training. It was very difficult just to be doing that. And then the long hours and no sleep, very high stress. It was hard.

MR. LOFGREN: Did you get any sort of read on how the MPs felt about it?

SPEC. PANFILI: Most of the corps are staff sergeants or above. It's only if you are training that you're a specialist. So a lot of the MPs are, of course, PFCs [privates first class] or specialists themselves and to be working with staff sergeants or sergeant first classes and be telling them what to do was sort of uncomfortable for them. But I think after awhile, because we continued doing the MP duties about a week and a half, . . . they got more comfortable with us. We started to figure out slightly more what we were supposed to be doing. There was a good working rapport. They didn't try to demean us because we were just fife players or bugle players or whatever. A lot of the MPs, the Old Guard MPs, they don't actually do regular MP duties, a lot of what they do is with the ceremonies, involved in the ceremonies. For a lot of them it was something rather new as well. . . .

MR. LOFGREN: So you're searching under the cars with mirrors.

SPEC. PANFILI: With mirrors, going through people's purses and checking their trunks and looking for weapons, checking engines and—I learned what a lot of cars' engines look like. Some of the things that were found when I was on duty, one car pulled up and in the trunk there was a machete a good foot and a half long. Given the conditions lately, even if you're just going to the PX [post exchange] or something, most people would tend to leave that out of the car.

* * * *

The chow hall was open twenty-four hours so that helped out. . . . But on our shifts often we weren't able to take a break long enough to go and eat. People were generally pretty good about bringing us food at the gates, but it was often things like brownies, donuts, chips, nothing healthy.

MR. LOFGREN: People in the unit or just people—

SPEC. PANFILI: Like the Salvation Army or the Red Cross. Also we had some generals' wives who would make chili and cookies and things and brought them in to all of us. Just really nice gestures. But still it was just—for it to be my first week in the real Army per se, I was rather traumatized. And actually my group leader did take note of that and did what he could to actually get me out of the rotation and have me actually finish in-processing and do a little bit of training instead of doing regular guard duties that the rest of the unit was doing. So for that I am incredibly thankful. I was able to get a car so that I could take care of my needs and not have to be asking people to take me to the grocery store. For him to do that for me it was very helpful.

MR. LOFGREN: Who was that?

SPEC. PANFILI: Sergeant White is my group leader. But I think in the madness and everything I was just kind of forgotten about and they realized, "Hey, she's only been here three days, she might be having problems." The corps actually got together a bunch of things that they thought I might need and just anonymously donated a bunch of things to me like bed linens and some dishes and things. It was really very nice. . . .

Especially just coming straight from basic training where I was standing at parade rest for a sergeant and then to be talking to staff sergeants or master sergeants, yes, it took me a long time to just relax into the atmosphere of the corps. But kind of in a different way it was actually really good for me to get to know a lot of the people that I'm working with now in a completely different situation. I was doing guard duty with bugle players and drummers who on a day-to-day basis I don't really have much contact with here. . . . Everyone kept telling me, "It's really not like this. This really isn't normal. Really, we've never done this ever before." And there were people who said that they've been here for twenty years and the Fife and Drum Corps has never had to do anything, pull MP duty or anything like that. . . .

There were a lot of positive aspects to it. The whole corps really pulled together to get the job done. It was definitely a team effort just from within the corps. . . . No one really likes doing guard duty for twelve hours a day for ten days in a row, however long it was, but if you have to do it you go and you get the job done, try to keep a good attitude. I think it went really smoothly considering our lack of preparation and everything. It was good. I felt that we were really actually helpful and not just in the way. None of us really wanted to be there but . . . just the realization that not only are we members of the Fife and Drum Corps but we're also in the Army and we did take that oath. . . .

The community support was amazing but I think I said that. Just some of the stories a lot of people will tell you are just really nice. Just regular people coming by like one guy came by and gave us all Girl Scout cookies. Just people walking by and saying, "God bless you, you're doing a great job. Thank you so much for everything." Just little things that people would do that they normally wouldn't on a day-to-day basis. I think as a country it was kind of a wake-up thing. We did wake up.

Assistant Fire Chief James H. Schwartz was Assistant Chief of Operations for the Arlington County Fire Department.

CHIEF SCHWARTZ: So security was acutely on our mind from the first hour or two. It's hard to describe the feeling as we were standing there in South Parking. You know, I know that most of America had various feelings of emotions, given what we were going through on that morning. Standing in that parking lot on that morning with fighter jets flying over top and somebody telling me that the World Trade Towers had just collapsed and as many as four hundred brother firefighters had perished as a result, hearing the reports that a bomb had gone off at the State Department, thinking at least at that time that the second plane here had gone into Camp David, you know, we didn't have time to be emotional. But we were certainly unsettled by these events. And not knowing when the next shoe was going to drop, we were trying to get as much in place as we possibly could. So security discussions were happening very early in the incident.

One of the things that I said to the FBI early on was that I wanted a badging system. And originally, I had wanted a badging system that identified or was capable of identifying people for work periods. Because one of the things that for me was going to be very important was, you know, for many guys this was the event of a lifetime. And corralling them and not letting them overwork themselves was a real consideration for me. And so I wanted some way to say, "You're supposed to be here now and you're not." You know, some visual identification. We never really did get to that level. But those are the kinds of things we were thinking about in terms of security. . . . The FBI lost all of their resources to New York—all of their logistical capabilities deployed to New York almost immediately. But, obviously, they have other contacts. So they made a contact to the Secret Service and the Secret Service brought their badging—I don't know if it's a badging center, but it's a rather large setup. I mean, computers and cameras and badge-making machines and those sorts of things. So it was the U.S. Secret Service that provided the hardware and the "peopleware," if you will, to operate the system. It was managed by the FBI.

In the early stages essentially anybody who provided a valid ID, which in most cases was a driver's license, got a badge. Okay. There were a lot of people that were very clearly identified as having some legitimate need to be there. In the early stages we weren't doing such a good job of trying to separate those that we probably could have figured out in the early stages did not belong there. In fact, again, as an anecdote, there was an evening, I think either the second or third evening, probably the third evening. . . . I sent my aide to get dinner. And he came back all frustrated because the line of people there to get badges, you know, just went on forever. And we hadn't called for any more resources, okay? And most of our resources, certainly the fire and the EMS resources, by that time we were bringing them into our training academy, putting them on buses, bringing them up. They'd relieve their counterparts at the end of a work period. Those guys would get on a bus and go back to the training academy.

So a lot of these people, we had systems in place, you know, to that point. And unfortunately, the folks doing the badging, they didn't know how to sift through these people. They didn't know how to make those determinations. So I went over to the badging center—I didn't step out of my role as the incident commander too many times. But, you know, I was walking around this line of people saying, "Who are you and what are you doing here?" And, oftentimes they were nice people who wanted to volunteer. But we had to get a handle on this. And so many times my answer to them was, "Thank you very much, but I don't need you right now. Go to logistics, leave your name and phone number, and we'll call you if we need you." You know, we upset a lot of people, I think, by doing that. But I didn't need any more hangers-on at that point. I mean, we had some significant issues security-wise, safety-wise, incident management-wise. You know, this is the headquarters of our military establishment. You know, it wasn't lost on me that the sensitive nature of what was going on here and the potential risk far outstripped what we normally deal with. So we were trying to get a handle on that, as best we could.

So the initial badging system really was, if you had a valid ID they gave you a badge. That was the piece where the FBI came back to me and said, "You know, it's out of control. There are too many badges out there. What do we do?" And so we set about to devise a plan where we would shrink the perimeter and put up a hard line. We had [a] fence up, but, you know, the perimeter was out on [Route] 27, okay? And there were armed guards there and you had to have an ID to get in there. But once you got in there, you could go anywhere. You could walk into the Pentagon, you know, if you tried hard enough. Now, we did have some other, I'll call them security measures, mostly incident-management pieces, that would stop people from doing that. Nobody was walking off alone without somebody saying, "Who are you and what are you doing here?" But they could roam rather freely inside that perimeter. So what we did was we made a decision and set about to enact a plan that would shrink down that perimeter and make it a harder border than we had had before. And the way that we did that was, we had a database now of people. We printed out all the databases based on organization, because you not only had to give your name, you had to give your organization, which was a cluster in itself because—I'll give you a great example. The USAR [urban search and rescue] guys alone, okay, would say, "I'm from the Fairfax County Fire Department." Other guys would say, "I'm from USAR." Other guys would say, "I'm from Station 23." Okay? Whatever they said is what got put on the badge, even though they were all a part of the same group. So that took some work.

But essentially what we did was we got the database by organization or by affiliation. All of the fire and rescue people came to the command post. All of the law enforcement went to FBI. And at least at that macro level, we culled through those lists and we said, "They don't belong here anymore. They don't belong here anymore. They don't belong. They're okay. They're okay. They're okay." With those lists we went back and they put into the database or they printed out from those new lists a red badge. Same configuration, but they were able to change the color. Now you couldn't get inside that inner perimeter unless you had a red badge. Again, we put armed guards at those checkpoints. And at that point they became really good. I mean, they looked at everybody's badge. It wasn't, "I see red, go on in." It was, "I want to see that picture." And that perimeter got a lot harder, and hopefully security got a little bit better. In concert with that, you know, we were constantly trying to de-escalate, you know, from a standpoint of what resources don't we need here anymore? What's not important to be here? And so we were saying, you know, "These people can go home. These people can go home. These people can go home." And that's how we tried to manage some of those security issues.

Deputy Bob McFarland was Deputy Chief of the Arlington County Sheriff's Office and an aide to the sheriff. He was interviewed by M. Sgt. Donna Majors of the 46th Military History Detachment on 23 May 2002.

MR. MCFARLAND: The state police had two dogs at the scene, and these dogs are trained to sniff for explosives. And every vehicle—whether it be the little golf carts or whether it be a truck that was bringing in supplies, and there were lots of them—had to be sniffed by the dog. Whether it's the same person driving the same golf cart, how-many-ever times a day, they had to stop and the dog had to sniff or smell the vehicle. Well, in September the weather was extremely hot, and these poor dogs could either stay in the handler's vehicle—but here again that would be hot and so forth—or the dogs would have to get outside. But the pavement was extremely hot, the blacktop. And the dogs would literally be dancing on the pavement because the pavement was hot and their paws would get hot, burned, and they would physically be just stepping, stepping, stepping, stepping. Then somebody came up with the idea of putting down one of these large blue plastic tarps, putting ice—we had plenty of ice—just throw ice out there to cool that off. The dog would then stand on this blue tarp, on the ice, and he would stand there and it wouldn't burn his feet. So then the dogs got so they liked it so much, they'd eat the ice, and then they'd lie down and cool themselves on this blue [tarp]. Looking back on it, it was sort of a funny little experience, but here these dogs are dancing around on the blacktop and then they got this blue tarp and were able to cool their paws.

Thomas N. Kuhn was the Acting Director, Casualty and Memorial Affairs Operations Center, U.S. Army Personnel Command. He was interviewed in his office at the Hoffman Building, Alexandria, Virginia, by Frank Shirer of the U.S. Army Center of Military History and Lt. Col. Robert Rossow of the Office of the Deputy Chief of Staff, G–1, on 8 February 2002.

MR. KUHN: I was in my office and one of my NCOs came over and said, "You've got to come see this." I said, "What?" He said, "Some idiot just flew his plane into the World Trade Center." Of course, over in the operations center they have CNN on all the time because that's how we find out about a lot of things is through CNN. . . . So I went over there and could see the aftermath of the first aircraft in the World Trade Center and the fire and all that, and everybody speculating what was going on. And while we were standing there we watched the second aircraft come around and hit the other building. And my immediate thought was, "This is not an idiot. This is planned. Somebody's doing something." And then as we were watching this, and it's all unfolding, what, twenty minutes later or whatever, CNN—and the telephone rings at the same time—and CNN is saying that there's been an explosion in the Pentagon. And the phone rings and is telling us that an aircraft had crashed into the Pentagon. And at that point in time I just mustered everybody and said, "That's it. Call in the augmentees. We're going to be here awhile." And we were, that first day. Well, the first week, we were here.

MR. SHIRER: The augmentees you said you mustered, who were they? . . .

MR. KUHN: We have a group of soldiers throughout PERSCOM [U.S. Army Personnel Command] who are pretrained and are tagged by name that we pull in when we have what we call a mass casualty. We pulled these soldiers in and we brought them up here. And we go to twenty-four-hour—we're already on twenty-four-hour operations all the time . . . but at very low levels of manpower—when we bring them in we're at twenty-four-hour operation with a lot of manpower. And we were able to work the issues.

I'll tell you, there were a lot of wide-eyed people running around trying to figure out what had happened and how were we going to handle this. And I just knew we were going to get a lot of guidance from on high. And we did. We got a lot of guidance.

MR. SHIRER: Now we were told that the [Hoffman] building was evacuated—you went to an off-site location.

MR. KUHN: Yeah. That happened a little later, where people started to be concerned about the potential attack on these two buildings. And then we were told, "Okay. Prepare to evacuate." And then we were given the order to evacuate. And we have what we call a "fly-away kit." And we're able to operate from anywhere. As a matter of fact, I ordered everybody out. The building was evacuated. And when we evacuate the building, we have a predetermined spot that we go to. It's like when we do a fire drill, there's a certain place you go and then you have a muster of everybody to make sure everybody's out of the building. So I told everybody to go to that position, told all the officers and NCOs to gather their folks up and get them out there to that position.

We went out to our position and they had the fly-away kit and I told them to set it up, see if they could get commo [communications], and be prepared to work from the parking lot and do whatever needed to be done from the parking lot. That didn't work well. And the reason it didn't work well is because Verizon failed. We could not use our Army phones because we couldn't get through. But I turned around and picked up a personal phone. It either was MCI or AT&T or one of those, you know, Sprint or something, and got right through. . . . And [the Army phones] failed at a time that we could not afford to—we had to have commo. And I couldn't call from the parking lot across the street into the building, on my cell phone. But I could use an MCI or a Sprint [phone] and get into the building. . . .

Once we got out in the parking lot, we were out there for a couple of hours until we determined that they weren't going to let us back in the building. So we had to try to find a place to go. My initial reaction was to set up in the Holiday Inn. . . . The problem would be that . . . the rooms are just not big enough to put everybody in that we would need. And, of course, you've got a lot of civilians wandering around. The security is not there. So we started thinking this, that, and the other thing. And a buddy of mine works down by the Springfield Metro. He's got a new building. And I thought about, well, you know, I wonder if he's got some room that he can put us down there because he has government contracts. His folks are cleared and all that. So in thinking of getting a hold of him it came to mind that, "Well, Fred Simmons is down there as well"—the GSA contractors that we use for our systems. And we got a hold of them and they said, "Absolutely. Come on down." And we went down there and we set up in one of their spare rooms. . . . And that was our COOP [continuity of operations] site for about six hours or so. . . . But they were very accommodating. . . . We set everything up and had phones and they gave us computers. And it was really great. And we were there until early evening and then we got the word that we could move back to the [Hoffman] building. . . .

MR. SHIRER: Once you got back here in the building and you had your fully manned operations center, what were the key things that you had to make sure happened?

MR. KUHN: Well, we had to make sure that the names [of victims] were not inadvertently disclosed. We had to make sure we knew who was over there [at the Pentagon], who was in the building. And I will tell you that that was very difficult to do because we had to rely on the offices in the building to tell us who was at work that day. And they do not do a personnel asset inventory very well in the Pentagon, especially at the secretariat level. That was the most difficult one, was at the secretariat level, because most of them were civilians. We received a couple of lists of names, and we had to scrub the lists. And it was a continual thing of scrubbing lists to find out exactly how many we had that were missing. And I want to use that word "missing" not in the legal sense but in the sense of they were unaccounted for. Probably a better phrase is "unaccounted for." And that first day and second day, the 12th and the 13th, were days that were full of list scrubbing, additional names, taking names off, putting names on, finding people who were—"Oh, he's on leave. He's out in California." And those sorts of things. Very frustrating, very hard to do, very difficult to do. But we finally got it down to the seventy-four names. . . .

The other thing that was difficult is as we found these names and tried to verify that they were, in fact, unaccounted for, is to notify the families. Because the majority of those folks that work in the Pentagon, their families were here and they saw it on TV. And TV was very definitive about where the plane hit. So people knew where their folks were. "My husband or my wife or my son or my father works on the other side of the Pentagon. So chances are he or she is okay." . . . People knew that they were working on that side of the Pentagon. And that made it very much more difficult because families were finding things out or surmising things before we had a chance to do the official notification that their loved one was unaccounted for. That was very difficult.

We had to mobilize around town. We had casualty area commands that we go to and do the actual notification, go out and they do the notification. And they assign the casualty assistance officers. And in this case we knew right away that these people lived here. So they either came under [Fort] Belvoir or Fort Myer and potentially Fort Meade. But it was all Military District of Washington [MDW]. And those are the three casualty area commands we have here in the Military District of Washington. So we notified Fort Myer on the 11th and had them stand up and go to twenty-four hours and bring their augmentees in and start bringing in people to train for CNO duties, the casualty-notification-officer duties, and for casualty-assistance-officer duties, CAO duties. We also told Belvoir to do the same thing. And we gave a heads-up to Fort Meade that they would need it. And these are all concurrent actions on the 11th and the 12th. They did that. They had people standing by. . . .

Another thing that was difficult was finding out where the wounded were, and getting a handle on the wounded. . . . The commander at Walter Reed, [Maj. Gen. Harold L. Timboe], assumed responsibility for all the injured and sent casualty liaison teams, or they sent patient administration teams, to the local hospitals to police up as much information as they could on people that were being brought into the local hospitals so that they could watch over that. And initially that was very difficult to do. Again, everybody was in some state of panic and everybody's trying to do everything right. . . . And the first responders, of course, stay out of their way, let them do the things that they needed to do.

And then we had to start thinking about and start planning what are we going to do once the fire is out? What do we do? How do we recover the remains? How are we going to recover the personal effects out of the building? And then what are we going to do with them? The Air Force stood up Dover [Air Force Base] mortuary. And the decision was made by the Armed Forces Institute of Pathology and the Armed Forces Medical Examiner that the remains would go to Dover. . . . So they were all transported to Dover. As we found them they were transported up to Dover.

So we had to start to plan for "What are we going to do once the fire is out?" Well, about that time along comes our buddies from the Federal Bureau of Investigation, who say, "This is a crime scene and you can't go in." So initially we were prohibited from going in to the crime scene. . . . The FBI brought in their own forensic folks plus criminal investigators. And they went into the building. And we offered them military support. They would not let the military into what they called the crime scene, the areas that they had not investigated. But as they would clear a small area, they would let the military in there. And what they did is they packaged up the remains and they passed them to the military. And the military brought them out of the building. So when the television saw people bringing remains out of the building and saw soldiers bringing remains out of the building, they didn't see the FBI bringing remains out. They saw soldiers bringing remains out of the building. And the leadership thought that was really good. Soldiers were taking care of soldiers.

Eventually, over a period of weeks, the FBI finally allowed us to go in and do whatever we needed to do. The FBI, the forensic specialists, recovered remains as best they could. Some remains, they declared evidence. In fact, initially all the remains were declared evidence. And then there were things that they found in the building that they declared evidence. And they sequestered them away. Down in Crystal City they had a place where they put pieces of the airplane and the luggage and those sort of things. . . . Then the remains they allowed to go up to Dover. . . . And the FBI had a liaison at Dover. They were . . . watching what was going on at Dover, too, so in case there was any evidence that popped up at Dover that they'd be there and be able to take it.

When the fire finally got out, we had the 3d Infantry from Fort Myer who were the initial soldiers that we used to bring the remains out of the building. They were not doing recovery. They were bringing the remains out. Then we brought in the 54th Quartermaster Company from Fort Lee, which is a Mortuary Affairs Company. . . . They went to work over there to do recoveries and to recover personal effects and that sort of thing. Then we . . . order[ed] up the 311th Quartermaster Company out of Puerto Rico, which is a reserve component, a United States Army Reserve outfit. Their primary function is to recover and catalog and warehouse personal effects. So we brought them up here, and they went to work over in the building. . . .

We were very fortunate in that we were fixing to have a fairly large mortuary affairs meeting here at the time. And we had experts from CILHI [Central Identification Laboratory, Hawaii], from my identification laboratory in Hawaii, and we had *the* mortuary officer from USAREUR [U.S. Army, Europe] here. And the ones from CILHI were not a problem because they work for me, so I just extended them here and kept them. And we went back to Europe and asked Europe if we could keep Mr. Roth, who is their mortuary officer. And, of course, they said yes. And he basically was the senior forensic expert on the ground at the building working with the 311th and the 54th to do the recoveries. . . . And he was instrumental in this thing going right. . . . And I had two officers from CILHI who also knew what they were doing, they were over there. And they set it up and ran a 24-hour operation. . . .

At the same time, I was calling up my individual mobilization augmentees [IMAs] that I needed to work this. . . . I released my PERSCOM augmentees and let them go back to their regular jobs, bring my IMAs in. . . . They took over in the reporting section over here. They took over those other functions. And I brought them back into my mortuary affairs, and they started to set up and get prepared to manage the funerals, the funeral homes, the movement of remains, casketing, anything. As soon as Dover would release a set of remains, my guys back here are the ones that work all those other actions, shipment, the remains and all those things. I had liaison. I put three people from my staff at Dover to manage that end of it. As the remains were identified and released, then my people had three people up there who would organize the shipment and all those things along with coordination here. And they were running twenty-four-hour operations up there at Dover, initially.

My IMAs that I brought in here—we would set up systems, along with PCC [Personnel Contingency Cell], how to track the funerals and all the viewings and memorial services and all those things. Because the leadership—and when I say the leadership I'm talking about the Chief of Staff of the Army *personally*—wanted to know, as did Mr. [Joel] Hudson [Administrative Assistant to the Secretary of the Army] and lots of other folks in the building, but the chief wanted to know when all the funerals were going to be, when all the memorial services were going to be, and he ordered that a general officer and an SES would attend each one. And I'm not so sure that he needed to order that. I think that would have happened anyhow. Mr. Hudson tried to attend all the funerals of his people personally. He didn't make that, but . . . it was either him or [Mrs. Sandra Riley, Deputy Administrative Assistant to the Secretary of the Army]. . . . They went to all of the memorial services. The chief went to the ones that he could go to, that were here in the area. And then if we had funerals that were a distance from here, and there were a number, there were general officers that either traveled from here or general officers in the local area that went to those funerals. And we had a big, elaborate system to track all of these, these rosters and everything to track all these to make sure.

And an unsung hero in all of this was the chief of the general officer management office, Colonel [James N.] Delottinville. . . . He personally handled all the general officers here in MDW, to attend the funerals here. . . . And it didn't make any difference what time of day or night it was. He personally did it, Jim Delottinville. And that had to really be excruciating. Because when we set this thing up, we said, "Man, how is my sergeant first class going to call some three-star and tell this three-star, 'You will be at'"—Delottinville said, "He doesn't need to. I'll do it. You just tell me when the funeral is and I will get a general there." And he did. And then the SES office jumped in and then they did it for SESes. They said, "You tell us when the funeral is going to be and we will have an SES there." So that part, once that started working that went pretty good. That went pretty good. And like I said, the vice and the chief both tried to attend as many of them as they possibly could.

At the same time that we're planning on what are we going to do in the future, part of our plans had to be, what are we going to do with the personal effects that we take out of the building? Because we're going to have personal effects, literally personal effects, glasses, rings, things that are in people's desks, handbags, all that sort of stuff, briefcases, whatever, coins, coin sets, pictures, all the things that you look around an office and you just kind of, you know, the "I love me" walls and all of those things. You look around an office and everything that is not government in nature is a personal effect. And so what are we going to do with them? Where are we going to put them? Because we don't have a warehouse just standing here waiting for us to show up. And then what do we do with the government stuff, computers, chairs, other things that are government in nature?

Well, we went over—this was the MDW commander's problem, but since I have the experts it really became our problem—so our IMAs went over to talk to the folks over in MDW. And my IMAs who handle personal effects, trained to do this, explained basically what we were looking for, the kind of a building that we would need, the kind of security we would need and that sort of stuff. MDW fell right in line and they were really great. I've got to commend [Maj.] General [James] Jackson's whole staff. They did a splendid job, really did a great job from our perspective. Never a hassle. Yes, there were discussions, but there was never a "No, you can't have" type of an attitude. They were really, really good about all this. And they gave us the buildings on Fort Myer. In fact, the PE [personal effects] depot is still there. It's still set up. And they gave us the buildings, and they put money into the buildings for us to help get them ready the way we needed them and to help us configure the inside of the buildings. . . .

We had all the personal effects that we collected out of the Pentagon. We had a deal with the property guys in the Pentagon on what to do with the government stuff, and basically they said they wanted to take the government stuff because some of the computers apparently had classified hard drives. And so they didn't want to let them out of the building. And we said, "It works for us. Just so it's not something that personally belongs to someone who is either unaccounted for, or dead, or living." Because the living—we have to collect up the personal effects in the area that was affected, because at the time we're collecting it, we can't tell if it belongs to somebody who's alive or not. So we collect it all. . . . It goes over to the personal effects depot. And they clean everything. They catalogue everything. They record where it was found in the building. It's very, very detailed. And it is all boxed up, photographs were taken of all of it. Another thing I've got to tell you, the Army photo lab—there's a photo something or other that belongs to the Army over there in the Pentagon—and the DOD photo folks, absolutely magnificent. They gave us photographers. Never questioned it. Gave us photographers to work over in the PE depot. And just super, just super. Everything just fell into place. So anyhow, all of this is cataloged and will be at some point in time returned to the living and then returned also what we know belongs to the dead, we'll return to the families.

But there's another set of PE, and the FBI had it because . . . the FBI had gone through the building first and taken everything that they considered evidence. So they had boxes and boxes and boxes of stuff as well, which they were going through from an evidentiary point of view. And then they will turn that over to us and we will catalog it and photograph it and do everything to it, make sure it's clean and all those things and return it to the proper people. So an incident like this doesn't end once we clean the building out. It goes on and on and on.

1st Sgt. Steven Stokes was a member of Company C, 1st Battalion, 3d U.S. Infantry (The Old Guard), which helped to recover bodies in the Pentagon. He was interviewed by Stephen Lofgren of the U.S. Army Center of Military History on 25 September 2001.

1ST SGT. STOKES: The FBI had gone in with the dog teams and there was a symbol they would spray paint on a room with orange florescent spray paint. And it would be an X, and then in the top quadrant of the X, there were the initials of the team that cleared the room, and then the right quadrant of the X would be how many bodies were in that room, and then there was some sort of code on the other two quadrants for the location of the body, which I never—I never broke the code on that. But there would be the four-man litter team and we'd move with an FBI agent or two, and then a FEMA [Federal Emergency Management Agency] guy or two. So probably like seven or eight people would be searching for a body, and then somebody would find it. They'd tell us, "It should be right over here somewhere," and, at which time, we'd locate it. And then once we located it, then we'd bag the body and get it out, which was very, very physically demanding.

In the inside of the room it—it was like walking through a swamp, but instead of brush, it was just steel, just twisted steel and rubble everywhere. You were probably standing on two or three feet of

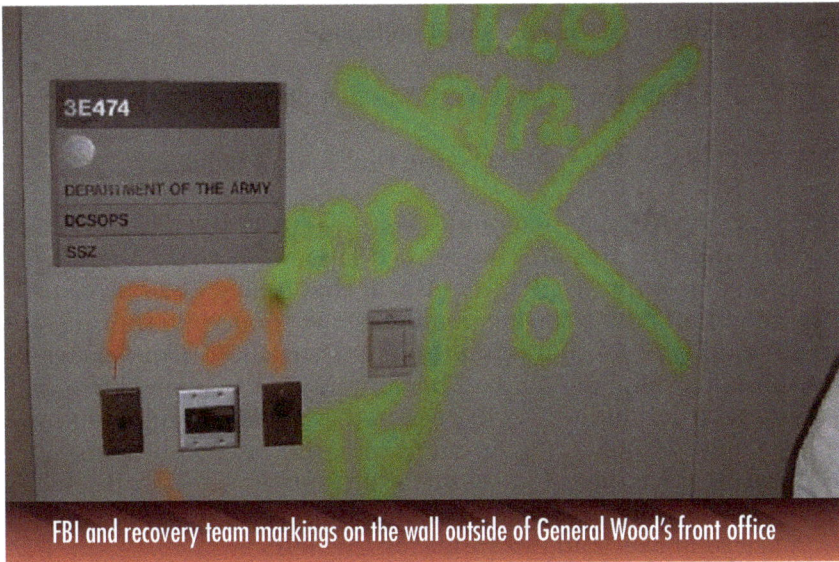

FBI and recovery team markings on the wall outside of General Wood's front office

debris, with this chemical suit on, trying to walk, and there were still ankle-high fires. So it was tough to see and very tough to breathe. And then once we'd get to the body, the FBI guys would actually handle the body. And we might help them physically by trying to pick up a limb, and four of us trying to get it in the bag, but without disturbing the bodies as much as—well, actually, the first thing that would happen is they'd take pictures, take pictures of where the body was at. And then there'd be an FBI guy with a clipboard who would write up a tag of the location and the number of the body. And once that was done, then we'd move the body, and had real hard times getting the first bodies out. . . .We ended up breaking up the four-man teams just to make a human chain going in and just trying to pass the bodies up over the rubble to the next guy and the next guy, and then you'd peel off and get back in the line, just to get the guy out. Until we smartened up and we'd pass a litter back. Probably the second body we realized the litter was the way to go, that the other way wasn't going to work. And then we'd just hold the litter high and just try to pass the litter over the rubble to get them out. And then once you got to the hallway—the hallways were relatively clear, just flooded—then the four guys would take the litter back down. So the four-man litter team would get broken up as soon as they got there, and whoever just happened to be at the end would be the guys who actually brought the body back downstairs to the refrigerated truck.

MR. LOFGREN: So this area had collapsed?

1ST SGT. STOKES: Oh, it was—it was just devastation.

MR. LOFGREN: But it hadn't—the roof hadn't fallen in?

1ST SGT. STOKES: At that point, we were—we didn't have problems with the structure. A couple days later we realized there were problems with the structure. But at that time we had probably a little more faith than we should have. We ended up shoring that area up later on. But just, just total destruction. The ceilings—I think that the building had been renovated so many times, they probably left old wiring in place rather than remove it, and just ran new wiring. And the same with the air conditioning and heating ducts. So there was just stuff, you know, two or three feet high, and then wires just hanging down from the ceiling—very hard to move—and just rubble everywhere.

MR. LOFGREN: How long was a team in the building at a time?

1ST SGT. STOKES: It would depend. . . . We were short of respirators. That was the show-stopper. I think we only had like twenty-two respirators that first day for the actual litter teams, and we probably had forty people suited up. So when you came out, you'd make the call whether you wanted to go back in or give up your respirator and take a break, in which case, you'd just wait for the next team to come out and grab one of their respirators and go back in, which later caused a couple guys to get an upper respiratory infection. We—about two or three days later, people started getting sick and we realized it was because we were passing the respirators back and forth without properly—

MR. LOFGREN: Picking up germs up from each other?

1ST SGT. STOKES: Right. I mean, within a few days we all had our own, but, I mean, obviously they didn't have that many just—because we weren't the only effort. I mean, there was our effort and there was another effort on the other side of the building doing the same thing. . . .

Now one thing that we were conscious of that first day is we knew we didn't need everybody to go in. We knew we only needed about half of the people to go in. So I don't know if we did the right thing or not, but rather than just say, "First Squad, you go," we told each platoon, "Give me four teams of four." And we told them, if there was a guy who probably—who was showing some apprehension, it wasn't important for them to go in. The labor wasn't the show stopper, it was the respirators, though. We weren't going to send a guy in who—who wasn't up to it. And some guys wanted to stay. Some guys would not take a break. But where some guys just kind of, just never—when you said, "We need four"—they just never—you know, four guys would come forward and they never did. So no hard feelings. . . .

We did the retrieval, probably intense retrieval, for three or four days, and then like on the Saturday, it turned into labor details, shoring up the building. At that point, we still hadn't gotten to the—no one had gotten to the fuselage, which is where we wanted to be. . . . Now we were on the first floor. . . . And we came in this corridor. . . . Corridor 5, and we went down—I don't know if it was E or D . . . and we just started from the outside, and the fire departments were cutting eight-by-eight timbers, probably eight feet long, eight inches by eight inches by eight feet long. And we were just bringing those in, and we just started shoring up the pillars that had been damaged. And as we shored pillars, we recovered bodies as we went. And that took about three days to actually—of doing that, I would think—to get to the actual fuselage, to the worst part. But some guys . . . had gone in the service road and there were some remains in the service road. There was some landing gear from the aircraft. . . . There was debris in that road, and remains in that road. And we were using, actually, the company truck to retrieve those remains, the company Humvee to retrieve those remains for the FBI. And then, later—I mean, the XO [executive officer] never came back that second night. He worked through that second night with the Humvee and one driver, taking aircraft parts and remains to the FBI, who was setting up in the North Parking lot. So then we started shoring the building, and then it just turned into a labor detail from that point up. And then from that point, you'd come across bodies, but that wasn't the prime mission. It was shoring up the building so the FBI could get in there.

And that went on for a few days until—then it just became debris removal. We'd have wheelbarrows. We'd just pick up cinder blocks and we'd—and other debris—and walk it back to Corridor 5, dump it in the hallway, and they had that little bobcat, baby tractor, pushing it outside. So once we started doing that, we really started making progress. And it—it wasn't a day—that didn't even take a day until we could completely get to the aircraft fuselage. We got there pretty quick once we started doing that, clearing out. That's basically what we did . . . and by Saturday I think the first floor looked like an empty warehouse. It was completely clear of rubble and debris, Saturday the 22d. . . .

MR. LOFGREN: The water all evaporated?

1ST SGT. STOKES: Everything is out. I mean the first floor looks like an empty warehouse. Every pillar is shored up. Everything is out.

MR. LOFGREN: I'm thinking with all that water they were dumping on there, there'd be a small lake in there somewhere.

1ST SGT. STOKES: Well, they were pumping it. . . . Yeah, they were pumping the water back out. And some of the companies working on the second floor—I didn't get back up to the second floor, but they said it was pretty well cleared out also. So I think it went pretty quick, actually. I think we got a lot done real fast.

* * * *

MR. LOFGREN: If you had to assess your company's performance overall . . . ?

1ST SGT. STOKES: We're a better company for it. We're a ceremonial unit. We nitpick at each other all the time, you know? We find fault and—a medal being off by an eighth of an inch that no one is really going to ever notice anyway. And we kind of got to roll up our sleeves and go in there, and junior leaders got to be junior leaders. Everybody—I mean, unfortunate incident, obviously—but people got to go in there and be a leader. People got to go in there—

MR. LOFGREN: In something other than a training exercise?

1ST SGT. STOKES: Right, and we really are ceremonial units and we really don't spend much time in the woods. So for us it was— it was a—in my opinion, you know, it definitely changed some people: some for the better, some for the worse. But, you know, there's some guys who rolled their sleeves and just did not take a break, and even—we had a guy who was AWOL twenty-nine days, thought it was thirty, so he thought he'd get released at thirty, counted wrong and came back, and we're like, "Oh, my goodness, this guy." But that guy went down there, and knowing he has an R-15 pending, and just worked like a dog. You know, so you saw some good in some people, a lot of good in people. . . . But the positive thing was people that didn't have anything invested in it or they just wanted to go down there and do all they could do to help. So I think we're a better unit for it. . . .

MR. LOFGREN: When you look back at this a year from now, or five years from now, any dominant impressions? "Memory photographs" is what I always think of.

1ST SGT. STOKES: Sure . . . like my baby, I always put her little shoes on the stairs next to our little shoes, my wife's and my shoes on the stairs. And her little cute little shoes are there. And I did find a baby's shoe with remains in it when I was down there. I mean, so that's probably, you know, a negative memory. . . . But honestly—I mean, if it had to happen, I'm glad I was there to help. I think that's definitely a huge part of American history, and to be able to have gone down there and help people out is—makes you feel good that you could go down there and help.

Capt. William Besterman was Commander of Company A, 1st Battalion, 3d U.S. Infantry (The Old Guard). He was interviewed at Fort Lesley J. McNair, Washington, D.C., by Capt. Timothy Frambes of the U.S. Army Center of Military History on 3 October 2001.

CAPT. BESTERMAN: We got a mission on the 12th to go assist in the humanitarian assistance at the Pentagon with the rubble removal, and the removal of remains of the people that were victims of the attack. . . . I went up and I reported to my Regimental Commander, Colonel Laufenberg, and Sergeant Major [Aubrey] Butts was there, and so was the deputy commander. We talked, and they gave me what my mission was going to be. The purpose wasn't specifically spelled out that way, but what it was—more or less—[was] based on the other company that was there. It was Charlie Company that was there. I went and talked to the company commander who was on the ground. And what they had been doing was they put the guys in a sterile suit. . . . Tyvek suits they call them, with work gloves on top of a set of sterile gloves, and also the yellow dishwashing gloves, and on top of that, a work glove. Then a respirator and a hard hat, and boot covers, too—or you could have fireman's boots. It was a couple of different sets of boots. At that point, they had a company that was there working on one side of the building—on the right side over there by that magnolia tree—that was where they were coming in and out of the building. There was still a lot of debris. It was smoky. You could smell it very heavily there, so I don't know if the fire was completely out, but it was safe at that point.

CAPT. FRAMBES: What was the purpose of the Tyvek suit?

CAPT. BESTERMAN: The purpose of the Tyvek suit was to prevent you from being exposed to biohazards—from the remains or some type of asbestos stuff or the aluminum that—they were concerned about the levels of that inside the building.

CAPT. FRAMBES: Who gave you this kind of gear?

CAPT. BESTERMAN: Our medics had all of this stuff. . . . The Old Guard medic, Sergeant Haggerty, medical platoon sergeant, somehow he had gotten all this stuff. . . . Initially they didn't have a lot of it, but they had enough to get in there and do what they had to do.

But, as I said, I was getting in there, I did my recon, I saw the area of the building, I saw what they were doing. The ATF and the FBI people would identify human remains, they would tag it with a number, they would record what it was they found. The way I understood it was, at the end of this whole thing, they were going to be able to put it into a program in some computer. . . . They were going to come up with a three-dimensional-type logging of where everything was in the building, and where every set of remains was, so they could come to some agreement about whose remains . . . they found, if they had some trouble with identification. They were also interested in not only remains recovery but also the collection of evidence from the hijackers, and what not. . . . But initially, we had a group of eight go in, they'd assess the situation, and they'd come out and say, give me two sets of litter bearers. On the initial recon they would drop the body bags with each of the set of remains. Sometimes the FBI and ATF people would bag the remains, and other times, just to save time, we would do it as well. I got my introduction. I said, "Okay, I got it." It's traumatic, but it's not a hard mission from a soldier's standpoint.

CAPT. FRAMBES: What did you think of to cut back on some trauma? What did you think of right then, that you needed to tell your soldiers?

CAPT. BESTERMAN: What we needed to tell our soldiers was, "We are assisting these fallen comrades and we're going to try to repatriate their remains out of this building and get them out of there and that's what our mission is. If you've got a weak stomach or if you feel like you don't need to be doing that, you need to raise your hand and say so because we're going to be handling some remains." But the other thing that we did was—they kind of developed this system before we got there . . . Charlie Company commander told me this is kind of leader intensive. You don't want your eighteen-year-old soldier up in here looking at this. You want some experienced guys that you know you can trust, probably you and your leaders or what have you.

CAPT. FRAMBES: What were the respirators for, the smell and things like that?

CAPT. BESTERMAN: The smell was just charred. I wouldn't say it was like a burnt body smell. It was more of a fire smell—and it was to protect the people in the building from any kind of contamination or asbestos—

CAPT. FRAMBES: Did you have anybody in that group that had combat experience or that had any disaster experience?

CAPT. BESTERMAN: [1st Lt. Robert] Wolfe was a veteran from DESERT STORM. He was a staff sergeant in the engineers during DESERT STORM and he went to OCS, or actually got a Green-to-Gold [scholarship] and got his commission that way.

CAPT. FRAMBES: Any veterans from the Green Ramp group at Fort Bragg? Anybody that had been involved in that?

CAPT. BESTERMAN: Yes, Sergeant Major Butts had been involved in that and he was a big Bragg guy; he had seen the destruction from that thing at Bragg and seen the burned people down there. So he'd seen it before. And he'd been pulling bodies out of there all day. So he prepared us—I don't know that there was any way to prepare a person for what we saw in there, but we did the best we could based on what he was able to tell us.

* * * *

When we went in the building, it was right there along the edge of that side where it had collapsed, and the structure was still holding, and they had shored it up with some initial shoring. As I said before, it was about four-plank structures they put in there. So we went in there in between those plank structures and there was significant guidance from the rescue workers and the structural engineers about where to come in. A couple of times they'd pull us back and say, "Don't go in this way because it's not stable," so we were constantly looking up to make sure it wasn't going to come down on top of us. I think we pulled out about three remains out of that location. The reason we did that is because they were concerned that the building might come down, and they had found them there and they wanted to get them out as quick as possible. . . . These were whole remains, basically burned beyond recognition. You could not identify them—man, woman. Maybe from weight you could identify them one way or the other, but you couldn't identify who they were, Army, Navy, whatever. They were burned that bad. They were the first three that we pulled out. . . . The FBI, they would mark the remains, they would photograph it, and they would record it on a paper. And then what we would do is, we would provide them with a body bag and they would put the remains in a body bag sometimes, and sometimes I assisted them in putting the remains in the body bag, and several times we had to do that.

CAPT. FRAMBES: And you were just picking up the person and you were putting them in the bag? Anything around them, anything like that?

CAPT. BESTERMAN: In one instance, one of the people that was a victim, his shirt had come off, and physically, I put the shirt—it had a nametag on it—I put it inside the bag with the guy because I knew it was his shirt and I wanted to make sure that the nametag went in with it. But we went in there, we pulled those three out of that location right next to the blast area and then immediately they pulled us out of there and they continued to work on the shoring and that. Then we moved down towards the left-hand side of the building, down there at the Pentagon Fire Station, that little structure outside, and we were down past that—where we came in, that entrance. And we went up to the second floor and began pulling remains from there. That night we pulled out, I'd say, another five remains out from the top floor.

* * * *

CAPT. FRAMBES: What's the most striking thing . . . that you remember?

CAPT. BESTERMAN: [The first] bodies [we saw] were completely burned. . . . You couldn't really discern that it was a human. The troubling part of it was when we got to the other side there were some of the bodies that were burned on one side and not on the other. Some of them were identifiable somewhat. I found one. . . . I assume that he had gone in there to try to help people, and he maybe was overcome by smoke. It appeared to me his last act as a live human was to grab his Pentagon badge and cover it in his hand and hold it up over his head so that he would be identified if he was burnt. He had his wedding band right there; you could see his wedding band. That really struck me, as it was not something that you—that upset me. . . .

All the computers, all of that stuff was completely—in the section that I'm talking about. . . . it was completely melted like a slice of cheese on a hamburger. It was really—unbelievably hot in there. They said it was two thousand degrees [Fahrenheit] where the blast occurred. I don't know what it was up there where the rest of them were. It was amazing to me, though, that the Pentagon structure was in as good a shape as it was. It just shows that building was a fortress to withstand an aircraft flying into it full of fuel and that's all the damage it did. It was pretty amazing.

* * * *

We sent a platoon up to the North Parking lot to assist them with evidence sorting. They would put the stuff out of the building into a big long dumpster. They'd put up a forklift, hook it back up to the truck, take it up to the North Parking lot, dump it and then they would move it with heavy equipment. Then they would get rakes, get down on hands and knees, and they'd be sorting through all that junk trying to find anything. . . . The FBI was running that whole part. At times we had—we assisted them the first night. The first night they started that up there we assisted in number one, guarding the perimeter, and also sorting the evidence. Then eventually it just became where we were guarding the perimeter and the FBI was sorting the evidence. . . . You don't take anything out of the building; it's all evidence. Don't take anything out of there. We were told if you find colors that are—we found a set of national colors in there that were all jacked up—and we didn't want to let them be there in that disgraced state. So what we did is we pulled that out and we turned it over to the DPS [Defense Protective Service] people. So everything in that building was considered evidence. . . . We took all that stuff out of there. Everything that came out— basically the three floors that we worked on in that building, we worked the first, second, and third floor, and that building was whistle clean. It was spotless. Everything in that building was pulled out of that building. We're talking like—I don't know how many tons of rubble that would be—but it was like tons and tons and tons of file cabinets, desks, concrete, soot, all of it. All came out of the building in a dumpster, they took it out there, they dumped it, they sifted through it with a water hose and with rakes and everything; and they went through and they took it all. . . .

We wanted to help and the soldiers were motivated about helping; and we know probably more than anybody about the handling of remains respectfully because we do that in the cemetery.

CAPT. FRAMBES: Usually in a casket though.

CAPT. BESTERMAN: Yeah, it's in a casket and you're not usually in close contact with it. But I'll tell you right now that I think everybody that saw something in that building will forever respect people that sacrifice for this country, because all those people in that building, as far as I'm concerned, are heroes because they are basically what started this whole campaign.

* * * *

As I said, the civilian agencies, they were really happy with the way we performed. They just said, "You guys are tireless, you do all the backbreaking work for us," and that's what we were doing there. We were there to help, so we did.

I'm very proud of the way the soldiers in this company worked together down there, and it was a difficult job; it wasn't really pleasant, especially in the middle of the night. But the other part was towards the end of the operation, when people were getting a little tired and getting cranky, I just told them, "We're not deploying to Afghanistan this week, we're not victims of this attack. You could easily have been a victim of this attack, so be happy that we're not and just be focused on what your mission is because people paid the ultimate sacrifice here. We're at war and we don't have much right to be really upset about too much because we're able to see our families."

Capt. Lance Green was Commander, Company H, 1st Battalion, 3d U.S. Infantry (The Old Guard). He was interviewed at Fort Myer, Virginia, by Capt. Timothy Frambes of the U.S. Army Center of Military History on 4 October 2001.

CAPT. FRAMBES: All right, so let's go . . . to your initial impressions.

CAPT. GREEN: Yes, I was expecting to go down there and see a plane, the rear end of the plane hanging out from this building. I had no idea that it caused this much damage and I definitely, just by looking at it, saw how the building was burned. I could just imagine, the plane had hit, the building collapsed on the plane, probably simultaneously as it went into flames and all the heat and flames and the explosion just spread through the building, just down each side.

CAPT. FRAMBES: So what was the condition of the building when you first got there? Was it still on fire? How long had it been from the attack?. . .

CAPT. GREEN: It was either one day or two, but it was still smoking when we went down there, and there was a fire team spraying water up onto the ceiling, the roof area.

CAPT. FRAMBES: And did you go in the building right away?. . .

CAPT. GREEN: I went in that night. I didn't go in until that night with my guns platoon. . . .

CAPT. FRAMBES: Walk me through what happened.

CAPT. GREEN: Well, they went from the basic shoring mission the first day they had the job, or the first day they had the tasking, and it rotated between guns and drill team, each night a different platoon would do it. And where they started working with the outside shoring, then they actually went into the building to do a lot of the rubble removal. I understand that a lot of engineers and FBI personnel had already been into the building, after it was determined it was safe, the structure was sound and they had marked, tagged, photographed a lot of the rooms, identified the bodies that were visual. . . . I guess the Alpha Company soldiers and some of the other soldiers of the regiment had already been removing some of the bodies. So we went in and we were doing the exact same mission, removing the large rubble, areas where the small bobcat-type vehicles could not remove some of the debris. They went in and they were removing the large-type debris. Everything being saved for later examination by the FBI, and there were bodies. Me, personally, when I was with the soldiers, I never was with them when they located bodies, but our soldiers did locate some of the people that were in the Pentagon. They also located a lot of classified information. All that stuff was gathered, given to the right authorities and all that was saved, but the majority of it was removing large rubble and everything else in the building and along the way, yes, they found body parts, a lot of body parts.

CAPT. FRAMBES: Were your guys in protective clothing?

CAPT. GREEN: Yes, before they would go in, they would suit up in their white suits, the boots. The suits were taped at the boots. They had the gloves, the masks, the helmet. They would go in, they would do their job and then they were deconned [decontaminated] after they were finished and they were coming out. If they ripped a suit while they were in, they would come back out and go in with a new suit.

CAPT. FRAMBES: Did you have any guidance to say, if you had any soldiers decide they didn't want to go in or if they felt emotionally—

CAPT. GREEN: No, I had every soldier in the company volunteer. They wanted to go down there and be a part of it. I had caisson soldiers that wanted to go down and be a part of it, headquarters element wanted to be a part of it, tomb sentinels as well. Everybody wanted to be a part of it. But at the same time we had to do our mission here, so it made it a little bit difficult. . . . I think initially when they went in and they were removing a lot of the big stuff, it was hard work, but it really didn't affect them or bother them at that point. It's only when they removed a lot of the big stuff and they started shoveling a lot of the stuff out and they were finding personal remains. Like there was a small stuffed animal, and just by looking at that stuffed animal, me, personally, I could tell that was probably sitting on some secretary's desk. What it signified I don't know. I don't know if her daughter had given it to her or what. There were planters, there were pictures, a lot of personal effects, and that's when you really realized that these were people and they just came to work that day and just seeing all these things, it made it a lot different. It really, really did.

CAPT. FRAMBES: Emotionally, I mean did you run from sadness to anger, what kind of things did you feel?

CAPT. GREEN: First it was anger when this whole thing got started, but I could tell, me, personally, when I got down there and started working, I really felt, I felt pretty bad there for a good week and a half to two weeks. I can't really explain how I felt—I just didn't feel good about myself. I felt pretty bad. It wasn't because I was worn out and tired from working long hours. . . . We would talk a lot before each of the platoons would go on shift and I would just flat-out tell them, "Look, if you've got soldiers that don't want to do this, just let me know."

CAPT. FRAMBES: But you never had that problem?

CAPT. GREEN: Never had that problem.

CAPT. FRAMBES: And did you rotate guns platoon one night, the next night would be your? . . .

CAPT. GREEN: It rotated like that for the first maybe six days, then it went strictly guns platoon doing Pentagon work. Drill team was doing security here at Fort Myer. The requirement for security on Myer increased, not only at platoon, but they had to have people manning the gate and standing at the wall at ANC [Arlington National Cemetery], so the drill team took that mission. And then after about, I'd say six or seven days, it really started to wear on the guns platoon down there. It really, really did.

CAPT. FRAMBES: What kind of support down there did you have for those guys when they came out? Obviously, you said that

they got deconned. Did folks talk to them about anything that they saw?

CAPT. GREEN: Yes. . . . And then right there, where we were at, in that little tent city, there was everything we needed as far as food, water, and chaplains. Anything and everything we needed was right there. Red Cross, Salvation Army did an outstanding job of helping us and the soldiers, so that was really good.

CAPT. FRAMBES: Did you keep all your soldiers here or did you allow them to go home?

CAPT. GREEN: For the first four days we were all pretty much all here.

CAPT. FRAMBES: So the first four days was like being in the field?

CAPT. GREEN: Exactly, we were here. We were definitely here and then at that point, we allowed them to go home. Let me rephrase that. The first three days I don't think anyone left. I really don't. I think everyone was here, and then on the fourth day we went ahead and had soldiers—we could release them and send them home.

* * * *

The last site mission, I believe was the night they had the small tornado down at the Pentagon. . . . They did security and a National Guard Unit or a Reserve Unit, the 311th [Quartermaster Company], from Puerto Rico, they were assisting the FBI down there with that. Interesting note, the night of that tornado—and I don't remember if it was Wednesday, Thursday, or Friday of last week—I had a platoon leader and platoon sergeant, First Lieutenant Gage Smith was the platoon leader and Sergeant First Class Bobby Springfellow, the platoon sergeant. This tornado started blowing through there and they evacuated that North Parking lot site and got everybody under the underpass. And it might have been maybe two minutes before that small tornado came through that parking lot, they realized, you know, "I don't think we checked that sleeping tent that the 311th [Quartermaster] guys were sleeping in." . . . So they raced to the tent, got two soldiers out and as they were running back, this tent just collapses and rolls and it hit with such a force that it broke all the wood beams in the tent pretty much. . . . And it crushed quite a few cots in that tent.

CAPT. FRAMBES: But they got everybody out?

CAPT. GREEN: They got everybody out.

* * * *

CAPT. FRAMBES: Out of all the things that have happened—you talked about the small stuffed animal—what stands out in your mind the most that's either going to be hard to shake or something that you'll remember for a long, long time?

CAPT. GREEN: I found a guy's planner in there and I still remember his name. It had his picture with his girlfriend or fiancé in the planner. With his planner, there was a backpack with ties, T-shirts, shaving kit, and stuff like that in there, and at the time I thought, you know, this was a contractor, civilian contractor in there and he probably lost his life. You know, I saw a picture of him and his girlfriend. I still remember the guy's name and probably—

CAPT. FRAMBES: Was he on the casualty list?

CAPT. GREEN: No, thank goodness. And I came back here and looked on the casualty list and he was not on the list, which is really good. That was really good, but at the time, I thought he probably was, so for some reason that like etched in my mind, his name, and I was really concerned and really bothered with it until that list came out, so I was pretty relieved when I found out he wasn't on the list. Just all the things like that, that was probably the worst thing, seeing personal effects, personal items, coffee cups. There were so many coffee cups, personalized coffee cups in there. Stuffed animals, framed pictures, planners, personal planners, name plates for desks, stuff like that. That was probably the worst thing. If those things hadn't been in there or I hadn't came across those things, maybe it would be different, but when you see those little things like that.

CAPT. FRAMBES: Daily life reminders.

Steven E. Beck led the Network Operations Team for the Army Information Management Support Center (IMCEN) in the Pentagon. Michael E. Shea

was the Program Manager for BTG, which was the principal contract support provider to IMCEN. They were interviewed by Stephen Lofgren of the U.S. Army Center of Military History at the Pentagon on 12 October 2001. Also present were June Kronholz of the Wall Street Journal *and Lt. Col. T. Ryan Yantis of the Office of the Chief of Public Affairs.*

MR. LOFGREN: Can you tell us what you were doing Tuesday morning?

MR. BECK: Tuesday morning I was over in another part of IMCEN . . . across the hall in a meeting and we had heard that morning earlier about the attack to the Trade Center. I did not know at that point that it was a terrorist attack. For all I knew it was an airplane accident. About 9:30 we heard a loud boom. The room shook, things fell over, one of the light fixtures fell out. There was perhaps thirty seconds of people looking out into the hall wondering what to do and people were shouting, "Get out, get out, get out." Which we did. We split up pretty quickly. No one in my area was hurt. We were in 1D624 area. And we went out an exit in the wall where the plane struck. What I could see—there was a large fireball. Because that's near the helicopter landing sites, I assumed a helicopter had crashed on landing or take off. We could not see that something had actually penetrated the wall of the building, or I could not see that. And of course, we were directed away from that area. I tried to link up with other IMCEN people and [was] particularly looking for the people in my own section. And the areas we could get to kept changing. We couldn't walk around the outside of that, we had to keep moving further west up Route 27 direction, or around the outside of the Pentagon toward the Potomac. I eventually linked up with everyone except two from my organization. . . . It was when we reached the bank of the river that I found the last two; one of those had actually seen the plane hit. He'd been walking in from the parking lot. That was close to 11:00. And that was the first I knew that there had been a terrorist attack. . . .

[We] wound up down at the Crystal City Metro stop about 3:00. . . . We started about 11:15. It was a long trip. I rode back to Springfield a little after 4:00. I didn't think we were going to be able to get back into the building for days at least, so I got on the phone, called my boss, several of my people, and started making arrangements. I was on the phone for a good part of the rest of the evening. Later found out that we could get back in and set a meeting time, 6:00 the following morning, to decide how bad

Heading home; *below*, the scene in South Parking

the damage was and what we had to do. I went in a little earlier than that, gained access to where our servers were; this would have been about 5:30 a.m. on Wednesday morning. The area had been taped off. I found a portion where the tape was not there so I figured that was okay to go in. Went downstairs, there was no power, very smoky, and there were about two inches of water on the floor from the firefighting efforts. Beside the power and network being out, I didn't see any sign of bad damage to the server areas I could get access to, which wasn't much, by the way. The user areas were, again, just smoke and water damage. The air was very bad. Went back and met with the management about 6. At some point, Mike and I were put in touch with DISC4 [Office of the Director of Information Systems for Command, Control, Communications, and Computers].

MR. LOFGREN: Colonel Quinn?

MR. BECK: Quinn . . . who, with whom we went back down into the areas I visited that morning. We actually broke in the door to the main server room, just to see how things looked, and it looked in pretty decent shape. Things were smoky but otherwise okay as far as we could tell.

MR. LOFGREN: Do you know what room number that was?

MR. BECK: 1D644. We also went over to one of the new rooms where the Pentagon is being renovated, and we had servers in the second and fifth floor of the renovated area. We were able to enter the second floor of what we call the APEX Room, 2B400. It also looked okay. The rest of the day was spent in getting network services running again. We worked closely with the Network Infrastructure Service Agency, NISA, to actually get the physical network conductivity wherever we could— that's an ongoing thing. We are still working those issues. We had a number of servers available to us; there was one of the five server farms that had not been affected except for some power issues. We did get servers out of that room, got them up elsewhere. . . . We were given space down in NISA, in BG849, to start assembling servers and getting those back up such as we could get at. Although Mike and I had been in—well I had been in twice, Mike had been in once that morning—we soon found that access to that area was being considerably restricted by the FBI, by Defense Protective Service [DPS], by MPs in some cases. . . . There were differences of opinion as to who was in control of those areas and who [would] be allowed access. . . . Our main concern was to get going and get the servers out and get them up and running again. Several shifts would go in, work for brief periods, and be told to leave. . . . We did get a large group of servers out Wednesday and Thursday and moved them in—and my people, Network Operations folks, worked literally through the night to get those back up and running. We found the damage to them to be minimal, fortunately.

MR. SHEA: Just yanking them out . . . finding power cables, everything else to get them working, was, I think, amazing. It normally takes a while to stand a server up, and then just to pull them out like that, drag them somewhere, put them back into operation, is pretty fantastic.

MR. BECK: We didn't have all the servers. So servers were jury-rigged to provide some of the services on the servers that [they] were not necessarily designed for. What did we pull out? All told . . . we pulled out about a hundred and forty to a hundred and fifty IMCEN servers, and we also assisted several other Army organizations up to, I'd say, about another sixty servers. Getting them out, getting them down to BG849, getting them up and running again. And they also assisted us, too. Shared manpower, going in, pulling servers, putting them in the cart, wheeling them down the hall, that stuff.

MR. LOFGREN: What was your failure rate on the ones you were pulling out?

MR. BECK: Frankly it's been zero so far. Everything that we were able to get out, we were able to get up and running. . . .

MR. SHEA: The fifth floor was extensively damaged with water. We pulled them out, didn't even bother to bring them down to BG849—just put them aside to another area in the Pentagon so they wouldn't get mixed up, and someone slap a wet server into a hot rack, and get fried. . . .

MR. SHEA: [*Speaking to Beck*] You also got the SAN [storage area network] out [of] there.

MR. BECK: That's right. Large IBM storage area network.

MR. SHEA: Million-dollar piece of equipment that we rolled out. . . .

MR. LOFGREN: Mike, where were you Tuesday morning?

MR. SHEA: I was in the same room as him. My wife was calling, told me a plane hit the World Trade Center. She called me up fifteen minutes later, screaming that another one had hit. And I pretty much, you know, "The first one was an accident, the second one, it was deliberate." And we were watching it on TV and we heard a "whish—woom," people getting knocked over, stuff getting knocked off the walls. [I] stayed there for about thirty seconds and started yelling, "Get out!" I went out heading toward the closest exit I knew, which unfortunately was on the same side as the plane hit. As I got out the door, we had stuff—I had parts of the roof burning to my right, and I saw daylight [*pointing*] that way, I didn't even look that way. I just went to daylight. Got out, sixty seconds, ninety seconds after the attack. Murphy had a cell phone. I got through to my wife, like instantly—too soon, because she thought I was in the building. So I spent the rest of the day writing names on paper, anybody I saw, I wrote their name down, just trying to get accountability. Ran into an old friend directing traffic in the middle of the street there, I guess a vehicle must have got hit with a piece of the plane. This young lady was pretty much in shock. And a chunk, didn't look that big, but it had caved in the whole side of her vehicle. [We] had to go all the way around the Pentagon. . . . There was a CP [Command Post] set up at Crystal City, so I was trying to make my way there to see what I could do. By the time I got there, they pretty much had decided to send the folks home, get accountability. I was pretty much on the phone till about 11:30 that night, working my corporate folks and working with the government folks just trying to account for my people. By the end of the day I had two missing and they were killed in the attack. One on this contract and one on another DCSPER contract. That was it. I've always worried about planes coming into the Pentagon to begin with—Reagan [Airport] there—I just didn't think it would be deliberate. . . .

We went back the next morning. . . . I just looked down there, there was nothing left. Just burned out. Just concrete piles sitting there. Spent the next three days, "Hurry up, you can go in" . . . grab everybody that's available to get in, grab garbage carts. [If] we didn't have them, we would have been seriously hampered. We just dumped the stuff in the garbage carts and hauled it back to the computer room. After about three days, we were fighting with the sanitation guys, because they needed them to do their job. So they followed us back to the room, we'd empty the computers out and they would go and do their business. . . .

MR. BECK: Where the plane hit was the worst place to hit as far as the servers. . . . Now, at least in my unexpert opinion, it was also the best place for the plane to have hit to avoid loss of life, because you were right there in the renovated section, people were just moving back into it. And next to it, there were places that people were already getting out, moved out. But it just happened to catch just the right part, to hit all five of our server centers.

We already knew about the [NISA] data center and the fact that it was underused, quite a lot of empty space down there. That was the logical place for us to go up.

MR. SHEA: Some SASS [System/Application Support and Services] folks have moved . . . over to the new area in the old BMDO Missile Defense Organization area. So they . . . had space for twenty-two there; we had a hundred and fifty operating over there. So we spent Wednesday also getting the phones hooked over so that when people called the help desk, it went over there. And we started taking calls to get people working again. So that guys—the techs working twelve, fifteen hours a day, just getting . . . people with new computers up because we lost a lot of computers in the fire. Just kept working, fixing people's machines and putting new ones in and just helping them out. . . .

MR. BECK: You had the help desk up and running . . . Wednesday morning. . . . I had my network operations guys in here that morning, too, trying to salvage what they could salvage and get the network up right away. Everybody on the operational side, your guys, my guys, people, were working minimum twelve-hour shifts, many of them more.

Some of the administrative folks were, as many people in the Pentagon were, actually told to stay home: "There is no office for you," "There is nothing you can do right now, so stay put." They were contacted later . . . as there was something for them to do and some place for them to go.

MR. LOFGREN: Moving all these servers down there. I've seen the end result but can you describe what's involved with standing [them] up?

MR. SHEA: I can tell you moving. His guys were the ones who set up. Looked like a gypsy caravan going on down there. We had garbage bins, we had anything that wasn't nailed down that had wheels on it. We collected it and put servers on it and moved them down. Everybody worked. We had different contractors, normally competitors and everything, but everybody was helping each other out, moving them down there and getting people operational. It was frustrating because we are trying to get the job done—the customer operation. We have Defense Protective Services and everyone doing their job trying to secure what was considered a crime area. There was a lot of confusion and some frustration. I didn't hear a lot of shouting matches, but there was a lot of frustration. We would get in, and get our guys suited up, and go off into a server room. They get up there, and they say, all of a sudden this mysterious voice would come over the radio, "Uh-uh, they're not allowed in there, move them out." And they [security] would pull them out and they would have half the servers sitting in that hallway ready to go. And then another two hours of negotiation and back in again. So it's just back and forth all day long.

MR. BECK: Yes, at least one instance I know of where there was a whole bunch of stuff just left sitting out there, where it shouldn't have been sitting. . . .

And also to pick up on something you just mentioned. There were other people involved besides just the Network Operations and help desk folks. Some of the administrative folks that I mentioned—Requirements Analysis Division. Many of them not technical, but they were there, carried servers, they came in and helped. It was a joint effort.

MR. SHEA: It was pretty much a "Hey, you" thing. When we got word we went in. It was like whatever bodies were available, and we could explain to them. After a while we got even more of an idea of what was in there. They had asbestos and lead, and everything—that's when we suited up. But prior to that we basically [had] gone in there—a gauze mask and that was it.

MR. LOFGREN: How did you get the suits?

MR. SHEA: Once OSHA [Occupational Safety and Health Administration] got involved in it . . . and said you are not allowed without the suits, they were provided by the government. They had to mask up, tape up, and all this stuff.

MR. LOFGREN: Was there a certain place you picked them up?

MR. SHEA: Yes, in one of the hallways. . . . Eventually, you had to go in, and had to have a monitor on you when you went in. But as the weeks went on, that happened. The first couple days, it was gauze mask. Then I found out what I was walking through. . . .

I had a set of clothes sitting on my back porch that's probably going to go in the garbage. Once I found out, especially that one morning I went through some stuff, that, just, you know—I stripped in the back, hope the neighbors didn't get offended—went in my house with my shorts, because there was too much nasty stuff on there. You're talking about asbestos, lead, all these other things. Once you identified what the issue was, as long as they felt comfortable with adequate protection, they went in. . . . There were probably thirty people that went in and out all week long just to get the job done, to get the customer back operational. Everybody felt they wanted the Army Staff operational so they could do what they had to do. There was no question about how many hours we had to work, or working weekends, or working nights or whatever, it was just what do we have to do to get the job done.

MR. BECK: I don't know how your averages worked out. Everybody in my group, I think the first couple of weeks anyway, averaged out between fourteen to sixteen hours a day. I was working about fourteen hours a day, and I know some of my guys were working more than that.

MR. SHEA: Guys like Bob Shaeffer, we were sending them home because they were getting to where they were wanting to stay to work—but we had to kick him out the door for him to go and get some rest.

MR. LOFGREN: Can you [tell] . . . someone like me who doesn't know anything about servers, what's involved in hooking up a couple hundred of them?

MR. BECK: You have to have a place to put them, for one thing, you can't just stack them upon the floor because of the air flow issues and heat issues and all those. You also have to make sure you have enough power. Well, where we put them didn't have enough power, didn't have enough network connections, didn't have enough air conditioning, air flow either. The NISA folks immediately started remedying that. They got the power people in there to bring more power cables in. Basically turned up the air conditioning, ran more network cables in. We got the servers on racks, got them plugged in, brought them up, made sure they were doing what they were supposed to do, made sure they were working with the rest of the servers, the way they were supposed to work. We have certain servers do some things on a network, and other servers depend on those servers to do those certain things so they can do their thing. And we had some real issues the first couple days about that. I'll just throw out the techno language, you can cut it out if you need to. We have different domains and you have to decide who can get in to what. It's a permissions-access issue. And certain machines are domain controllers. So they've got an account for you and they know your access level. You need to put in the right password, and go into your account so you can get access to it. That machine does that, this machine holds your files, this machine holds your e-mails. They have to talk all together. The number one priority is to get e-mail up for everybody because that's what the whole headquarters runs on, e-mail. More important than the file services, certainly more important than printing. The rest of it could wait. So for each server, of the hundreds we brought in there, that procedure had to be gone through. Plug it in, and get it on the network, bring it up, make sure it's running okay, make sure it is talking to the other servers all right.

MR. LOFGREN: How many people did you have in there hooking the stuff up—it was just like a sea of cable?

MR. BECK: Yes, it was. . . . Network Operations would have as many as ten working and then NISA would be in there with people doing the network. And of course, while that was going on, we still got other people just moving boxes around. There are another couple of sections of IMCEN—we would have people in there doing that kind of work. I drew temporarily from some of those other sections [that] didn't have to have their stuff up right away. So I pulled in five people from the other sections temporarily. So I guess it would be more like network operations had ten, fifteen people. And I had five, plus the movers.

MR. SHEA: All of us went from a five-by-twelve support to twenty-four hours, seven days a week. So you would have my staff—we were staffed for twelve hours daily, now we had to do it twenty-four hours a day. So we had to adjust our schedule and pretty much, that's where the twelves came in and they had to provide that support. We were staffing right now to provide that coverage, but still it's been a stress on everybody. You are basically tripling the number of hours you need to provide support and you don't have the bodies to do that. So it's quite the challenge. . . .

MR. LOFGREN: None of the servers you set up have failed?

MR. BECK: That's correct. I thought the smoke would do something.

MR. SHEA: They said thirty to forty-five days. It's been forty days. Let you know in fifteen days. . . .

MR. BECK: Hardware is a lot faster to replace [than people]. Our management has been under a strain because of that very fact, the loss of people. . . . And the people who stepped up, stepped up magnificently. But now they are doing two peoples jobs.

David A. Nanney was a customer account manager with the Network Infrastructure Agency–Pentagon. He was interviewed by Stephen Lofgren of the U.S. Army Center for Military History on 27 November 2001.

MR. NANNEY: By six o'clock that evening [11 September], we had some people in the building reconstituting the networks, starting to bring up the core. The core never failed as I understand it, but . . . so much was damaged of the Army network, Army lost a lot of connectivity. Like almost all. But, by six o'clock, we were back in working. We support joint services. All the backbone in the Pentagon and some of the services never went down at all. Some of the OSD, some of the Air Force, much of JCS [Joint Chiefs of Staff] didn't go down hardly at all, which is remarkable.

* * * *

By the next morning, we had already heard the President's message saying that they wanted us to return to work and so, we all came back into literally a burning building. There was fire going on both sides of the building on the roof. . . . The significance for us was that—one is, of course, the burning. Trying to assess what was going on. We started getting our first reports from IMCEN [U.S. Army Information Support Management Center] asking could they bring some servers into our data center. . . . Got a call from IMCEN saying they had about twenty servers they wanted to bring in and the answer is, of course, "no problem." Because in the data center, we had been planning for a server farm and actually had some racks up and had power to those racks, planning for some internal server consolidation and for some [servers] from OSD.

So, in the crisis, the answer was, "Sure bring them on down." Well, about an hour later, it's somebody else has six more. About an hour later, there's ten more. I think we ended up after about a week having a little over three hundred servers—I'm not sure of the exact number—that had been basically pulled out of the burned and other space, brought into the data center and just loaded up into that area. The significance there was we had the data center ready, wired, air conditioned, and everything else and while it put a strain on our resources, it was the perfect place for them to come. And within a matter of days, we had the e-mail up and a couple of days after that, we had full functional capability for almost all of the staff who could get to a network. Now, the key there is there were over two thousand Army people who were homeless, who lost their offices and had no place to go. They set up all over the Washington metropolitan area and so, we had to reestablish . . . those networks and those offices, but basically we had for almost all of the Army, almost all of HQDA [Headquarters, Department of the Army], within a week, most of their functional capability. You talk about a miracle. That was phenomenal. . . .

Of course, there's the emotional thing as I'm finding out who got hurt. We lost many people that I knew that were Army customers. . . . And as the days went on and you learned more and more about who got lost, at the same time, you're trying to do the mission. . . . I worked something like seventy-some hours that first week and I was a slacker compared to what some other people did.

* * * *

MR. LOFGREN: Was there a conscious decision or did somebody make a formal decision that, you know, we should go looking for servers and not wait for them to come to us?

MR. NANNEY: That's a really excellent question. What was going on is there was a formal management that was standing up. Every morning at eight o'clock and at three o'clock, we were meeting in our conference room and because we had the backbone communications, it was like we became the central focus of the [restoration] even though organizationally we don't have the command line for all the functional users. . . . We had DISC4 [Director of Information Systems for Command, Control, Communications, and Computers] at our table. We had a two-

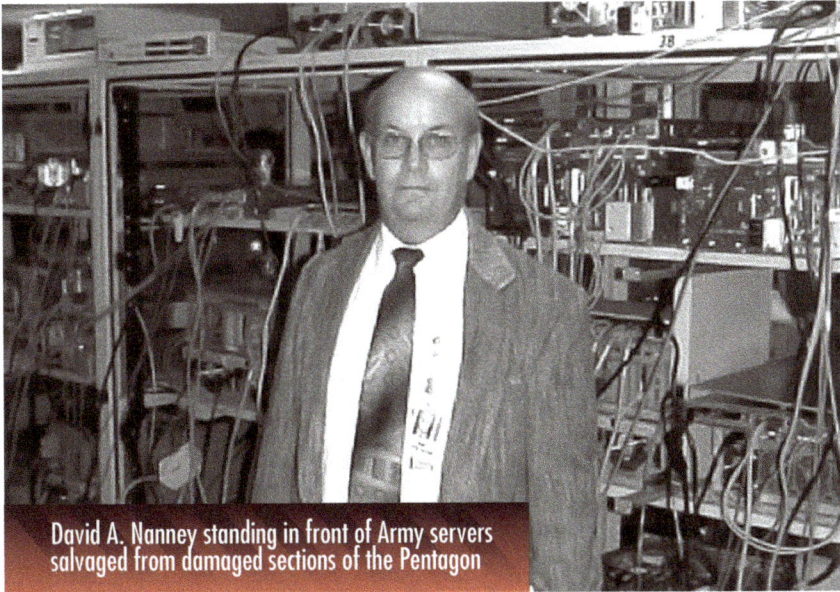

David A. Nanney standing in front of Army servers salvaged from damaged sections of the Pentagon

star general. . . . Daily, we had close to forty to sixty people in that room at our eight o'clock stand up, breathing heavy, and all of the reporting was done by the various teams, Team Army, Team Air Force, Team JCS. We had organized our teams that way.

But, from a management standpoint on the Army servers, that was happening in the back room. We were reporting progress in the—at the formal meeting, but in the back room [was] where you had the technicians, assistants, administrators from everywhere, our engineers who were hooking up the communications to the server racks. We're all working—you know, "What's the functional requirement?" and "That's who I was working with." . . . It's "What's the need right now?" and a systems administrator from IMCEN would say, "We need *this* to go make e-mail work." We'd had [the Office of the Assistant Secretary of the Army for] Financial Management show up saying, "I have six servers that are in room so-and-so. If you could get those, we could do our mission." So, we started hearing what the needs were.

We have a Seth Werbin who is a Lockheed Martin person who informally set up contacts with the FBI and the federal police and so tried to bring some organization to our access. Because we basically—a systems administrator would say I need to do a room and they'd go to the room and if it was unguarded, they would just pull everything they could. So—

MR. LOFGREN: So, the access to the damaged area wasn't [shut down]?

MR. NANNEY: We got a lot more done in the first couple of days before they got the security in. And as the security shrunk— tightened down, it got to be harder and harder to get things out, and that's when we went more and more to Seth and the organization with the FBI. We had several individuals who got in hot water, both with our agency and others with the FBI, because we were going into a crime scene, which is what they declared it after a couple of days. But, we had to get our technology out. So, there was a real push/pull, and if they left a door open or if they left a corridor open, people were going in. It was an incredible thing and it was very much in the technical informal management. You know, we were doing the formal stuff with the generals and then we were the guys who were doing the work. . . .

You could see as—you know, everyone was so focused. Probably the—you know, if you want to say—the proudest hour of my entire career, professionally and personally, was being a part of what went on in that first week because of the total focus on trying to undo what was done to us to get the capability back up. And within two days, we were able to get the e-mail back up. The psychological benefit, beyond any mission, to people who could sit down at their desks and get all the messages from all over the world—I mean, you can't believe how many people sent letters saying, "I hope you're okay." I heard several of the young enlisted people being really just overwhelmed by how many people cared about them. You know, as you're older, you understand your circles of support, but for some of these young kids who might have taken a troubled path to get into the Army, all of a sudden [they] find out that they've touched a bunch of lives. Incredible.

Maj. Willis T. Leavitt was the Assistant Chief of Forensic Psychiatry Services at Walter Reed Army Medical Center. He helped run Operation SOLACE, a program that provided stress management assistance and other mental health

services to Pentagon personnel in the wake of the 11 September attack. He was interviewed at the Pentagon by Stephen Lofgren of the U.S. Army Center for Military History on 23 July 2002.

MAJ. LEAVITT: I know that shortly after the planes had hit . . . the chief of psychiatry [at Walter Reed Army Medical Center] had called all the psychiatrists over to the main hospital so that we could have a pow-pow, as it were. He took about ten of the senior staff and we got into a room, and we discussed the game plan of what needed to be done. . . .

MR. LOFGREN: When did some decision get made about sending people down here [to the Pentagon]?

MAJ. LEAVITT: The Army has had in place SMART teams. That's S-M-A-R-T. I think it's stress management reaction team. . . . These are teams that are pre-identified so that in case of traumatic incident they can pick up and fly to wherever to take care of the problem. Walter Reed had a SMART team; I think about twelve members on a team. And it was clear at that point that one SMART team was not enough. So the idea was to kind of enhance the SMART team with the staff from Walter Reed: psychiatry and psychology, social work, psychiatric nursing, occupational therapy, and chaplains. . . . On the 12th it was set up that there would be three shifts composed of a variety of different disciplines that would go [to the Pentagon], and I think it was about eight folks in each shift. . . .

MR. LOFGREN: Can you walk me through what you've been doing since?

MAJ. LEAVITT: During the first, I believe it was the first week, I was part of one of the teams down here. The initial emphasis was to take care of the first responders on the outside of the building. Those are the people who were taking the bodies out, sifting through the rubble, et cetera. It became clear that there was also a need inside the building—the people who were exposed to smoke, the panic. They lost people that they knew or had familiarity with. Communication networks had broken down, et cetera. But in some cases leadership, you know, perished. So there was also this emphasis that we had to take care of the inside as well. And we had to take care of those people who were in portions of the damaged part of the Pentagon that had been displaced to outside facilities.

So I was part of the team that worked within the Pentagon. And the plan was rather simple. We would split into small groups. We would be held responsible for floors in the Pentagon. And then we would go door to door, desk to desk, to provide information about the services that we offered, the mental health services, to provide surveillance of individuals as well as the office, to get the sense of, is this office, as a system, is it functioning well? Is it coping well with the stresses? Or do we need to come in and do a work group intervention? The individuals that we meet, was the individual coping well, or does that individual need a one-on-one session with us for a more in-depth assessment of their needs? Do they need to be referred to a higher level of care or a more comprehensive evaluation, et cetera? So that's what the team was doing, these small little teams within the Pentagon, and I was one of the members of that [effort]. During the course of the day, a team would visit approximately twenty offices and each individual would have contact with about fifty or sixty persons. And by the end of the day we'd see quite a few people. In total, at the most, we had about thirty or thirty-one mental health providers working at one time on the teams inside and outside the Pentagon. So it was a pretty big staff to oversee.

After about a week I was asked to step in and organize and provide leadership to the groups within the Pentagon, so that there would be a more systematic coverage of the offices to set up a pattern of communication, so anything that was identified as a problem for an office or an individual was reported back to me, so that we could start making better oversight of the work. During the first week it was kind of like people were just doing whatever they could to take care of the situation. And it's in the second week that things just became more of a group, more cohesive, more followed and tracked. . . .

Since then, we moved from a phase from September to the beginning of December when the teams down here were primarily Army and Air Force personnel. . . . [They] worked on the teams and did the office-to-office, desk-to-desk mission, provided the individual evaluations when necessary. And then in the December timeframe, then we moved over to an all-civilian staff. . . .

The mission is that we will have no post-Pentagon syndrome. We had a lot of concern that, following this event, if we did not attend to the needs of this population, many people would advance into post-traumatic stress disorder or [have] other unexplained, mysterious, somatic or physical complaints that couldn't be explained through just routine medical evaluations, but instead were symptoms related to mental stress. The goal is to provide pre-clinical and clinical mental health services. . . . And the emphasis is prevention, support, surveillance, and education. . . .

There's always been a stigma, a mental health stigma, or stigma against seeking mental health [care]. And that's not necessarily true just of military, but it's true with our culture in general. But within the military there is a reasonable concern, "If I see somebody for mental health, will this affect my career in a negative way?" So many soldiers, officer or military service members, will avoid seeking a mental-health consultation or evaluation. So that was a big stigma that we knew that we had to face, especially here in the Pentagon where everyone is high functioning and very successful in their career by and large. And then the other reasonable concern was, "Well, if I see somebody for mental health, will this affect my ability to maintain my security clearance?" Because one of the questions in the security clearance process—

MR. LOFGREN: Sure. "Have you ever consulted [a mental health professional]?"

MAJ. LEAVITT: Yeah. So we knew that these were obvious barriers to access care. So the way to skirt that problem was to make it very clear that we maintain the highest confidentiality, provide at least four sessions in which we won't document anything unless we're mandated by law to do so. For instance, if somebody told us that they were suicidal, homicidal, were beating their children, et cetera, we would be mandated by law to report that to authorities. But otherwise, keep it as confidential as possible. How do we do that? We just don't take their name and social security number. Okay?

And so with that policy in effect—which is unlike anything we've done, at least in the United States Army—it opened the door so that we could start seeing officers. I can tell you just from my personal experience as a psychiatrist who has served at Walter Reed and the 1st Infantry Division, officers don't seek care. It's the general rule. We might see a captain on occasion. But very rarely will you see a major, a lieutenant colonel. There's like this gulf where we don't see these officers until they've retired. Interestingly though now, with this plan in place, the desk to desk, door to door, not taking names, not taking Social Security numbers, we've had many officers talk to us about how they reacted to 9/11, how they currently cope, the good things, the bad things. And we're able to provide education, support, and help them with coping.

MR. LOFGREN: How many people have you spoken with?

MAJ. LEAVITT: We have approximately thirty thousand contacts, meaning that we talk to a hell of a lot of people. It was mandated by the Surgeon General [Lt. Gen. James B. Peake] that we contact every person in the Pentagon. You're talking about approximately twenty-four thousand. That's a lot of people. And I can't tell you that we talked to absolutely every single person because we don't take names.

MR. LOFGREN: Right.

MAJ. LEAVITT: But I can say that we have swept through the building at least twice going desk to desk, door to door, meeting with the supervisors, asking for their support and their permission to meet with all their employees. We've marketed through the *Pentagram* [a Pentagon newspaper], through posters, through e-mail, through this direct face-to-face contact. We've set up support groups. We've gone to off-site federal facilities like in the Crystal City area, all those buildings that are associated with the Pentagon. We've met with displaced offices over there. We've met with just the offices that were originally there essentially doing the same thing, making sure that people knew that there was a resource available for the four sessions. And if they ever needed anything more, that they could come through us as a referral point for assessing information.

MR. LOFGREN: How many people do you think that have taken you up on your offer?

MAJ. LEAVITT: I can't give you a firm number, I really can't. Some of the referrals are just done on the spot. And that is something that we just haven't tracked. So, I mean, my social workers will have encounters on a daily basis, where they'll meet someone and someone will ask them, "Well, if I'm thinking about accessing mental health care, can I meet with you?" And they'll set up an appointment. Or, you know, they'll also be offered a variety of other different avenues to meet their needs. . . .

We also try to increase the likelihood of people who will access care through familiarity. So I've assigned social workers to particular buildings, to particular sections, to particular offices here in the Pentagon, so that the people in the offices see the same person come by, they encounter the same person. Okay? And once they feel that they do need to talk, then they can speak to that person that they've seen over a number of times. . . .

MR. LOFGREN: The Army talks a lot about, you know, soldiers and our people are our most important resource. So, here's an example of following up on that.

MAJ. LEAVITT: Which is impressive because I have to admit, I mean—and I don't want to sound cynical—but there's certainly a political part to Operation SOLACE, too. And it's that message that's conveying that we *do* care, you know? But it's also a way of demonstrating that the Army does take care of its own. . . .

MR. LOFGREN: This was the Surgeon General's idea?

MAJ. LEAVITT: Yeah, yeah. I think it's really based on lessons learned from the Gulf War, because many people came back from the Gulf War with a variety of different complaints. Some mental health related and the others were these mysterious unexplained physical symptoms. And there wasn't a mechanism in place to respond to this. There was no Operation SOLACE or anything like that. And what happens, just going through the traditional medical care system, people receive an extensive physical work-up. They were feeling like no one cared for them. That people were blowing off their symptoms. And so this was a way to be able to respond immediately. One out of every seven soldiers that deployed to the Gulf has been evaluated for a Gulf War syndrome. That's a hell of a lot of people. Sixty thousand or so, isn't it? That's a lot, and the cost of doing that evaluation has been immense. So the idea was pay now, in a sense, by funding Operation SOLACE and it may decrease the likelihood of people manifesting these mysterious, unexplained symptoms. . . .

MR. LOFGREN: Is there something else . . . someone ten years from now would want to know? A general comment?

MAJ. LEAVITT: Well, I can say this. The Operation SOLACE model—
there are many within the leadership of psychiatry that do
believe that this is a model that can be extended beyond the
Pentagon that may be of use to soldiers or military service
members worldwide. The stigma that coming to see a mental
health provider is immense. . . . This could be a way to bring
people to see us before their problems become so apparent.
That's usually how things work right now. It's that a solider could
exist in a unit and have multiple problems. He might be in debt.
He might be drinking. He might have some abuse of his child or
spouse on the side. But it doesn't surface up to the commander
or his first sergeant's level until it really gets bad. The idea of
having a program similar to Operation SOLACE on the ground
in units is that we would have a chance to maybe identify these
problems before they reach the peak. Identify it, intervene, and
direct people to the right services so they can be addressed at a
very low level. . . .

This is an opportunity to perhaps change the face of at least Army
psychiatry, and so it's kind of like trying to ride that wave and
use the momentum that we've acquired here and then pushing
a bit further. There are many people that are excited by this.
And there is a potential, given that we have a Surgeon General
who is favorably disposed to taking care of problems before
they become, you know, immense, we do have the potential of
instituting some of the changes. . . . We'll see. I think time will tell.
I think it has a potential, though, of really making a difference.

*Sandi Hanish was a clinical nurse specialist at Walter Reed Army Hospital
and a member of the Operation SOLACE team that provided stress management
assistance and other mental health services to Pentagon personnel in the wake
of the 11 September attack. She was interviewed by Stephen Lofgren of the U.S.
Army Center of Military History on 23 July 2002.*

MS. HANISH: This is a pretty resilient population. They're pretty
tough in all senses of the word. They sort of get the Timex
award from me, which is, you know, "Takes a licking and keeps
on ticking." I think it's been really helpful that they—certainly
the active duty people—they know what they're here to do.
They knew on 9/11. I think that it helps people to be so clear in

their goals and their purpose and to not have the choice about whether you climb back in the saddle or not. And to keep on going. So they're very resilient. That's not to say that there's not a cost for that also to individuals. I'm not trying to say that. But they have been able to stay amazingly functional. The goal is to be able to keep them that way over the course of the next— well, for the rest of their life, really—but certainly over the next few years to make sure that there's no fallout. And that's pretty hard to do. There's no guarantee ever for anybody. But we try to get the word out about what symptoms for themselves to be worried about. Part of the problem is that they may have them, but they don't always have time to deal with them right now anyway, you know, because they've been very busy.

They're also kind of tough in another way, which is [they are] resistant to help, resistant to mental health [care] certainly. It took a lot of different ploys on my part when I was making these calls [to people who were in the building at the time of the attack] because, you know, there is a tendency to say, "Yes, yes. Thank you so much." And "I'm just fine." And so I had to teach a few people what the acronym FINE means, which is "fouled up, insecure, neurotic and emotionally unstable." And I did, if nothing else, I succeeded in teaching them not to tell me they're fine. Now when I see some of them in the hallway, they tell me they're "okay." . . . I found that humor was the way to work with these folks, and tenacity. And I finally said to a couple of them, "You know, you wouldn't let somebody else determine when your mission was over or accomplished. And I can't let you determine when mine is. So I'll be calling you back." I just couldn't let them have that control of my job. My job is to keep checking in and making sure they're okay. And after awhile it's fine. But initially, you know, I just met with some of that resistance. If they could get me to shut up and go away, well why not? I don't blame that . . . if they thought that that was going to help them. But I'm just more determined than that. And so I just hung in there and teased them. I told one of them one day, I said, "I'm going to sound like a combination of your mother and your third-grade teacher, and you're not going to like this very well. But here's the story." And then after we can break through, it worked really well.

* * * *

MR. LOFGREN: How do you judge the success of something like Operation SOLACE?

MS. HANISH: Well, sometimes you judge it by the absence of something, not by the presence of something. . . . And so you look at what the predictors might be for people who are demonstrating a lot of increase of stress. So what are the things that you expect? Well, you might expect an increase in domestic violence. You might expect an increase in substance abuse. You might expect an increase in psychosomatic disorders. You might—I mean, there's just different things that you know can be outcomes of people when they're under stress. Premature separations. Just all sorts of things. So we've gotten some of the data on that, you know. Certainly suicide and homicide can be outcomes, too, incredibly negative outcomes. And so we've been collecting data on those kinds of things. And, in fact, there's kind of a dip, which is kind of interesting. . . .

I'm certainly not trying to be so grandiose as to say that Operation SOLACE is responsible for a decrease in all of these areas. There could be many factors involved in that. But just maybe, you know, maybe we've been able to have some impact at least in letting people know that they have services available to them and letting them know that, maybe, it's okay to reach out and get those services. And, again, a lot of places are working very hard. It's not just here, you know? [Fort] Belvoir and [Fort] Meade and [Fort] Myer and everyone, they all have behavioral health services and they're all trying to serve the populations. It's not just the Pentagon any more that's affected. What about the National Guard and the reservists who've been called up and what that does in a person's life and the stress that *that* adds? So, you know, we're moving in that area to support those people because . . . they wouldn't have been called up if it hadn't have been for 9/11.

* * * *

One of the things that I have come to appreciate—and I thought this scheme in my own head as I have been dealing with people—is this whole sense of duty. But there's a hierarchy about duty, and it's been a problem for me, but it's been one that I've respected. And I'll explain. This is the way I kind of understand it. It's sort of like there's a duty to God and there's a duty to country and there's a duty to comrade and there's a duty to family and there's a duty to self. But anything that comes between family and self gets moved before self. And that's very difficult when you're trying to help people because everything comes before them. . . . It's just too easy to keep adding to the list and moving themselves down on the list. And so one of the things that I think that I try to do is to keep people focused on their stress management efforts, to keep themselves on the list, because if you're going to manage your stress you've got to keep yourself on the list.

Col. Roy Wallace was Chief of Resources Division in the Office of the Deputy Chief of Staff for Personnel. He was interviewed by Frank Shirer of the U.S. Army Center of Military History on 27 February 2002.

COL. WALLACE: [On 11 September] we carried [Lt. Col.] Brian Birdwell down to the Redskins' snack bar, which is at the intersections of the fifth corridor and sixth corridor in the A-Ring. . . . We dropped Brian Birdwell off. There was . . . some sort of medical person that was in scrubs maroon scrubs—[she] was female, long blonde hair. I don't know her name. But she started triaging Brian Birdwell. We took a pair of shoes that we had found. Or maybe they were his. I don't know whose they were. But we took the shoes. We took a black sweater and we rolled it up and we put it underneath his feet to start treating for shock. A week later when I went back into that area, those same shoes and that same sweater were still sitting there with the little police line across there just as we'd left them. So, it was kind of eerie.

Col. Marcus A. Kuiper was the Director of the Army Initiatives Group in the Office of the Deputy Chief of Staff for Operations and Plans.

COL. KUIPER: It took us a long while to get back in because of the damage. . . . And my office was a very interesting science experiment because, actually, I didn't know until later that the plane had gone underneath us. The floor had gotten incredibly hot, and so you could see where the support beams in the floor were because . . . all this carpet was like melted into the floor itself, and my briefcase was like fused to the floor. I had a case of Diet Coke tucked up underneath here, and that cooked off. Diet Cokes exploded, you know, that sort of thing. Interestingly, files that were inside metal drawers . . . did not catch on fire. So what you got was . . . smoke damage, and you got mold damage. But if it was inside a metal, a closed metal thing, it got hot, but it didn't catch on fire. It was just like it cooked it in an oven, but it didn't burn it up. So obviously it wasn't hot enough. . . . I keep some Triscuits and a thing of peanut [butter]—I had one of these in my drawer. It fused into one ball. This was one melted ball of plastic and peanut butter inside the drawer. But the paper files were still there. . . . Then the biggest thing was the mold, you know, growing on the uniforms, and some of the stuff, you couldn't get it out because of the intense smoke damage and then the mold on top of it. It was really, like I said, a very interesting science experiment. . . . So we went in. They made us wear respirators and gloves and that kind of stuff. And we went in. . . . Whatever you could stick in a box is what you could carry out, and then they had to clear it. They wouldn't let you take out things that they thought were severely mold-damaged or that you're going to bring out some kind of nasty spore or something.

Col. Joseph M. Tedesco Jr. was the Chief of the Focused Logistics Division, Office of the Deputy Chief of Staff for Programs. This is another excerpt from his written account.

22 September 2001—1120

FDL was about to *Go Home*. The Army had given us permission to attempt to reenter the space, which was once the proud home of DAPR-FDL. We were prepared with masks and helmets, and led into the torn and twisted Wedge One of The Building. We had decided that we would not send a small party, but that we would all go back in together. The stress management counselors thought it to be a good idea. As we approached our office, a peaceful surrounding pervaded an area, which had clearly been filled with mayhem and destruction only days earlier. We entered the first of our three offices. It looked *nothing* like our old home. We saw where the windows shattered, and the twisted

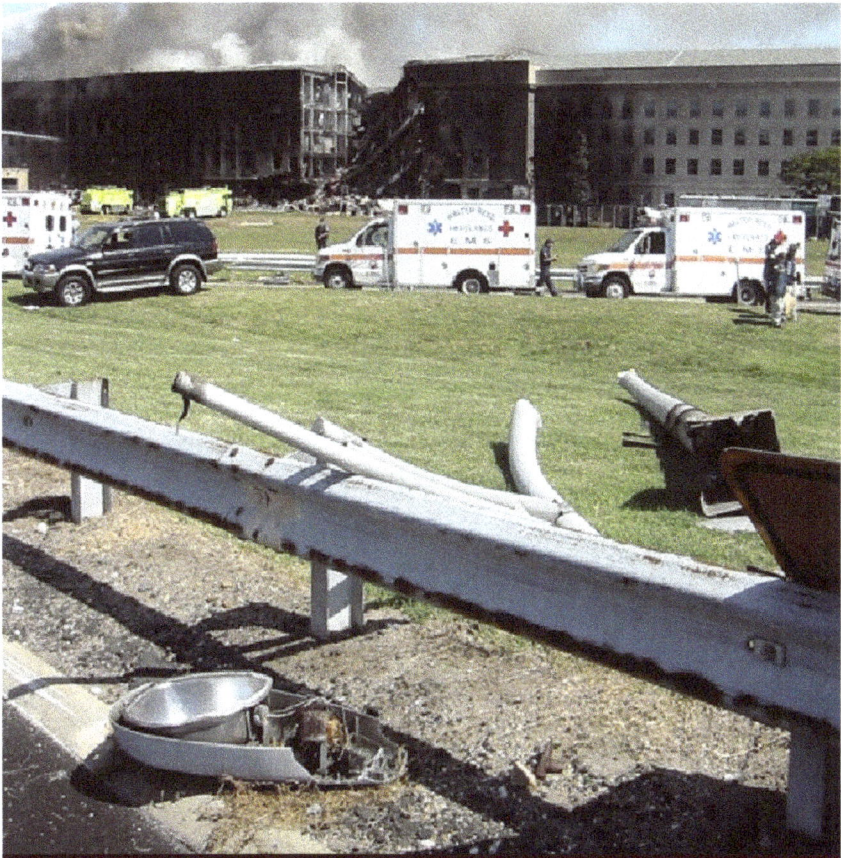

The angle of attack (*note the streetlight that the airplane knocked down*); below, dealing with the aftermath (14 September)

steel had imploded. We saw where the walls had buckled and collapsed around us. We gazed on Jim Randazzo's desk with pure amazement that he survived. We looked at the conference table where FDL was sitting . . . bored at 0937 on 9/11. The walls were collapsed around it. In the middle of the table was the half-eaten loaf of Tom Bortner's sweet bread . . . still intact . . . with the M&M candy pieces on top a little faded from the brave fireman's water . . . but still intact. We just had to laugh. We now joke about how that bread must still be preserved in our digestive tracts. Then we walked to my office. Stark reality is sometimes a bit hard to take. The blinds in my office had been pulled up to allow maximum light. There were no steel blinds to protect any occupants. Thank God we had not had our meeting in there (as we often did). The stark reality was that the steel from the window had pierced the chair at the desk. At that point in my life, I understood what we mean by the phrase *There, but for the Grace of God, go I.* American Airlines Flight 77's nose wheel had ended up only ten to fifteen feet below our conference table. Shocking! We gathered the pictures of our loved ones, our wallets and purses, and our databases to continue the Nation's bidding, and we left the old FDL for the last time.

Brenda Hirschi was Chief of Military Personnel, Army Division, in the Army Budget Office, under the purview of the Office of the Assistant Secretary of the Army for Financial Management.

MR. LOFGREN: When you think back about this ten years from now, what will you remember the most?

MS. HIRSCHI: I'll remember that at 4:30 in the morning on the 11th of September, the journal entry I made. That morning I wrote in my journal—for some reason, who knows—who knows how this stuff all fits together—I had calculated how many days I had left in my life. And I just can't believe it—you know, that I made it. It's a real awakening. . . .

MS. KRONHOLZ: Have you been back in the building?

MS. HIRSCHI: Yeah.

MS. KRONHOLZ: So have you seen the offices?

MS. HIRSCHI: They took us. One day last week, they took us on a tour of the area and showed us from the B and C corridors. You know, we were down on the ground level. They showed us. I mean, it's just a hole.

MS. KRONHOLZ: So there's nothing—

MS. HIRSCHI: There's nothing. No. There's nothing that you could see.

* * * *

Leona G. Shaw worked in the Office of the Assistant Chief of Staff for Installation Management.

MS. SHAW: I will never forget the image of Mr. Mike McCarley, formerly Chief, ACSIM Management Support Office, desperately moving away from the Pentagon Child Care Center and crossing the roadway with a toddler under each armpit. All of the children from the Center were taken down by the river on the opposite side of Boundary Channel Drive. That image will continue to burn in my mind as long as I live.

Maj. Jeanette K. Stone worked for the Environmental Law Division, U.S. Army Legal Services Agency.

MAJ. STONE: The following week, I ran into a chaplain on the Metro who recognized me from that day. We talked, and in the course of doing so I shared with him some of the more disturbing aspects of the event that were bothering me; specifically, the idea that the personnel inside were awaiting a rescue from their units, peers, and coworkers that never came. He then told me that he had been allowed inside the following day, and had seen for himself that most of the victims had died right where they presumably were at the time of impact—at their desks and in their workspaces—and so they probably never even knew what was happening. Although I think that he was probably shading the truth a bit, I want to believe him. I really do.

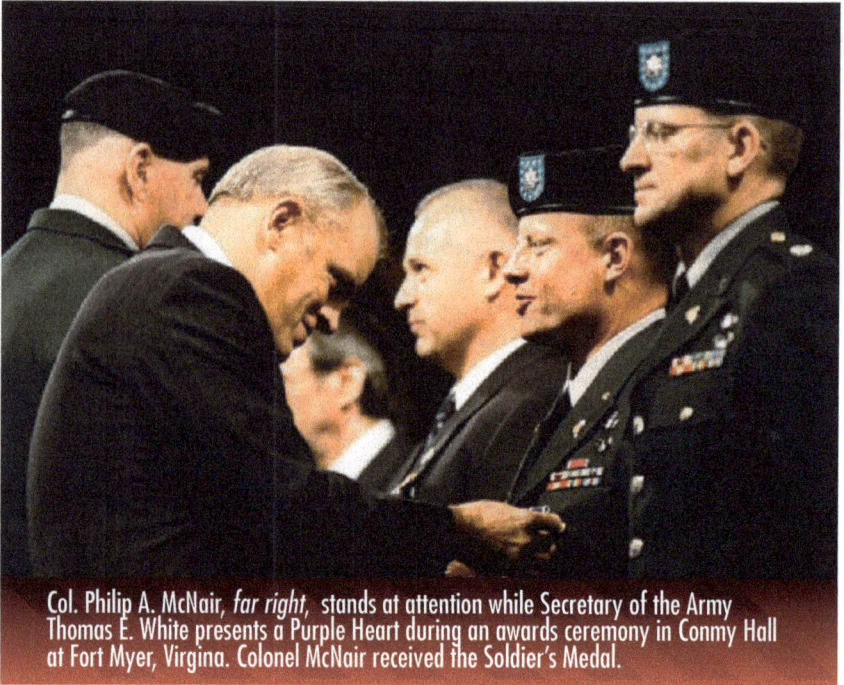

Col. Philip A. McNair, *far right,* stands at attention while Secretary of the Army Thomas E. White presents a Purple Heart during an awards ceremony in Conmy Hall at Fort Myer, Virginia. Colonel McNair received the Soldier's Medal.

Sheila Moody was an accountant with Resource Services–Washington.

MR. SHIRER: Is there anything else that you would like to add to this interview?

MRS. MOODY: Just my gratitude to all the people that have helped me. The people here at the hospital have been so wonderful, and then the Army community—I've had the Secretary of the Army come in and check on me, and Mrs. Rumsfeld, the wife of the Secretary of Defense, come and see me. I've had two four-star generals, General [John M.] Keane and another general come and check on me. And just their gratitude—President Bush sent flowers. And I've gotten teddy bears and I got flowers. And my little friend Stephanie. There's a little girl from an elementary school that sent me a card with my favorite thing attached, with chocolate on it, you know. So I just appreciate all the prayers and all the love and all the care that people are showing. It's just been a wonderful show of love and everything, and I'd just like to thank people for that.

Lt. Col. Isabelle Slifer served in the Office of the Deputy Chief of Staff for Personnel.

LT. COL. SLIFER: I have received so many e-mails, so many phone calls from friends, family, people that I hadn't seen in years that wanted to know about my well-being and which truly, truly humbled me and in some cases flattered me. . . .

There was one phone call in particular that I'd like to reference, and that was from a Mr. Brad Gallagher, who lives in Peters Township, which is south of Pittsburgh, Pennsylvania. He was my neighbor for three years. We still have our home there. However, he called me Wednesday evening and what was so endearing about his phone call is the fact that he was a highly decorated NCO from the Battle of the Bulge and, as most of those greatest generation soldiers, did not brag about it. It was one of those things that I found out living next door to him quite by accident. But he called and he said, "Isabelle, I'm calling to find out how you are." And I said, "Oh, Mr. Gallagher, what I went through pales by what you endured when you were fighting in the Battle of the Bulge." And he put it this way. He said, "Well, Isabelle, let me put it to you that every day I went into battle I expected to get hit. You went into your office area at the Pentagon never expecting what you went through, and there's the difference." And I guess that is the difference. We went on like it was any other day, never expecting, obviously, that a plane would hit you by coming into the building.

Col. Marcus A. Kuiper was the Director of the Army Initiatives Group in the Office of the Deputy Chief of Staff for Operations and Plans.

COL. KUIPER: I spent thirteen months in Bosnia, you know, walking around a country full of land mines and dealing with paramilitaries and thugs and all kinds of people who might want to do me harm. I also spent six months in Kosovo. I was down in Albania during the air war. So I've been places where bullets were flying around and people might want to kill me. I never thought that probably my biggest chance of getting killed in uniform was going to be sitting in my office in the Pentagon. That I was going to become a bigger target there than I was in Bosnia or Kosovo. . . .

It's very surreal to be sitting in the office and you're watching an event on television. They're replaying the plane flying into the World Trade Center again and again and again. And so you're a spectator, an observer, watching this event happen. And then all of a sudden you're a participant. All of a sudden you are *in* the event. All of a sudden *you're* the terrorist act, you're on fire. That was a very strange transition.

Martha Carden was the Assistant Executive Officer in the Office of the Deputy Chief of Staff for Personnel.

MS. CARDEN: [On 11 September,] people were so helpful and they were so concerned. And I can't tell you how many people came to me with cell phones saying, "Ma'am, can I call somebody? Can I get you water?" There were so many people who wanted to help. And you felt—well, I said to the vice chief of staff—he spoke at an AG [Adjutant General's Corps] regimental breakfast that I attended a few weeks ago. And he talked about what he knew about the 11th. And he told about some of the heroic actions. And so he asked for questions at the end. Nobody had any questions. So I raised my hand and I said, "Sir, I don't have a question. But I would like to tell you that I, too, was in that conference room, and a Lieutenant Colonel Rob Grunewald got me out of the building." And I said, "I was in the courtyard and out on the lawn with all these people." And I had said—and I had, this was pretty much the truth—I had told many people, "If I am ever again in a catastrophic event, please God, let me be in the midst of the Army." And to that group I said, "Because you are the finest." And they are. . . . Well, not just the Army. There was Army, Navy, Air Force. There were dentists, doctors, chaplains. They were just all wonderful. You just could not imagine. . . .

MR. LOFGREN: When you think about this ten years from now, what will be your strongest memory?

MS. CARDEN: Well, we just had so many heroes that day. Rob, of course, number one in my heart. Colonel McNair, our XO that you were just talking to across the hall, he just did unbelievable things to save at least seven Navy personnel who were on the first floor. Sergeant Major Tony Rose, Colonel Karl Knoblauch. They are incredible human beings in my view. In their view they would tell you, "That's crazy. You know, I did what anybody would have done." But they're amazing. They are amazing. That's a true hero, I guess. But they just performed so admirably. That will be my everlasting enduring memory.

ABBREVIATIONS

ACSIM	Assistant Chief of Staff for Installation Management
ADCSOPS	Assistant Deputy Chief of Staff for Operations and Plans
AG	Adjutant General's Corps
ANC	Arlington National Cemetery
AOC	Army Operations Center
ATF	Alcohol, Fire, and Tobacco
ATOIC	Antiterrorism Operations Intelligence Cell
BLS	basic life support
BMDO	Ballistic Missile Defense Organization
BRAC	Base Realignment and Closures
CACO	Congressional Affairs Coordination Office(r)
CAO	casualty assistance officer
CAP	Combat Air Patrol
CAT	Crisis Action Team
CILHI	Central Identification Laboratory, Hawaii
CNO	casualty notification officer
COOP	continuity of operations
CP	Command Post
CW5	Chief Warrant Officer 5
DA	Department of the Army
DAS	Director of the Army Staff
DCSLOG	Deputy Chief of Staff for Logistics
DCSOPS	Deputy Chief of Staff for Operations and Plans (now the Deputy Chief of Staff, G–3/5/7)
DCSPER	Deputy Chief of Staff for Personnel (now the Deputy Chief of Staff, G–1)
DCSPRO	Deputy Chief of Staff for Programs (now the Deputy Chief of Staff, G–8)
DEA	Drug Enforcement Agency

DISC4	Director of Information Systems for Command, Control, Communications, and Computers (now the Chief Information Officer/Deputy Chief of Staff, G–6)
DMPM	Directorate of Military Personnel Management
DPS	Defense Protective Service
EMS	emergency medical services
EMT	emergency medical technician
ERT	emergency response team
ETA	estimated time of arrival
FAA	Federal Aviation Administration
FBI	Federal Bureau of Investigation
FEMA	Federal Emergency Management Agency
FORSCOM	U.S. Army Forces Command
GSA	General Services Administration
HQDA	Headquarters, Department of the Army
IMA	individual mobilization augmentee
IMCEN	Information Management Support Center
IMO	Information Management Office
JAG	Judge Advocate General
JCS	Joint Chiefs of Staff
LAN	local area network
LAW	light antitank weapon
MASCAL	Mass Casualty
MDW	Military District of Washington
MOS	military occupational specialty
MP	military police
MP OBC	military police officer basic course
NCO	noncommissioned officer
NCOIC	noncommissioned officer in charge
NISA	Network Infrastructure Service Agency
OCLL	Office, Chief of Legislative Liaison
OCS	Officer Candidate School
OSD	Office of the Secretary of Defense

OSHA	Occupational Safety and Health Administration
PA	physician's assistant
PCC	Personnel Contingency Cell
PE	personal effects
PERSCOM	U.S. Army Personnel Command
POAC	Pentagon Officers' Athletic Club (an older name for the Pentagon Athletic Center)
PT	physical training
PX	post exchange
QDR	Quadrennial Defense Review
RPG	rocket-propelled grenade
SACO	staff action control officer
SAN	storage area network
SASS	System/Application Support and Services
SES	senior executive service
SGS	General Staff Secretariat
SITREP	situation report
SMA	Sergeant Major of the Army
SMART	stress management reaction team
SOP	standard operating procedure
TDY	temporary duty
TOC	tactical operations center
USAR	Urban Search and Rescue
USAREUR	U.S. Army, Europe
VTC	video teleconference
WHS	Washington Headquarters Services
XO	executive officer

INDEX